MOUNT ATHOS

MOUNT ATHOS

Microcosm of the Christian East

Edited by

GRAHAM SPEAKE

and

METROPOLITAN KALLISTOS WARE

PETER LANG

Oxford · Bern · Berlin · Bruxelles · Frankfurt am Main · New York · Wien

Bibliographic information published by Die Deutsche Nationalbibliothek
Die Deutsche Nationalbibliothek lists this publication in the Deutsche Nationalbibliografie;
detailed bibliographic data is available on the Internet at http://dnb.d-nb.de.

A catalogue record for this book is available from the British Library.

Library of Congress Cataloging-in-Publication Data:

Mount Athos : microcosm of the Christian East / Graham Speake and
Kallistos Ware (eds.).
    p. cm.
Chiefly papers delivered at a conference held in Feb. 2009 at
Cambridge University.
Includes bibliographical references and index.
ISBN 978-3-03911-995-0 (alk. paper)
  1. Orthodox Eastern monasteries--Greece--Athos--History--Congresses.
2. Athos (Greece)--Church history--Congresses. 3. Orthodox Eastern
monasticism and religious orders--Greece--Athos--History--Congresses.
I. Speake, Graham, 1946- II. Kallistos, Bishop of Diokleia, 1934-
  BX385.A8M695 2011
  271'.81949565--dc23

                        2011040242

ISBN 978-3-03911-995-0

Cover image: the tower of the Amalfitan monastery on Mount Athos,
seen from the north in winter. Photo: Gerald Palmer.

© Peter Lang AG, International Academic Publishers, Bern 2012
Hochfeldstrasse 32, CH-3012 Bern, Switzerland
info@peterlang.com, www.peterlang.com, www.peterlang.net

Printed in Germany

IN MEMORIAM JEREMY BLACK

Contents

viii

Acknowledgements

The Friends of Mount Athos would like to acknowledge with thanks the generous sponsorship that they received from the Leventis Foundation and the Eling Trust in support of the conference at which most of the papers collected in this volume were presented. The editors in their turn would like to thank the Friends of Mount Athos for generously contributing towards the costs of its publication. A further, not insignificant, contribution was provided from the collection taken at the funeral of the late Jeremy Black. Jeremy was for many years a staunch supporter of the Friends of Mount Athos, he served as a member of its Executive Committee, and he expressed his love for the Mountain in many ways, not least by regularly accompanying path-clearing expeditions and by remembering the society in his will. This book is dedicated to his memory in all humility and with deep affection.

GRAHAM SPEAKE AND KALLISTOS WARE

Introduction

Most of the papers collected in this volume were first delivered at a conference entitled 'Mount Athos: Microcosm of the Christian East' which was held by the Friends of Mount Athos at Madingley Hall, Cambridge, in February 2009. Both the speakers and the delegates were drawn from all corners of the Orthodox world and, as far as was possible, the presenters were chosen to speak about the traditions which they themselves represented. All the same, there were gaps in the coverage and, in an attempt to fill them, we have commissioned a number of additional papers which are now included in the volume. We are conscious that the collection here presented is still not entirely comprehensive, but we hope that it does at least convey something of the remarkable diversity of traditions that has characterized Mount Athos throughout the 1,200 years or so of its existence as a holy mountain.

Holy mountains were a not uncommon phenomenon in the Byzantine world. There were notable examples in various parts of Asia Minor such as Mount Olympos in Bithynia, Mount Latros near ancient Miletus, Mount Auxentios near Chalcedon, and Mount Galesion near Ephesus. But as the Byzantine empire contracted before the advance of the Seljuq Turks, all these monastic centres went into irreversible decline and, after the disastrous Byzantine defeat at Mantzikert in 1071, most of them were overrun and their monks either enslaved or expelled. All this meant that Athos acquired an ever-increasing prominence, since it emerged from the period of the Latin empire (1204–61) as almost the sole survivor. Since that time it has been known throughout the Orthodox world as *the* Holy Mountain, and so it will be referred to in this book.

The significance of monasteries in the Byzantine world-view should not be underestimated. Jonathan Shepard has recently described the restoration of the capital in 1261 as signalling 'the rehabilitation of Constantinople as a locus of God-blessed authority on earth'. He continues:

> If the imperial capital provided one conduit to God's kingdom, Byzantine monasteries offered another. The veneration and awe they generated as microcosms of the celestial order had come increasingly since the mid-tenth century to focus on the Holy Mountain of Athos.[1]

From the start, the monasteries enjoyed imperial patronage. Indeed monasteries on such a scale could scarcely have been founded without it; and for the patrons, to be commemorated in perpetuity as 'founders' of a monastery on Athos was a sure route to immortality. But, as Shepard points out, imperial patronage also ensured privileged status for the monks, which may have accounted in part for the speed with which Athonite monasticism developed in the tenth century.

From the start, monks were drawn to Athos from all over the Byzantine empire and even beyond, though many had already made their monastic profession elsewhere. Among the earliest ninth-century hermits, for example, St Peter the Athonite and St Blasios of Amorion had both become monks in Rome, St Euthymios the Younger on Bithynian Mount Olympos, and Joseph the Armenian, the friend of Euthymios, had also clearly travelled a long way from home. After the foundation of the Lavra in 963 there seems to have been what Rosemary Morris calls a 'quantum leap' in Athonite recruitment,[2] not just in numbers but also in the geographical spread of their origins. Within fifteen years of its foundation, for example, the Lavra is said to have housed as many as 500 (though this figure probably included lay workers as well as monks); and by 985 monasteries had been founded for both Georgians (Iviron) and Amalfitans. 'At first glance', writes Morris,

1   J. Shepard, 'The Byzantine Commonwealth 1000–1550', in M. Angold (ed.), *The Cambridge History of Christianity*, vol. 5: *Eastern Christianity* (Cambridge, 2006), p. 14.

2   R. Morris, 'Where Did the Early Athonite Monks Come From?', in R. Gothóni and G. Speake (eds), *The Monastic Magnet: Roads to and from Mount Athos* (Oxford, 2008), pp. 21–40 (p. 32).

it might appear that the arrival of Georgians and Italians on Athos (evident by the end of the tenth century) marked a major expansion of the geographical extent of the spiritual magnetism of the Mountain. In fact, however, many of the newcomers passed through regions where Athonite monasticism was already well known. Mount Olympos, where Georgian monasticism had long been established, was the most important ... Another such was Constantinople ... It may, in fact, have been via the capital that the first Amalfitan monks came to Athos.[3]

But even if some of the first Athonites came via the traditional monastic 'stopping-off' points, there is no doubting the fact that in one way or another they travelled great distances in order to avail themselves of the seclusion and tranquillity that Athos was known to offer. Just as monasteries were regarded as 'microcosms of the celestial order', so the Mountain itself quickly became a microcosm of the Christian East. The story, or rather the many different stories, of that development are told in the papers that follow.

Averil Cameron's opening chapter on 'Mount Athos and the Byzantine World' sets the scene by positioning the monasteries of Mount Athos and their influence in the context of the Byzantine empire. She demonstrates that, as the fortunes of the empire waxed and waned, and its borders expanded and contracted, so Athos came to symbolize stability and to embody not just the cause of Orthodoxy but also the essence of Byzantium. Indeed, as the political and economic situation of the empire grew increasingly insecure during the Palaiologan period, so the monasteries of Athos flourished as the beneficiaries of donations of land and other favours not only from Byzantine emperors and aristocrats but also from rulers of other states. The two key elements that support the subsequent emergence of Byzantium as a 'commonwealth' are seen to be, first, the authority and enhanced worldwide religious role of the Patriarchate and, second, the authority and increasing autonomy of the Holy Mountain. When finally the empire fell and there was no longer in Constantinople an anointed defender of all Orthodox Christians, the transnational community of Athos was well positioned to become an alternative source and symbol of divinely ordained religious authority that would itself pave the way for the future role of Orthodoxy worldwide.

3   Ibid., pp. 33–5.

Georgian monks first became active on Athos in the decade of the 970s, as Tamara Grdzelidze describes in her chapter. Through his close friendship with St Athanasios the Athonite John the Iberian first obtained a number of cells for Georgian monks near the Lavra and subsequently was given permission to build the monastery of Iviron. Iviron provided a link between the royal house of Georgia and the imperial court in Constantinople which the former was able to exploit for political ends. The monastery became a centre of learning and translated Christian texts into Georgian which were then shipped back to Georgia to provide spiritual nourishment for the Georgian people. But Georgian prosperity on Athos was short-lived: gradually their monastery was infiltrated by Greek monks, by the twelfth century it contained two distinct communities, and in 1357 the Georgians finally lost control of it. Today there are no more than a handful of Georgian monks on the Mountain, none of them at Iviron, but the memory of the monastery as a national spiritual symbol lingers on.

In his chapter on the Bulgarians Kyrill Pavlikianov concentrates on the period from 980 (when at least one Bulgarian-speaking monk is known to have been on the Mountain) to 1550. A minor Slav-speaking monastery known as Zelianos is referred to in several documents of the eleventh century and may have been connected with the Bulgarian population of Halkidiki. The monastery of Zographou was in existence by 980 but seems not to have become Bulgarian before the second half of the twelfth century and not to be commonly known as 'the monastery of the Bulgarians' before the late thirteenth century. The only Bulgarian saint of the Byzantine period known to have been a monk of Zographou is St Kosmas the Zographite who is said to have died in 1422, though another saint of Bulgarian origin, St Romylos of Vidin, lived as a hermit near St Paul's monastery for about twenty years from the mid-fourteenth century, and several other Bulgarian monks were active as copyists at Megiste Lavra at this time. A group of Bulgarian monks is known to have occupied and restored the deserted monastery of Koutloumousiou in the first half of the sixteenth century, but by 1541 they had been replaced by Greeks. The Bulgarian Athonites have produced no major spiritual figures, attracted no spectacular royal donations, and aroused no particular interest on the part of the medieval Bulgarian Church. They have been content to maintain a low profile throughout, but they remain in control of Zographou which has shown modest signs of renewal in recent years.

The Serbian tradition on Mount Athos begins in the year 1191 with the arrival of Prince Rastko Nemanjić (later St Sava), as Vladeta Janković recounts in his chapter, and is formally established in 1198 with the completion and consecration of the katholikon of Hilandar monastery. In that year the founders appealed to the Emperor Alexios to grant Hilandar the status of an independent monastery on the lines of the already existing Georgian and Amalfitan monasteries. The request was granted and a chrysobull was issued stating that the monastery was to be 'a gift to the Serbs in perpetuity'. Hilandar rapidly grew into one of the wealthiest and most influential monasteries on Athos as well as representing the spiritual heart of medieval Serbia. Serbian influence on the Mountain was at its height during the second half of the fourteenth century when at one point the Serbian state stretched from the Danube to the Peloponnese. At that time several other monasteries, such as St Paul's, became largely Serbian, and Serbia used its own resources to revitalize a large number of other monasteries such as St Panteleimon, Simonopetra, Xeropotamou, Karakalou, Esphigmenou, Konstamonitou, and Philotheou. Hilandar may be described as Serbia's best diplomatic 'envoy' to Byzantium, it has always enjoyed (and continues to enjoy) a 'special relationship' with its neighbour Vatopedi, and the Serbian tradition remains deeply rooted in Mount Athos today.

The inclusion of a chapter entitled 'Latin Monasticism on Mount Athos' may come as something of a surprise, but Marcus Plested writes about the flourishing existence of a Benedictine monastery of the Amalfitans on Athos for some 300 years from about 980 to the late thirteenth century. This was a major house with a large community that celebrated the Latin rite and followed the Benedictine rule. The reasons for its eventual decline are unknown but there is no suggestion that there was any objection to its liturgy or theology. Other contacts between Athos and the West have been less glorious. After the Fourth Crusade the Mountain was systematically pillaged by its Latin masters. In the late Byzantine period there were various attempts at reunion with Rome which were not necessarily always opposed by the monks, even though nothing came of them. Again in the seventeenth century the Jesuits were asked to revive the idea of reunion between the Mountain and Rome, and again nothing came of it, but a Jesuit school was founded at the Protaton. Such contacts have little chance of being revived in today's climate, but the Latins have played a significant part in the history of Athos over the years.

Unlike the Latins, the Romanians have never had a monastery they
could call their own on the Holy Mountain, as Fr Constantin Coman
laments in his chapter entitled 'Moldavians, Wallachians, and Romanians
on Mount Athos'. Romanian monks are first recorded as present on the
Mountain in the fourteenth century when a significant number of them
settled in the monastery of Koutloumousiou but, although the Voyevod
Vladislav I was given the title 'owner and founder' of the monastery in recognition of the support he had provided, the monastery remained under
Greek jurisdiction. The Romanians also missed an opportunity at Esphigmenou in 1805 when it was suggested to the Metropolitan of Moldavia that
the monastery could become a 'settlement of that nation', but for reasons
that are obscure the offer was rejected. Between these dates and indeed
until the formation of the modern state of Romania in 1859 the Romanian
principalities were unstinting in their support of the Athonite monasteries
and there is scarcely a house that did not receive some form of assistance
from them, often in the form of monasteries in Romania that were dedicated to Athos. And yet the status of the Romanian monks on Athos has
remained humble and they have had to be content with the two sketes of
Lakkou and Prodromou. These are once again flourishing centres of spirituality, and there are a good many Romanians scattered among the ruling
monasteries. All together there are now about 200 Romanian monks on
the Mountain and, though they have no monastery of their own, they do
in fact form the largest ethnic minority on Athos today.

In a paper entitled "The Ark of Hellenism": Mount Athos and the
Greeks under Turkish Rule' Graham Speake picks up and develops Averil
Cameron's suggestion that after 1453 the Holy Mountain was able to represent a symbol of the continuity of Orthodox culture and of divinely
ordained religious authority. Rather than attempt a general survey, he takes
two snapshots of Athos, in the sixteenth century and in the eighteenth
century, and focuses on two pairs of parallel lives. Perhaps the clearest
indicator of the continuing prosperity of the Mountain in the sixteenth
century is the foundation in 1541 of the monastery of Stavronikita, accomplished with the assistance of Ecumenical Patriarch Jeremias I. Needing an
artist to embellish the newly built katholikon and refectory, the Patriarch
turned to Crete to commission the most celebrated iconographer of the
day, Theophanes. Athos was still the place where artists' reputations were

made and as a result of his work not only at Stavronikita but also at the Lavra Theophanes found himself setting a style that became the model for Orthodox church art for the next two centuries. Scholars too were attracted to Mount Athos at this time and it was no doubt with a view to accessing the contents of its library that the learned Michael Trivolis in 1506 became a monk of Vatopedi with the name Maximos. Ten years later Maximos was invited to Moscow to translate patristic texts into Slavonic. Drawn into the controversies that divided Muscovite society and refused permission to return to Athos, Maximos fell foul of the authorities and was charged with heresy, sorcery, and treason. After spending more than twenty years in prison he was finally released in 1548 and allowed to reside in a monastery near Moscow for his remaining years. Venerated as a holy martyr and 'Enlightener of the Russians', he was finally canonized in 1988. Further examples of Athonite outreach may be identified in the eighteenth century when the Holy Mountain was at the centre of an intellectual and spiritual revival. At the suggestion of the monks an academy of higher learning was established on a hillside overlooking Vatopedi with the brief to train leaders both for the Church and for the Orthodox world as a whole. As its director the Patriarchate appointed a scholar of international reputation, Evgenios Voulgaris, but after only six years in the post this star of the Enlightenment found that his supporters had turned against him and in 1759 he resigned. Some years later he was invited to join the court of Catherine the Great in St Petersburg where he developed a political philosophy that envisioned an enlightened Christian monarchy being re-established over the Orthodox peoples of south-eastern Europe. St Kosmas the Aetolian had studied at the academy on Athos before becoming a monk of Philotheou. Later, with the blessing of the Patriarch, he embarked on a series of missionary journeys, preaching, teaching, and founding schools the length and breadth of Greece. Dubbed the 'equal to the Apostles', he was suspected of harbouring political ambitions against the Ottoman authorities and in 1779 he was hanged. It is a tribute to the vitality of Athos that two men so completely different from each other as Voulgaris, doyen of the Enlightenment, and the arch-traditionalist Kosmas could be accommodated on the Mountain at more or less the same time. The lives of all four show that Athos has never lost its ability to attract men of outstanding ability and send them out into the world as ambassadors of its traditions.

In his chapter entitled 'The Russians on Mount Athos' Nicholas Fennell demonstrates that the Russian presence on the Holy Mountain, which has lasted for well over a thousand years, has experienced many vicissitudes, at times manifesting conflict, envy, and rivalry, at other times inspiration, mutual support, and spiritual revival. For most of that millennium their numbers rarely rose above 200 and for most of it relations with the Greek majority were harmonious. The most influential Russian Athonites have been models of piety, humility, and asceticism, notably St Antony in the eleventh century who is regarded as the father of Russian monasticism and went on to found the great monastery of the Caves in Kiev, St Paisy in the eighteenth century who was at the heart of spiritual revival both on Athos and subsequently in Moldavia and Russia, and indeed Fr Sophrony in the late twentieth century who founded the monastery of St John the Baptist in Essex. Relations became more complicated in the second half of the nineteenth century when the Russians regained control of the St Panteleimon monastery and expanded its brotherhood to almost 2,000. There is no doubt that among the Russian spiritual fathers there were holy men, who acted as a magnet for the thousands of Russians who flocked to Athos. For a time the Russians even outnumbered the Greeks on the Mountain. Moreover the Russian houses attracted great wealth from their many supporters and pilgrims. All this inevitably aroused envy and suspicion, and previously good relations with the Greeks deteriorated into competition and conflict. The situation resolved itself with the Revolution of 1917 and the consequent severing of ties between Russia and Athos. Since then numbers of Russians on the Mountain have dwindled to earlier levels and relations have improved, but memories are long and there is plenty of evidence to show that the Greek authorities have taken every opportunity to reduce the flow of Russian monks to the St Panteleimon monastery to a trickle.

In a concluding chapter, 'The Holy Mountain: Universality and Uniqueness', Kallistos Ware attempts to answer the question what makes Athos, if not unique, then certainly exceptional and distinctive. He makes no claim to be exhaustive in offering a fourfold answer. First he discusses the physical reality of the Mountain itself and its intrinsic sacredness. Many have commented on the astonishing natural beauty of Athos, and since beauty transforms the world into a sacrament of the divine presence, the natural beauty of Athos possesses more than a purely aesthetic importance. But there are many such places of natural beauty in the world: what gives Athos its special sanctity? A second distinctive feature is its universality. From its very beginnings as a monastic settlement until the present day Athos has always been a spiritual centre for all Orthodox. It is not unique in this respect either, since there has been an international element in Christian monasticism from its beginnings in fourth-century Egypt; but the pan-Orthodoxy of the Mountain, assisted by its membership of a supranational Orthodox commonwealth persisting long after the fall of the Byzantine empire, has been proudly proclaimed throughout its history. Furthermore, in the third place, Athos can claim to be a microcosm of the Christian East, not just because of its pan-Orthodoxy, but also because it embraces, as it has always embraced, all three forms of monastic life that are found there, namely the cenobitic, the eremitic, and the 'middle way' or semi-eremitic. Thus there are monks that choose to live a common life in the so-called 'ruling' monasteries, all of which are now coenobia; there are monks that live as solitaries, mostly in the desert at the southern tip of the peninsula; and there are monks that live in small cells housing between two and six men either in independent locations or grouped in the idiorrhythmic sketes. Each serves the world in the best way known to him, but above all by prayer. Finally Athos enjoys a uniquely privileged position in being under the special protection of the Mother of God. It is her garden and she is the patron of its creative silence, its stillness, its *hesychia*. Mary is the model for all hesychasts and her creative stillness is one of the most precious qualities of the Mountain. In conclusion Metropolitan Kallistos considers the extent to which these distinctive features of Athos are secure and he is dismayed to find all but the third under some sort of threat. Those of us who value the Holy Mountain must be vigilant in its defence, though we do well to avoid unsolicited interference and to bear in mind the Mountain is not without its own powers of endurance.

* * * * *

The following table presents the predominant nationalities (and significant minorities) of the ruling monasteries (including sketes and other dependencies) at different points in time.

		1489*	1725/44*	1903†	2010
1	Great Lavra	Greek	Greek	Greek	Greek
2	Vatopedi	Greek	Greek	Russ/Greek	Greek
3	Iviron	Georgian	Greek	Greek	Greek
4	Hilandar	Serbian	Serbian	Russ/Bulg	Serbian
5	Dionysiou	Serbian	Greek	Greek	Greek
6	Koutloumousiou	Moldavian	Greek	Greek	Greek
7	Pantokrator	Greek	Greek	Russ/Greek	Greek
8	Xeropotamou	Greek	Greek	Greek	Greek
9	Zographou	Wallachian	Bulgarian	Bulgarian	Bulgarian
10	Docheiariou	Serbian	Greek	Greek	Greek
11	Karakalou	Greek	Greek	Greek	Greek
12	Philotheou	Albanian	Greek	Greek/Russ	Greek
13	Simonopetra	Bulgarian	Greek	Greek	Greek
14	St Paul's	Serbian	Serbian	Greek/Rom	Greek
15	Stavronikita	[Greek]	Greek	Russian	Greek
16	Xenophontos	Greek	Serb/Greek	Greek	Greek
17	Grigoriou	Serbian	Bulg/Greek	Greek	Greek
18	Esphigmenou	Greek	Greek	Greek	Greek
19	St Panteleimon	Russian	Russian	Russian	Russian
20	Konstamonitou	Greek	Russian	Greek	Greek

* according to the Russian monk Isaiah

** according to the Russian pilgrim Vasily Barsky

† according to the Greek historian Gerasimos Smyrnakis

AVERIL CAMERON

Mount Athos and the Byzantine World

If we try to position the monasteries of Mount Athos and their influence in the context of the Byzantine world, our first problem is to define what that world actually consisted of. It is notoriously difficult to grasp the geographical limits of Byzantium at any one period – Byzantium was an empire, or perhaps we should rather say a state (for at some periods in its existence it did not in the strict sense exercise imperial rule over foreign populations), which itself increased and decreased dramatically in extent over time. This was so even if we leave out of account the powerful influence it exerted on neighbouring states (which of course themselves also expanded and contracted). Thus anyone who looks at a handbook or atlas of Byzantium will find a whole series of maps representing the extent of Byzantine rule at various periods with lines of various sorts – heavy, dotted, with shading, etc. – to mark changing boundaries and borders.[1]

In fact of course ancient and medieval states generally did not have clear borders or ethnicities, any more than their citizens had passports. As one of my colleagues used to say, over its long history the Byzantine empire was like a concertina – it frequently changed its shape as a result of warfare, conquest, and the rise of new states around it, and its borders went in and out almost on a regular basis.[2] Byzantium in the tenth century, when the first of the great Athos foundations took shape and the empire

---

1   See the very useful maps for different historical periods in John F. Haldon, *The Palgrave Atlas of Byzantine History* (Basingstoke, 2005).
2   For Byzantium's changing size and the validity of its claims to be an empire see John F. Haldon, 'The Byzantine Empire', in Ian Morris and Walter Scheidel (eds), *The Dynamics of Ancient Empires. State Power from Assyria to Byzantium* (Oxford, 2009), pp. 205–54.

of Constantine VII Porphyrogennetos seemed both large and impressive, was very different from Byzantium in the fourteenth, when Mount Athos's prestige in the extended Byzantine world was extremely high but the Palaiologan state based on Constantinople itself was tiny and its world fragmented. This change is something of a paradox, and I will explore it further in what follows.

If the Byzantine empire itself rose and fell, and therefore changed its territorial extent and its actual power, what of the 'world' beyond its borders? The monastic world of Mount Athos was by no means all Greek, even before the fall of Constantinople, and its relations with the Byzantine empire were merely one part, even if the most significant part in the eyes of many, of a complicated network of influence and interests. One aspect of my topic is the question of how the peoples and states beyond the borders of Byzantium themselves perceived the Holy Mountain, and how and why they associated themselves with it; the other is the nature of their involvement with Byzantium through the medium of the monastic communities of Mount Athos, and what this amounts to in relation to Byzantine authority and political and religious influence. Why and how was Mount Athos so important for Byzantium itself? Was this influence purely religious, a matter of Orthodoxy, or did it really also mean, in Dimitri Obolensky's famous formulation, that Mount Athos was the key to something that can properly be called a Byzantine 'commonwealth'?[3]

Let us start with Byzantium in the tenth century, the century not only of St Athanasios the Athonite and the Great Lavra, but also, in an amazing rush, of Iviron, Xeropotamou, Xenophontos, Esphigmenou, the original St Panteleimon, Hilandar, Vatopedi, and perhaps also Zographou. By the beginning of the next century the number of Athonite houses was very large, and the peninsula welcomed new foundations, whatever their background. In the tenth century, in the age of the Emperor Constantine VII Porphyrogennetos, Byzantium recovered territory in the east which had

---

3   Dimitri Obolensky, *The Byzantine Commonwealth. Eastern Europe 500 to 1453* (London, 1971); see recently the important chapter by Jonathan Shepard, 'The Byzantine Commonwealth, 1000–1550', in M. Angold (ed.), *Cambridge History of Christianity*, vol. 5 (Cambridge, 2006), pp. 3–52, in which Athos is discussed in some detail (and see map 2, p. 13), and further below.

been lost since the Arab invasions of the seventh century; that was how the great Mandylion, or Image of Edessa, was brought to Constantinople in 944 from its home in the east after three centuries under Islamic rule, to be greeted with full imperial pomp and veneration. The territorial gains and restoration of Byzantine influence also extended to Greece, Thrace, and Italy, a development which was to be particularly important for the later prosperity of the great monasteries on Mount Athos.

By the next century, after the conquests of Basil II (958–1025), the empire was at its greatest size. But this was still a period of fluidity or early state-formation for its neighbours, including the states such as Serbia which were to be prominent in the later history of Mount Athos. Constantine Porphyrogennetos's treatise *On the Administration of the Empire* laid down guidance for dealing with some of these emerging peoples, with diplomacy as the key, but the detailed information the text seems to contain about their location and development is very variable in its reliability for a historian today.[4] Yet this was the great period for Byzantine court life and the diplomatic system, and if there was the idea of a commonwealth we can say that this period was when it found first expression, when Byzantium had recovered from the struggles of iconoclasm, when it began to experience military success, and when the life of the court was rich, well regulated, and immensely impressive to foreigners.[5] According to Garth Fowden, Justinian's sense of the interconnection of politics and mission in the sixth century in the Caucasus and round the eastern arc of the Mediterranean all the way to Nubia had constituted a 'first Byzantine commonwealth'.[6] But since then the Arab conquests had intervened and Byzantium's influence had been cut off; even Constantinople was not safe in the face of Arab sieges of the city itself in the seventh and eighth centuries. But now in the tenth century confidence had returned, and outsiders knew it.

---

4   Constantine Porphyrogenitus, *De Administrando Imperio*, ed. and trans. G. Moravscik and R. J. H. Jenkins, rev. edn. (Washington, DC, 1967, repr. 2009).

5   For this important side of Byzantine life see the essays in Henry Maguire (ed.), *Byzantine Court Culture from 829 to 1204* (Washington, DC, 1997).

6   Garth Fowden, *Empire to Commonwealth: Consequences of Monotheism in Late Antiquity* (Cambridge, 1993), p. 8.

To be sure, the Holy Mountain was not the only monastic centre. Alongside the monasteries on Mount Athos there were also other holy mountains and centres of monasticism – in Asia Minor Mount Galesion near Ephesus, Mount Latros near ancient Miletus, Mount Auxentios near Chalcedon, and Bithynian Olympos – as well as many individual major monasteries, which often developed around an original holy man, as the monastery of Hosios Loukas did around St Luke of Stiris. But mountains offered a symbolic nearness to God, as well as the advantage of inaccessibility. Paradoxically, and for these very reasons, they also attracted large numbers of monks. From the point of view of inaccessibility the Athos peninsula could hardly be bettered, as St Athanasios explained in his *typikon* for the Great Lavra:

> The mountain resembles a peninsula which extends towards the sea in the shape of a cross. The islands in the sea, Lemnos, Imbros, Thasos, and the rest, are a great distance away. Because of this, when winter comes, a ship is unable to sail from the mountain to the mainland to procure necessary provisions or to sail back from there to the mountain. It cannot find any sort of anchorage because the seashore on both sides provides no shelter. On the other hand, there is absolutely no way for a person to transport his own provisions by dry land, partly because the road is so long, and partly because the mountain is practically impassable for pack animals.[7]

Perhaps this is one of the main reasons why the monastic houses on Mount Athos grew and developed as they did. Not only were the monks protected from the influences of the outside world; the peninsula itself was self-contained and comparatively cushioned from the political and military incursions suffered elsewhere. This was certainly the case in the last phase of the Byzantine empire when Constantinople itself was under constant pressure from the Ottomans, and had even become, in the words of one scholar, 'an island in the middle of Ottoman territories'.[8]

7   Trans. George Dennis, in John Thomas and Angela Constantinides Hero (eds), *Byzantine Monastic Foundation Documents: A Complete Translation of the Surviving Founders' Typika and Testaments*, 5 vols (Washington, DC, 2000), vol. 1, p. 253.

8   Elizabeth A. Zachariadou, 'The Great Church in Captivity 1453–1586', in Angold (ed.), *Cambridge History of Christianity*, vol. 5, pp. 169–86, p. 169.

The shock of the Fourth Crusade in 1204, with the violent sack of Constantinople, led to the establishment of Latin rule in the capital and the fragmentation of the Byzantine ruling elite. Nevertheless the 'empire' set up at Nicaea in Asia Minor regarded itself as the natural successor state, and from here Michael VIII Palaiologos took advantage of Latin weakness to return to Constantinople in 1261 and reinstall Byzantine rule. But other Byzantine enclaves also came into existence – Epiros, Trebizond, Mistra. Thessaloniki was the scene of an early challenge to the emperor at Nicaea, and relations between these lordships or princedoms were complex, not to mention their exposure to external pressures from elsewhere – from Italians, from Anjou, from the Catalans, and from the Serbs, to name only a few. Despite some attempts to unite the various separate Byzantine enclaves, Epiros and Thessaly both fell to Stefan Dušan in the mid-fourteenth century, who styled himself 'emperor of Romania', and Mount Athos itself came for a time under Serb authority, remaining so for sixteen years after Stefan Dušan died in 1355.

In this confusing and fragmented situation, the Holy Mountain could symbolize stability and seemed to embody not only the cause of Orthodoxy, but also the essence of Byzantium. However it was not so clear what that meant in political or practical terms, when the reach of Palaiologan Constantinople was so limited in comparison with its earlier great days, and when it now had so many rivals for power. From the perspective of the Holy Mountain, the Palaiologan emperors must also have seemed to be locked into their desperate attempts to gain support from the west at the cost of union with the papacy. Michael VIII followed his perhaps unexpected restoration of Byzantine rule to Constantinople almost at once with an attempt to achieve union, culminating in the Union of Lyons in 1274, which divided both the Church and the lay elite down the middle. Serb, Tatar, and Turkish incursions, civil war, and plague were further negative factors for Byzantium in the fourteenth and early fifteenth centuries. But the divisions over union were to undermine the emperor's relation with the Church, from which the patriarch was to gain, and this too was a factor in the longer-term fortunes of the Holy Mountain.

One of the amazing aspects of this late period in Byzantium's history is the flowering in this small circle of Palaiologan art and intellectual culture, with its complex connections with Italian intellectual trends and its vigorous internal disputes and literary production.[9] But in other respects, after a period when the Byzantines had been driven from their own city, Constantinople and its court could hardly recapture the reputation it had had during the tenth century and before 1204, when it had undoubtedly been the greatest and most splendid city in the known world and a source of admiration and envy. Palaiologan Constantinople still attracted admiring travellers, like the English and Russian pilgrims who marvelled at its religious processions and its great icon of the Hodegetria. But Thessaloniki was a rival city, and both cities were riven by political, and especially religious, conflict. This was a very different Byzantine world from the empire in which St Athanasios had established the Great Lavra.

The changed world of late Byzantium and its increased number of players brought economic opportunities to the Holy Mountain. The aristocracy of late Byzantium, especially after the middle of the fourteenth century, engaged in trade as well as holding land, and had close and complex economic relationships with Mount Athos.[10] Thus great Athonite monasteries also owned land, with villages and *paroikoi* (dependent peasants), and even ships; they had *metochia* and employed agents and intermediaries to conduct their trade. Their records, somewhat paradoxically, are

9   I. Sevcenko, 'Palaiologan Learning', in Cyril Mango (ed.), *The Oxford History of Byzantium* (Oxford, 2002), pp. 284–93, p. 285, counts about 150 literati, spread over the various Byzantine centres of the period; this does not sound very many, but such examples as the very learned emperor Manuel II (1391–1425) or the members of the entourage of John V at the Council of Ferrara-Florence, which included Gemistos Plethon, Isidore of Kiev, and Bessarion, are enough to demonstrate the depth and vigour of their intellectual activity. The Byzantine encounter with western scholasticism was part of the background to the hesychast controversy of the fourteenth century and the intense debates in late Byzantium about the respective merits of Plato and Aristotle which went side by side with the debates about union: George Karamanolis, 'Plethon and Scholarios on Aristotle', in K. Ierodiakonou (ed.), *Byzantine Philosophy and its Ancient Sources* (Oxford, 2002), pp. 253–82.

10   For a very good recent survey of the bibliography on this topic see Dionysios Stathakopoulos, 'The Dialectics of Expansion and Retraction: Recent Scholarship on the Palaiologan Aristocracy', *Byzantine and Modern Greek Studies*, 33.1 (2009), 92–101.

our best evidence for the economic life of late Byzantium, so little having survived to show the economic organization of the secular state. Some of their lands and villages had suffered or even been abandoned during the period of Latin rule; Iviron, for example, set about trying to restore them, while Koutloumousiou was one monastery which gained by the transfer of land from elsewhere.[11] Turkish incursions were a serious threat in the early fourteenth century, which led to Gregory Palamas leaving the Holy Mountain, but Mount Athos adopted a realistic policy towards the Ottomans which helped it to survive and even prosper, while in turn it seems that the Ottomans extended some protection to the Holy Mountain.[12] The number of donations increased for a range of reasons, partly indeed because Athos was felt to be more secure, and were also encouraged by the scheme whereby donors gained annuities (*adelphata*) in return. In the early fifteenth century the Emperor John VII handed over land to several of the Athos monasteries, which were evidently regarded as being able to work it and make it productive.[13] Nikolas Oikonomides points out that a number of major monasteries were in fact founded or renovated in the fourteenth and early fifteenth centuries, all of which are among the governing monasteries on Mount Athos today.[14]

11   For the importance of the Athonite archives for the history of this period see the excellent survey of Byzantine monastic life by Alice-Mary Talbot, 'A Monastic World', in John F. Haldon (ed.), *A Social History of Byzantium* (Oxford, 2009), pp. 256–78, pp. 269–73, with references; for the Macedonian period see E. McGeer, *Land Legislation of the Macedonian Emperors* (Toronto, 2000). Iviron and Koutloumousiou: Angeliki E. Laiou, 'Agrarian History, Thirteenth to Fifteenth Centuries', in Angeliki E. Laiou (ed.), *Economic History of Byzantium: From the Seventh through the Fifteenth Century,* 3 vols (Washington, DC, 2002), vol. 1, pp. 311–75, p. 313.

12   N. Oikonomides, 'Patronage in Palaiologan Mount Athos', in Anthony Bryer and Mary Cunningham (eds), *Mount Athos and Byzantine Monasticism* (Aldershot, 1996), pp. 99–111, p. 99; see also Elizabeth A. Zachariadou, '"A Safe and Holy Mountain": Early Ottoman Athos', ibid., pp. 127–32, eadem, 'Mount Athos and the Ottomans, c. 1350–1550', in Angold (ed.), *Cambridge History of Christianity,* vol. 5, pp. 154–68, especially pp. 156–8.

13   Laiou, art. cit., p. 315.

14   Oikonomides, art. cit., p. 100.

Sometimes the revenues of villages were granted to monasteries, and cereals, fruit trees, and timber were all products well attested in Macedonia. The landlord would receive tax directly from the peasants, as well as from the common land cultivated with peasant labour, and could also rent out further land.[15] The documents sometimes give firm numbers. Thus, to draw on the excellent survey by Angeliki Laiou, the annual fiscal revenues of the monastery of Iviron in the year 1320 are estimated at 1,250 gold coins, that of Esphigmenou at 500 gold coins, and that of Lavra, the largest and richest Athos monastery, at 4,000 gold coins.[16] In managing their estates, which might also include vineyards, the monasteries were in competition with the great landowning families such as the Kantakouzenoi. They were also exposed to the same problems, and in some instances, such as for the lands on Lemnos belonging to Lavra, Iviron, Pantokrator, Dionysiou, and others, depopulation in the early fifteenth century had led to a shortage of *paroikoi* and to abandoned villages,[17] which the monastery might try to deal with by distributing land direct to the *paroikoi*. Products also had to be marketed, and the Athos monasteries were helped by imperial favours: in 1408 Emperor Manuel II allowed special conditions to the monks in which to market their products. They were relieved of the obligation to provide wheat for the biscuit of the seamen, thus retaining more of their surplus than did other landlords. They were relieved of the payment of taxes on flocks, which means that the products of animal husbandry came cheaper to them than to others. They did not have to pay tax on their wine sold in taverns. They were allowed to sell their wine in Thessaloniki freely, overriding the usual privileges of the governor of the city.[18]

These few examples show not only the importance of their landhold-ings and economic activities to the Athos monasteries themselves, but also the fact that they were regarded by the state as a key element in the economy of Byzantium and its efforts to improve prosperity. This is one

15   Laiou, art. cit., p. 331.
16   Ibid., p. 349.
17   Ibid., p. 366.
18   Ibid., p. 369.

aspect, and an important one, of the wider alliance of the Byzantine state, as well as of individual members of the Palaiologan upper class, with the monasteries of Athos.

The connection of Byzantine emperors with the Holy Mountain is well known. On the most obvious level, emperors founded or regulated monasteries on Mount Athos, beginning with the Great Lavra, and the foundation documents of several still survive. Imperial chrysobulls, signed in the imperial hand, organized or regulated the lives of the monks. Other documents assigned or renewed privileges in relation to taxes and landholding. Rosemary Morris has provided a useful table of instances of imperial privileges to monasteries in the tenth to early twelfth centuries,[19] from which it is interesting to see how widely spread these instances were in the tenth century and how much Athos later comes to dominate. But the question *why* the emperors so often gave the monasteries of Mount Athos their patronage, and what this meant in practice, is less often asked. One rather prosaic reason for imperial monastic foundations is provided by the prestige they offered and the pressure of past custom; emperors had for centuries, indeed since the early days of the empire, founded monastic and other religious institutions and this continued in the case of Mount Athos. It was equally to be expected that foreign rulers would follow suit: modelling their clothes, their insignia, and their style of rule on that of Byzantium, the best model they could find, they also followed Byzantine precedent in founding and endowing monasteries. Perhaps the best examples here are the Serbian rulers, but as the *typikon* of Dionysiou, supported by Alexios III of Trebizond in 1374, stated, '*All* emperors, kings or rulers of some fame have built monasteries on Mount Athos for their eternal memory'.[20] Stefan Dušan also supported the Rus monastery of St Panteleimon and others, though he received a rebuff when told that Athonite prayers would go first and foremost to the 'emperor of the Romans' in Constantinople.[21]

---

19   Rosemary Morris, *Monks and Laymen in Byzantium, 843–1118* (Cambridge, 1995), Appendix.
20   Oikonomides, 'Patronage in Palaiologan Mount Athos', p. 101.
21   See Shepard, 'The Byzantine Commonwealth, 1000–1550', p. 20.

Besides the wish for prayers and personal spiritual gain, more practical calculations also entered in, such as the recognition that the great houses could play a useful role in politics, diplomacy, and economic life. Whatever the motives, and they were certainly multiple, Athonite monasteries benefited greatly at all periods from imperial favours. Iviron, for example, increased its landholding on a major scale as a result of a chrysobull of Basil II;[22] it acquired yet more later in the eleventh century, even if only at the expense of a tight imperial control. As Alan Harvey has argued, emperors could also bestow tax privileges and protection, and this could be worth as much as a direct grant. The Great Lavra, for example, consistently benefited in this way through the eleventh century, as its chrysobulls show.[23]

Thus the monasteries did not stay the same over time, and the lucky ones were those with imperial or royal patronage. New ones were founded, and then too it helped to enlist imperial support. But the process might not be so high-minded: for instance, an abandoned monastery could be bought and refounded to suit the purchaser. Fundraising by impoverished monasteries could then as now entail accepting the donor's wishes.[24] The donor was encouraged in a very clear-sighted and thoroughly recognizable manner to act like many other rulers before him, Serbs, Bulgarians, Russians, and Georgians, and obtain the right to be commemorated and honoured.[25] Everyone knew what was expected. Nikolas Oikonomides succinctly notes three reasons for such patronage in the fourteenth century: prestige; competition between states – a new factor in this period – and the desire for material security, the monasteries providing a good insurance policy.[26] Led as they were by the example of the Byzantine emperors themselves, Athonite patrons formed an exclusive club, and the donors,

22 Alan Harvey, 'The Monastic Economy and Imperial Patronage from the Tenth to the Twelfth Century', in Bryer and Cunningham (eds), *Mount Athos and Byzantine Monasticism*, pp. 91–7, p. 91.
23 Ibid., pp. 96 f.
24 Oikonomides, 'Patronage in Palaiologan Mount Athos', p. 101.
25 Ibid., p. 102.
26 Ibid.

as he notes, 'belonged to the top ranks of society'.[27] The monks for their part looked in more than one direction, and by the fourteenth century even their acceptance of the ultimate authority of Constantinople might lead them either in the direction of emphasizing the Patriarchate or of appealing to the emperor.

As we have seen, the status of Mount Athos as a kind of symbol of Byzantium and of Orthodoxy in the minds of Byzantium's satellite and neighbouring powers was at its height in the fourteenth and fifteenth centuries when the Byzantine state itself was fragmented and weak. It also naturally gained in prestige and importance through the loss of the great monastic centres of Asia Minor to the Turks, and it proved a magnet for Byzantium's Balkan neighbours. Here we find ourselves returning to Dimitri Obolensky's well-known conception of a Byzantine 'commonwealth', with Athos playing a key role in the way this commonwealth worked. Recently Jonathan Shepard has returned to this in several papers and book chapters, most fully in his contribution to the volume on *Eastern Christianity* in the Cambridge History of Christianity. In a book which is dedicated to the memory of Steven Runciman, Dimitri Obolensky, and Sergei Hackel, it is hardly surprising that he, or possibly his editor, Michael Angold, even chose to call the chapter 'The Byzantine Commonwealth, 1000–1550'.[28] The vision inherent in Obolensky's book saw Byzantium as being at the centre of a group of states and peoples who in their different ways looked to it as their natural leader or senior partner; the medium and conduit of this relationship was Orthodoxy and the role played by Mount Athos was at its heart.

This is an idea that has had an extraordinarily powerful influence and appeal. Paschalis Kitromilides, for example, has gone on to explore how it might still apply in later periods as the basis of an 'Orthodox culture' in the Balkans; one of his papers, dealing with Greco-Russian connections in the Ottoman period, makes the connection explicit by using the title

---

27 Ibid., p. 111.
28 See Shepard, 'The Byzantine Commonwealth, 1000–1550' (n. 3).

'From Orthodox Commonwealth to National Communities.'[29] To quote from the concluding paragraph of this paper: 'The last figure to give expression to the idea of the Orthodox Commonwealth, Joachim III, Patriarch of Constantinople, died in the year of the outbreak of the Balkan wars.' As Kitromilides argues, the end of the nineteenth century, with its rising national states, 'seemed to symbolize the end or the forgetting of a thousand years of shared past for the peoples of East and South-East Europe'.

The shared past he had in mind was the Orthodox world of Obolensky's Byzantine commonwealth. It is a matter for reflection that now we have seen a resurgence of Orthodoxy in states where the Church was at best barely tolerated or at worst persecuted or forbidden, while at the same time we have also seen a resurgence of a different kind of nationalism. But the notion of an earlier Orthodox culture in which Athos played a central and benign role derives directly from the powerful image of a Byzantine commonwealth, which in Obolensky's original book of that title ended in 1453, but which in further essays, including his equally classic Raleigh Lecture for the British Academy on 'Italy, Mount Athos and Muscovy: The Three Worlds of Maximos the Greek', given in 1981, he himself carried forward into the Ottoman and especially the Russian worlds.

It is also a conception which has had its critics. 'Commonwealth' is a British idea, after all;[30] perhaps the concept lays too much stress on whether the spread of Orthodoxy really was a deliberate policy of the Byzantine state itself; 'commonwealth' being a political term, how can it be applied in a religious context? Jonathan Shepard has restated it in our case as a 'force field', with Byzantium as the centre of concentric circles of influence, and with 'horizontal' as well as hierarchical strands of connection.[31] In some ways this influence resembles what is nowadays sometimes called 'soft

---

29   Paschalis M. Kitromilides, *An Orthodox Commonwealth. Symbolic Legacies and Cultural Encounters in Southeastern Europe* (Aldershot, 2007), ch. 6, p. 18. The subtitle of the paper is 'Greek-Russian Intellectual and Ecclesiastical Ties in the Ottoman Era'.

30   Evelyne Patlagean, *Un Moyen Âge grec. Byzance IXe–XVe siècle* (Paris, 2007), p. 387; see also C. Raffensperger, 'Revisiting the Idea of the Byzantine Commonwealth', *Byzantinische Forschungen*, 28 (2004), 159–74.

31   Shepard, 'The Byzantine Commonwealth, 1000–1550', p. 46.

power'. Shepard's formulation of the reason for this influence is that the prestige and influence of Byzantium in the wider world derives from 'its credible show of majesty and piety'. That is, the way that Byzantium itself was perceived by the wider group of neighbouring peoples was deeply connected both with the concept of the emperor and court and with its Orthodox religion.

This is not to suggest that late Byzantium exercised a straightforward political or formal connection with the Orthodox states around it. Rather, while the Byzantine state may well have hoped for such influence, the relationship came from its neighbours themselves, for whom Byzantium, symbolized by the imperial city of Constantinople, embodied the prestige of centuries of history. So the conversion of Serbian or Rus leaders might be seen as an outward sign of protection and advantage, like the conversion of Caucasian and other rulers centuries before. In the eyes of western visitors before 1204 Byzantium was a source of envy and amazement for its luxury, its exotic ways, and its continuous imperial tradition. Though it was much reduced in the fourteenth century, travellers from England and Russia still marvelled at it, and its religious processions were translated to other centres including Muscovy. Athos played an important part in the process of cultural transfer from Byzantium to newer states. The process was encouraged by the amount of travel and other contacts back and forth between the monasteries and the outside world. It is hardly surprising if other rulers found their models for imitation here, or wanted to associate themselves with this glittering symbol of imperial and court life and of the Orthodox faith. But the transfer was also between monks and monastic houses themselves, resulting in spiritual and personal contacts between Athos and the wider geographical area which included Bulgaria and Rus, and which expressed itself in the production and copying of Slavonic manuscripts and the translation of Greek texts, as well as through the use of Athonite monks to undertake missions directed by the Patriarchate.[32] Just in the same way provincial elites in the Roman empire had adopted Roman dress, Roman architecture, and Roman culture, or in our own day people

---

32   Shepard, 'The Byzantine Commonwealth, 1000–1550', pp. 36–41.

the emperor, but when there was no longer an emperor in Constantinople it was the ecumenical patriarch who still represented that shared consciousness, or, in the words of Kitromilides, who 'donned the ecumenical mantle of the Christian empire'. In these circumstances, as Constantinople itself became weaker and eventually fell, Athos was a gainer, as a connected but alternative source and symbol of divinely ordained religious authority. Again the relationship with the Byzantine centre was complex, and hard to disentangle; it was indeed interconnected.

Four of the fourteenth-century patriarchs of Constantinople had themselves spent time on the Holy Mountain. Athonite monks were also involved in political and doctrinal conflicts. The great St Gregory Palamas was a monk on the Holy Mountain before and during the controversy about hesychasm, and against the background of the civil war which brought John VI Kantakouzenos to victory in 1347 and his own appointment as archbishop of Thessaloniki in the same year. Although the excommunication laid on him earlier was lifted, it took another synod in 1351 to settle the matter finally. Thessaloniki, the city so near to Mount Athos, was the victim of civil conflict in the same period, and Palamas himself had been imprisoned in Constantinople. But the final vindication of his theology immensely increased the prestige not only of himself but also of Mount Athos. This was another factor that released the Holy Mountain to stay an Orthodox powerhouse when the emperors in Constantinople were no more. In fact the hesychast 'movement',[38] which involved many of the Athonite monks, and which sometimes involved opposition to the emperors in Byzantium, was itself a contributor to the sense of universal Orthodox consciousness over and above attachment to Byzantium as a political entity. Mount Athos was already international, and when monks travelled, as they often did, their strong attachments of master and disciple carried this consciousness beyond geographical or political boundaries.

In the crucial fourteenth and early fifteenth centuries, therefore, the Holy Mountain was able to position itself in order to make the transition

---

38   See Shepard, art. cit., p. 39; Dirk Krausmüller, 'The Rise of Hesychasm', in Angold (ed.), *Cambridge History of Christianity*, vol. 5, pp. 101–26.

into the world after Byzantium; its history in that difficult period is one of resilience. As the Patriarchate found itself excluded from the Great Church and gradually confined to an enclave within the captured city, the Athonite monasteries themselves could now be a symbol of the continuity of Orthodox culture. The transnational community of Orthodoxy would be defined by common religion and common religious consciousness, a way that had already been well prepared in the Byzantine period by the internationalism of Mount Athos itself.

Bibliography

Constantine Porphyrogenitus, *De Administrando Imperio*, ed. and trans. G. Moravscik and R. J. H. Jenkins, rev. edn. (Washington, DC, 1967, repr. 2009).

Fowden, Garth, *Empire to Commonwealth: Consequences of Monotheism in Late Antiquity* (Cambridge, 1993).

Haldon, John F., *The Palgrave Atlas of Byzantine History* (Basingstoke, 2005).

——, 'The Byzantine Empire', in Ian Morris and Walter Scheidel (eds), *The Dynamics of Ancient Empires. State Power from Assyria to Byzantium* (Oxford, 2009), pp. 205–54.

Harvey, Alan, 'The Monastic Economy and Imperial Patronage from the Tenth to the Twelfth Century', in Anthony Bryer and Mary Cunningham (eds), *Mount Athos and Byzantine Monasticism* (Aldershot, 1996), pp. 91–7.

Karamanolis, George, 'Plethon and Scholarios on Aristotle', in K. Ierodiakonou (ed.) *Byzantine Philosophy and its Ancient Sources* (Oxford, 2002), pp. 253–82.

Kitromilides, Paschalis M., *An Orthodox Commonwealth. Symbolic Legacies and Cultural Encounters in Southeastern Europe* (Aldershot, 2007).

Krausmüller, Dirk, 'The Rise of Hesychasm', in Angold (ed.), *Cambridge History of Christianity*, vol. 5 (Cambridge, 2006), pp. 101–26.

Laiou, Angeliki E., 'Agrarian History, Thirteenth to Fifteenth Centuries', in Angeliki E. Laiou (ed.), *Economic History of Byzantium: From the Seventh through the Fifteenth Century,* 3 vols (Washington, DC, 2002), vol. 1, pp. 311–75.

McGeer, E., *Land Legislation of the Macedonian Emperors* (Toronto, 2000).

Maguire, Henry (ed.), *Byzantine Court Culture from 829 to 1204* (Washington, DC, 1997).

Morris, Rosemary, *Monks and Laymen in Byzantium, 843–1118* (Cambridge, 1995).

Nye, Joseph S., *Soft Power. The Means to Success in World Politics* (New York, 2004).

Obolensky, Dimitri, *The Byzantine Commonwealth. Eastern Europe 500 to 1453* (London, 1971).

Oikonomides, N., 'Patronage in Palaiologan Mount Athos', in Bryer and Cunningham (eds), *Mount Athos and Byzantine Monasticism*, pp. 99–111.

Patlagean, Evelyne, *Un Moyen Âge grec. Byzance IXe–XVe siècle* (Paris, 2007).

Raffensperger, C., 'Revisiting the Idea of the Byzantine Commonwealth', *Byzantinische Forschungen*, 28 (2004), 159–74.

Sevcenko, I., 'Palaiologan Learning', in Cyril Mango (ed.), *The Oxford History of Byzantium* (Oxford, 2002), pp. 284–93.

Shepard, Jonathan, 'The Byzantine Commonwealth, 1000–1550', in Angold (ed.), *Cambridge History of Christianity*, vol. 5, pp. 3–52.

Stathakopoulos, Dionysios, 'The Dialectics of Expansion and Retraction: Recent Scholarship on the Palaiologan Aristocracy', *Byzantine and Modern Greek Studies*, 33.1 (2009), 92–101.

Talbot, Alice-Mary, 'A Monastic World', in John F. Haldon (ed.), *A Social History of Byzantium* (Oxford, 2009), pp. 256–78.

Thomas, John and Hero, Angela Constantinides (eds), *Byzantine Monastic Foundation Documents: A Complete Translation of the Surviving Founders' Typika and Testaments*, 5 vols (Washington, DC, 2000).

Zachariadou, Elizabeth A., 'The Great Church in Captivity 1453–1586', in Angold (ed.), *Cambridge History of Christianity*, vol. 5, pp. 169–86.

——, 'Mount Athos and the Ottomans, c. 1350–1550', in Angold (ed.), *Cambridge History of Christianity*, vol. 5, pp. 154–68.

——, '"A Safe and Holy Mountain": Early Ottoman Athos', in Bryer and Cunningham (eds), *Mount Athos and Byzantine Monasticism*, pp. 127–32.

TAMARA GRDZELIDZE

The Georgians on Mount Athos

The Myth of Iviron

The period when the presence of Georgians had an influence on the Holy Mountain is a comparatively limited one. From as early as the second half of the twelfth century there were two communities in Iviron: Georgian and Greek. The Greeks worshipped in the church of St John the Baptist in Greek, the Georgians celebrated the Liturgy in the main church or katholikon. Both communities participated in the election of an hegoumenos (abbot), and by the mid-thirteenth century we already find the first Greek hegoumenos signing acts on behalf of the whole monastery.[1] It was in 1357 that the Georgians officially lost their monastery after Patriarch Kallistos I of Constantinople signed a document saying that Iviron was no longer in their possession. Nevertheless Georgian monks continued to be present in the Greek-run monastery until the nineteenth century when a group of Georgian monks was expelled from the monastery. The last Georgian monk in Iviron died in the early 1950s.

In the mid-1970s a small Georgian delegation visited the Holy Mountain and, although they were unsuccessful in their attempts to film Iviron, they were able to make microfilms of the Georgian manuscripts in the library. Today there are a few Georgians scattered across the Holy Mountain, for example at the monastery of Xeropotamou, where there are possibly three monks, and Hilandar, where a novice was registered a few years ago, as well

---

1   Helen Metreveli, *Philological-Historical Research*, vol.1 (Tbilisi, 2008), pp. 69–70.

as in Vatopedi and Zographou. Several Georgians have also been hired as workers, for example at the monastery of Dionysiou not far from the cell of Hilarion the Georgian.[2] This we know through visitors' accounts.

Today Iviron is in every sense a Greek monastery. Its Georgian origin is not always mentioned when a guided tour is given. On the other hand, the present inhabitants have expressed disquiet at the regular stream of visitors from Georgia who may show up unexpectedly and create an unwelcome disturbance over their special connection with Iviron. It is difficult to blame the modern Georgians for adopting such an attitude, even though it is of no relevance in practical terms. After all, Iviron became one of the most precious symbols of Georgia's Church and culture as well as playing a critical role in the political life of the Georgian people during a significant period of their history. The story of Iviron, as it is known and told by the Georgians today, may seem shrouded in myth. However, when it is demythologized by means of facts and documents, full credit must be given to the monastery as a remarkably powerful symbol for a nation as small as the Georgians.

Nationalism in a country like Georgia is an undesirable but inevitable phenomenon. For centuries the Georgians have struggled for survival as a nation and a state, suffering under the yoke of colonialism and totalitarianism, and they have become extremely defensive as a result. For the Georgians, any reading of their history has become a ritual of recalling their past glory, not because they have forgotten the endless wars and invasions, but precisely because of the painful memory of these lost battles. The survival of the nation has itself become a matter of honour. Under these circumstances nationalism in the Church is another inevitable result of the past centuries of oppression and struggle. And since symbols such as Iviron are not numerous in the history of the Georgian people, its past glory resonates strongly in the memory of the people. To understand these claims today, however, one must concentrate on the tenth and eleventh centuries.

---

2   Hilarion the Georgian lived in the nineteenth century and served in the imperial army in St Petersburg. He joined the monastery of Dionysiou but subsequently lived in a hermitage nearby.

The sources used for this essay are mainly the Lives of the three hegoumenoi of Iviron, John, Euthymios, and George: *The Life of Our Blessed Fathers John and Euthymios and Their Worthy Citizenship as Described by the Poor Hieromonk George (the Hagiorite)*, and *The Life and Citizenship of Our Holy and Blessed Father George the Hagiorite, described by George the Minor*.[3] The Lives provide evidence for approximately one hundred years of history on Mount Athos with glimpses into court life in Constantinople during the period from the reign of Emperor Nikephoros II Phokas (963–9) to that of Constantine X Doukas (1059–67). We have also the *Book of Synodikon*,[4] and the four volumes of *Actes d'Iviron*, published in 1985, 1990, 1994, and 1995 by Jacques Lefort, Nicolas Oikonomidès, Denise Papachryssanthou, and (later) Vassiliki Kravari with the collaboration of the late Helen Metreveli.[5] There are also a number of valuable colophons from Georgian manuscripts originating from Iviron as well as from other monasteries in Tao-Klarjeti (south-east Georgia). The latter were copied for the purpose of providing manuscripts for the newly established Iviron. These colophons together with the *Book of Synodikon* from Iviron contain some significant information about the Georgian monastery on Mount Athos.

3   See Tamara Grdzelidze (tr.), *Georgian Monks on Mount Athos. Two Eleventh-Century Lives of the Hegoumenoi of Iviron* (London, 2009).

4   Helen Metreveli, *The Book of Synodikon of the Georgian Monastery on Mount Athos* (Tbilisi, 1998). A *synodikon* is a book containing names of the departed who are to be commemorated in church services for their financial donations or contributions in kind to a monastery.

5   Archives de l'Athos, fondées par Gabriel Millet, publiées par Paul Lemerle et Jacques Lefort, XIV, XVI, XVIII, XIX: *Actes d'Iviron*, vols 1–4, édition diplomatique par J. Lefort, N. Oikonomidès, D. Papachryssanthou, V. Kravari, avec la collaboration d'H. Métrévéli (Paris, 1985, 1990, 1994, 1995).

The Beginnings

From the sources that are available to us today, whether published documents or critical writings, it is clear that from the late tenth to the early twelfth century Iviron was one of the strongest and most influential monasteries on Athos. During this period it took a leading role in providing new trends in Georgian church writings and correcting existing texts.

The Georgians started arriving on Mount Athos in the decade of the 970s and immediately acquired a certain authority which they managed to maintain for more than one hundred years. The reason for their authoritative presence on the Holy Mountain was a combination of personal contacts with the imperial court and with St Athanasios, the founder of the Great Lavra, and the capacity of the Chordvaneli family in Tao-Klarjeti to provide material and moral support. The Georgians foresaw the special role that Iviron could play in the spiritual and political life of Georgia and supplied the monastery with material goods as well as experienced or talented monks.

The main reason for this successful start lay in the personal friendship between John the Iberian and St Athanasios the Athonite. They may have first known each other through a Pontic connection: Athanasios's mother is believed to be from Pontos and John's family also had links there. Athanasios had a great respect for John the Iberian and fully supported the presence of the Georgians on the Holy Mountain.

The *typikon* of the Great Lavra mentions that Athanasios gave to John the Iberian on his arrival on the Holy Mountain first a shelter and then some kellia not far from the Lavra. These were to remain in his possession and that of his successors (probably no more than eight monks) for the duration of the alliance between the Georgians and the Lavra. The kellia could not be sold or given to anyone else, as the Life of Euthymios confirms:

> Thus, in the company of his son and a few disciples, [John the Iberian] went to the Holy Mountain, to the Lavra of the great Athanasios, and asked for shelter. He kept himself unrevealed and obediently did everything with humility and peacefully. For two years or more he served as a cook. [...] After a certain period of time, their presence on the Holy Mountain became known and the number of Georgians began

to increase there, and when this became clear to our fathers, who were filled with all manner of wisdom, they decided: 'It is not fitting for us to stay in the monastery because others come to stay and it is not possible to send them back.' Thus by the decision of Athanasios, at one mile distance from the Lavra, in a beautiful unsettled place the above-mentioned fathers built the church of St John the Evangelist with a number of cells and stayed there for many years as angels of God.[6]

The distribution of land on Mount Athos changed in the second half of the tenth century with the establishment of large monastic settlements together with their estates and farming economy where previously there had been only scattered cells and hermitages. The rule on the Holy Mountain was to assign property for temporary possession for a fixed term, sometimes up to twenty-nine years, without the possibility of selling or gifting it to anyone else. Although this practice was condemned by Patriarch Lukas in 1164, it continued until the fourteenth or fifteenth century.[7] This was the arrangement when the first Georgians received temporary possession of their kellia from Athanasios.

The building of Iviron, however, came later, in 981–3. In the war waged against the revolt of Bardas Skleros the Georgian monk John – the former general Tornikios – led an army against the rebel general and contributed to the emperor's victory over him in 979. In return for the victory John Tornikios received a vast amount of treasure and used it for building a monastery. It was the wish of the founder John that the monastery should become a dwelling place for Georgians, and one of his decrees was that hegoumenoi should be elected from the Chordvaneli family (to which he belonged) in Tao-Klarjeti.

Politically speaking, David Kouropalates, the prince of Tao, who contributed to the stability of the empire by providing an army in the fight against the rebel general Bardas, for his part supported the foundation of Iviron. The members of the Chordvaneli family who founded Iviron

6 T. Grdzelidze, *Georgian Monks*, pp. 56–7. This was the creation of a group of hermitages or a skete, also confirmed later in the text. The creation of Iviron, according to the chrysobull of Basil II, was decided in 979/80. *Actes d'Iviron*, vol. 1, p. 88.

7 Archives de l'Athos IV: *Actes de Dionysiou*, éd. par N. Oikonomidès (Paris, 1968), pp. 68–71. See also H. Metreveli, *Philological-Historical Research*, vol.1, p. 45.

together with John Tornikios and John the Iberian were well connected in Constantinople and were quick to seize the opportunity of obtaining support for Iviron.

In documents from the time of its foundation, Iviron was always referred to as a lavra or monastery of the Georgians/Iberians – *mone ton Iberon*.[8] The evidence for the foundation derives from analysis of the *Life of Our Blessed Fathers John and Euthymios* and other monastic documents. The Life describes it in quite simple terms. The Georgians chose a good site in the middle of the peninsula and there built a monastery with two churches, one dedicated to the Mother of God, the other to St John the Baptist. They bought lands in the surrounding area and, with the help of John Tornikios, the emperors Basil II and Constantine VII confirmed these acquisitions to the Georgians with a chrysobull of 979/980.[9]

> And similarly, because of his [Tornikios's] service and great deeds, any place or vil-
> lage [the Georgians] asked for, the God-serving emperors [granted to them], and
> all was confirmed by a chrysobull and [these places] were not only many in number
> but also very special, as befits this country.[10]

In reality, the foundation of Iviron was not as simple as it was described in the Life of St Euthymios; rather it became the cause of many exchanges between the emperor Basil II and John Tornikios. Instead of the monastery of the Iberians in Constantinople and the monastery of St Phokas in Trebizond, over which Tornikios owned rights, he demanded property nearer to Athos. Therefore, in exchange for these two monasteries Torni-kios received from the emperor an imperial monastery situated outside Mount Athos together with its numerous dependencies, a considerable fortune of estates in Macedonia, and the Athonite monastery of Klemen-tos, dedicated to St John the Baptist, a small establishment 11 kilometres

---

8   In 1035 a chrysobull of Emperor Michael IV Paphlagon refers to the Georgian monks
     of Athos.
9   This chrysobull is lost but its content is known through the act of Judge Leo (1059
     or 1074), *Actes d'Iviron*, pp. 11–13.
10   *Georgian Monks*, p. 60.

north-west of the Great Lavra.[11] This monastery of St John the Baptist was beautifully situated between the woods and the sea. The only disadvantage was that the area was not protected from the wind. This was the place to which the Georgians moved in the 980s when abandoning their kellia near the Great Lavra. According to the chrysobull of 979–80, Tornikios also received the monasteries of Leontia in Thessaloniki and Kolobou in Ierissos. The foundation of Iviron took place with the inclusion of all these monastic lands.[12]

Monastic rules, regulations, and statutes written by Euthymios comprised the first Georgian *typikon*. Although the document is lost, long excerpts from it are quoted in the Life of Euthymios by George the Athonite.

Economically, the Georgians contributed very generously to the Holy Mountain, as the documents verify, and not only to Iviron but also to the Great Lavra, a fact that does not necessarily demonstrate their inexhaustible wealth or extreme generosity as such but makes clear the role assigned to Iviron. In other words, the lavish supply of material goods by the Georgians to the Holy Mountain that was under the direct patronage of the emperor and the patriarch of Constantinople and was counted among the favourite places of the leaders of the empire served their long-term strategy.

Georgian Royal and Noble Families at the Imperial Court

The political situation in Georgia during the second half of the tenth century strongly supported the cultural orientation of the nation towards Byzantium. There had always been a tendency to find ways of creating and maintaining bonds with Constantinople. In this respect Tao-Klarjeti was

---

11   According to tradition, the Mother of God, on her way to Cyprus, landed on Mount Athos at the place known as Klementos.

12   *Actes d'Iviron*, vol. 1, pp. 24–6.

already linked to Constantinople because of its semi-dependence on the empire while, at the same time, being in a state of continuous confrontation because of territories which were received from Byzantium but then taken back again.

By the end of the tenth century a great many Georgians, both lay and ordained, were present in Constantinople, whether as diplomats, members of the nobility taken as hostages, or simply seeking patronage from the emperor.[13]

Iviron, like other monasteries on Mount Athos, was granted by the emperors large stipends or annual payments of money. In the middle of the eleventh century the monastery's properties amounted to approximately 10,800 acres with 246 peasant families installed on these lands. By the beginning of the twelfth century, the number of families had risen to 294, although the extent of the properties had been reduced through confiscations.[14]

At the time when Queen Mary, mother of the Georgian King Bagrat IV, was in Constantinople, George the Athonite, hegoumenos of Iviron, was also visiting the court in order to sort out some monastic affairs. Mary personally intervened with Constantine IX Monomachos (1042–55) to help Fr George overcome a problem of taxation.[15] This fact, described in the *Life of Our Blessed Father George*, is confirmed by the *Book of Synodikon* (no. 15, p. 209). Two members of the Chordvaneli family, Peter and John, also interceded with the emperor, together with Queen Mary, to change the existing regulation for taxation in a way more favourable to Iviron.

During the last quarter of the tenth century and the beginning of the eleventh, Iviron played a significant role in the development of Mount Athos, both politically, because of the backgrounds of John and Euthymios, and also John Tornikios whose family kept very close links with the emperors, and economically, because these individuals brought with them a great

13   Helen Metreveli, *Studies in Cultural and Educational History of the Athonite Establishment* (Tbilisi, 1996), p. 33.

14   Alan Harvey, *Economic Expansion in the Byzantine Empire, 900–1200* (Cambridge, 1989), p. 49.

15   *Georgian Monks*, pp. 118–20.

deal of wealth. Moreover, John and Euthymios were highly respected on Mount Athos: Athanasios spoke about them in laudatory tones and left them as the *epitropoi*[16] of his monastery.[17]

Nationalistic Aspirations of the Georgian Athonite Community

The Lives of the Georgian Athonite monks are full of venom against other nations, especially the Greeks and the Armenians, but the Georgians themselves also come under fire in the Life of Euthymios. There are different reasons for the criticism as the Lives attempted to prove a number of key issues, such as that Iviron was founded for the Georgians only, that the Church of Georgia had never been damaged by heretical teachings and the faith was therefore kept undefiled, and that any false teaching which may have been introduced via early translations, essentially from the Armenian, had been corrected.

The main reason for the offensive language used against the Armenians was their non-Chalcedonian Christology. In conversation with the patriarch of Antioch, George the Athonite, according to the author of his Life George the Minor, made the following statement:

---

16 *Epitropos* is interpreted in Byzantium as administrative head, but Helen Metreveli (*Studies*, pp. 34–5) says that Athanasios left John the Iberian and Euthymios as *epitropoi*, spiritual supervisors, of the Great Lavra and it led the Greek monks to dislike the Georgian presence even further. A conflict between the Greeks and the Georgians becomes clear also from the fact that none of the lives of Athanasios the Great mentions the presence and the role of the Georgians in founding the monastic settlement on the Holy Mountain. However, the eighteenth-century Greek description of the lives of the ktitors of the Great Lavra speaks about John the Iberian, John Tornikios, and Euthymios. Also, in the administrative centre in Karyes there is a fresco with eleven great saints of Mount Athos and two of them are Euthymios and George.

17 Archives de l'Athos, VII: *Actes du Protaton*, éd. par Denise Papachryssanthou (Paris, 1975), p. 84.

> Although [our nation] possessed the Holy Scripture as well as undefiled and true faith from the very beginning, our land was yet far from Greece. And the unkind Armenians, evil-doers and cunning, have been implanted among us as impure seeds and caused great harm to us. Although our flock remained pure and undefiled, [the Armenians] by proper and improper means or through temptation brought about that [the Georgians] translated a number of books from their [language].[18]

At another time, in conversation with Emperor Constantine Doukas while answering his question about the faith of the Armenians, George comments: "'Let the evil faith have no name." And the Armenian princes became ashamed in front of all.'[19]

Clearly, this is a very narrow interpretation of the historical reasons why the dogmatic positions of the Georgians and the Armenians became mutually exclusive. After the conversion of Kartli (western Georgia, at that time a separate kingdom under the rule of King Mirian) around the year 330, some of the first translations were made from Armenian as well as Greek and Syriac. After the seventh century, when the Churches of Georgia and Armenia became formal rivals, and later, when the orientation in the Georgian Church shifted towards Byzantium rather than the Holy Land and Antioch, new translations into Georgian were made mainly from Greek, while, as the Life of George mentions, the old translations were now also corrected to accord with the Greek texts.[20]

As for the Greeks, the reason for denouncing them was obvious: the Georgians were unable to run their community without the help of the Greeks. Iviron grew into a large settlement that required a great deal of labour for its maintenance. Thus the Greeks were welcomed as blacksmiths, carpenters, builders, vineyard workers, and sailors.[21] Very soon after its foundation, Iviron allowed the Greeks to reside in the monastery, even though this was against the wishes of the founders. One can imagine that the coexistence of the two languages and two cultures in one monastery would not be easy, especially since the environment on the Holy Mountain

18 *Georgian Monks*, p. 111.
19 Ibid., p. 145.
20 Ibid., p. 125.
21 Ibid., p. 60.

was predominantly Greek while Iviron had strong claims to its Georgian origin. Little by little the Greeks took over, while the Georgians dwindled in numbers as well as authority within the monastery and in the rest of the peninsula.

The Georgians themselves were not spared the critical eye of George the Minor when he explained the reasons for increasing the number of Greek monks in Iviron under Hegoumenos Gregory, who 'showed preference for them but he ignored and reduced the Georgians as incapable and unreliable. As all you know,' says George the Minor, 'we [the Georgians] easily change our mind and go from one place to another, thus causing some considerable damage to our own souls as well as to the community.'[22]

The years from 1029 to 1042 were the most difficult for Iviron. In 1029 Hegoumenos George the Varazvache,[23] from the house of Chordvaneli, was sent into exile and the Greeks were able to replace him with a new hegoumenos whom the Georgians called the 'evildoer'. In 1035 the monks of Iviron expelled the 'evildoer' hegoumenos and elected as his successor Gregory, another of the Chordvanelis, followed by two others from the same family, Symeon and Stephanos. In 1045 the leadership passed to George the Athonite, who also belonged to the Chordvanelis.

Intellectual Property of Iviron

When the first Georgian monks settled on Mount Athos, they worked out a strategy to make their presence as meaningful as possible. In the period when they were still living in the Lavra of Athanasios, the first programme

22 Ibid., p. 89.
23 There is an inscription by George Varazvache on the dome of the church: 'I, the Georgian monk George, fortified these pillars and dome so that they stand and do not move unto the ages of ages'.

for the Georgians was established by a group of about seven individuals.[24] Apart from the construction of buildings, they had to consider also the provision of books and senior clergy. The Life of St Euthymios refers to the fact that the founders of Iviron invited eminent monks to their new community. John the Iberian invited his old spiritual friends John Grdzelisdze and Arsenios of Ninotsmida to leave the Pontic desert and to join the first Georgian community on Mount Athos. John the Iberian sent a letter to the brothers:

> Holy fathers, your holiness has become known to us and we learned about your life there and we regret that you do not wish to come to this holy and eminent Mountain so that we also might receive your holy prayer. We entreat your holiness to come [here] so that we may reside together because, as you know, we too have been in a foreign [land].[25]

The importance of inviting spiritually advanced monks was emphasized at the very beginning of the Life of St Euthymios: God 'revealed to us our blessed fathers John and Euthymios, and John [ex-Tornikios] and Arsenios bishop of Ninotsmida, and John Grdzelisdze'.[26] Furthermore, when Tornikios returned from Georgia, he brought with him many *rasophores* and famous monks. In fact, Tornikios's wish was to accept only native Georgians into the monastery.

It is interesting to see how the activities of John the Iberian and his son Euthymios were viewed by their contemporaries. One of the manuscripts, the translation of theological texts by Euthymios (Ath. 13),[27] contains two colophons by the copiers John Grdzelisdze and Arsenios of Ninotsmida,

24   See Michel van Parys, 'La monachisme et sa signification pour l'identité européenne', in Gianpaolo Rigotti (ed.), *Dall'Oronte al Tevere. Scritti in onore del cardinale Ignace Moussa I Daoud per il cinquantesimo di sacerdozio* (Rome, 2004), pp. 297–308, p. 298. The article gives an exposition of eastern monastic spirituality based on the example of Iviron and compares the contribution made by the eastern and western monastic spiritualities to European identity.

25   *Georgian Monks*, p. 64.

26   Ibid., p. 53.

27   I. Pantsulaia, *Catalogue of the Georgian Manuscripts from the Monastery of Iviron on Mount Athos* (A Collection), vol. 4 (Tbilisi, 1954).

saying: 'Christ, bless and give rest to the soul of Fr John and bless our Fr Euthymios; they faithfully provided spiritual care for the Georgian people and reward for their work.' And then again:

> For remembrance of the soul of blessed John who is the cause of all these good things, who brought up and educated Fr Euthymios and made us worthy of such goodness, his soul is worthy of the immortal goodness. By the order of our God-bearing Fr Euthymios we poor sinners, Arsenios of Ninotsmida and John Grdzelisdze and Chrysostom, were deemed worthy to copy by our hands these holy books translated from Greek into Georgian by our holy illuminator Fr Euthymios for the comfort of all the Georgians and for prayers and to glorify Fr Euthymios who was revealed recently as equal to the first holy ones, Fr Michael and [Fr] George, our brothers in spirit and flesh.[28]

The miraculous scene of acquiring perfect knowledge of the Georgian language by young Euthymios illustrates the mindset of the first Georgian Athonites: they wished to bring the Georgian translations of the sacred books up to the Byzantine standard. As a child Euthymios was struck down by a severe illness and was close to death, being speechless and voiceless. His father feared that Euthymios would depart this world and went to the church of the Mother of God, prostrated in front of the icon of the Holy Mother, and prayed with fervent tears. When he went back to see Euthymios, he opened the door of his cell and immediately smelt a wondrous fragrance, which was the sign that the Mother of God had protected him. Euthymios was sitting upon his bed entirely healed and unharmed.

> 'What happened, my son?' And he replied, saying: 'A glorious queen stood up before me and spoke to me in the Georgian language: "What is it? What is wrong with you, Euthymios?" And I told her: "I am dying, [my] queen." And as soon as I said this, she came close, took my hand and said: "Nothing is wrong with you, get up, do not be afraid and [hence] speak the Georgian [language] fluently." And so I am fine, as you see.' And blessed John continued: 'Until then, his Georgian had not been good and I worried for this reason, but since then ceaselessly, like the spring water, [the Georgian language] purer than that of any other Georgian flows from his mouth.'[29]

---

28 Metreveli, *Studies*, pp. 113–16.
29 *Georgian Monks*, p. 67.

Clearly, the Georgian Church had not been without spiritual books before John the Iberian and Euthymios started their activity. The presence of Georgians in Palestine who translated the holy books is evident from as early as the fifth century. From the fourth to the ninth century translations were made from Greek of the *polykephalia*, lectionaries, writings of the church fathers, exegetical works, hagiography, and ascetical writings. The original texts of Georgian hagiography and hymnography were also developed in this period and some remarkable examples survive. Also from the ninth to the tenth century Georgians were present in Palestine at Mar Saba and on Sinai.

Before the Georgian community on Mount Athos established a programme to fill the gaps and enrich its spiritual writings, there already existed a rich body of translated and original Christian writings in Georgian. Despite this fact, both Lives place a special emphasis on the importance of the translations made by Euthymios and the intellectual programme worked out in Iviron in general. The previous translations had to be made purer and free of any possible heresy, so they were to be corrected and updated according to Byzantine standards. In this way, the Georgian community on Mount Athos was able to play an exceptional role in the life and culture of the Georgian Church.

In the Life of Fr George the theme of self-defence by the Georgians against 'false accusations' regarding their heretical teaching emerges a few times, which supports the most important message put across in the Lives of the Athonites: that spiritual leaders, whether in Georgia, Antioch, or Mount Athos, are concerned with improving the existing translations of church service books and other spiritual writings. The Lives reflect the eagerness on the part of the Georgian spiritual fathers to cleanse existing translations of all possible mistakes or corruptions. Both texts testify that Iviron had an efficient scriptorium where translations were copied and sent back to Georgia as well as to the Georgian monasteries outside Georgia. Iviron was also known for its collection of Greek manuscripts – twelve copies of Greek texts copied in Iviron by the Greek monk Theophanes have been catalogued in various libraries around the world. These are predominantly texts of a dogmatic or ascetic nature translated by Euthymios into Georgian.

Both Euthymios and George were translators of the highest class. Their texts often contain additional material, such as a list of contents with brief descriptions of the texts under discussion and commentaries. Today, Iviron possesses 2,192 Greek manuscripts, including a large collection of musical texts, and 94 Georgian manuscripts, of which 60 date from the period before the twelfth century.

Thus there occurred a fortunate combination of circumstances, and the opportunities were used in an inventive way by the Georgians to maintain a large and prosperous community on Mount Athos for more than one hundred years. Iviron received strong support from the Georgian kings and nobility in Tao and Kartli, and repaid this by improving the Georgian church books according to the Constantinopolitan standard and providing spiritual nourishment for the Georgians in their own country and abroad. For these reasons one Georgian historian has named Iviron 'the Georgian consulate in Constantinople'.[30]

Were the other monasteries as academically advanced as Iviron? Was it Athanasios who introduced this level of scholarship? Or was it purely Iviron's individual choice and orientation to intertwine in a creative way political and cultural ambitions and to create a national spiritual symbol that would resonate throughout the centuries?

Bibliography

Archives de l'Athos, fondées par Gabriel Millet, publiées par Paul Lemerle et Jacques Lefort, IV: *Actes de Dionysiou*, éd. par N. Oikonomidès (Paris, 1968).
——, VII: *Actes du Prôtaton*, éd. par Denise Papachryssanthou (Paris, 1975).
——, XIV, XVI, XVIII, XIX: *Actes d'Iviron*, vols 1–4, édition diplomatique par J. Lefort, N. Oikonomidès, D. Papachryssanthou, V. Kravari, avec la collaboration d'H. Métrévéli (Paris, 1985, 1990, 1994, 1995).

30 Shota Badridze, *Georgian Relations with Byzantium and Western Europe* (Tbilisi, 1984), p. 47.

Badridze, Shota, *Georgian Relations with Byzantium and Western Europe* (Tbilisi, 1984).

Grdzelidze, Tamara (tr.), *Georgian Monks on Mount Athos. Two Eleventh-Century Lives of the Hegoumenoi of Iviron* (London, 2009).

Harvey, Alan, *Economic Expansion in the Byzantine Empire, 900–1200* (Cambridge, 1989).

Metreveli, Helen, *The Book of Synodikon of the Georgian Monastery on Mount Athos* (Tbilisi, 1998).

——, *Philological-Historical Research*, vol.1 (Tbilisi, 2008).

——, *Studies in Cultural and Educational History of the Athonite Establishment* (Tbilisi, 1996).

Pantsulaia, I., *Catalogue of the Georgian Manuscripts from the Monastery of Iviron on Mount Athos* (A Collection), vol. 4 (Tbilisi, 1954).

van Parys, Michel, 'La monachisme et sa signification pour l'identité européenne', in Gianpaolo Rigotti (ed.), *Dall'Oronte al Tevere. Scritti in onore del cardinale Ignace Moussa I Daoud per il cinquantesimo di sacerdozio* (Edizioni Orientalia Christiana, Rome, 2004), pp. 297–308.

KYRILL PAVLIKIANOV

The Bulgarians on Mount Athos

The purpose of the present article is to offer the reader new knowledge about the presence of Bulgarian-speaking monks in the monasteries of the Holy Mountain during the middle and late Byzantine periods as well as during the early post-Byzantine period, that is, from 980 to about 1550. Although the late Ottoman period is also very interesting and quite rich with historical data and new spiritual phenomena, it would be very difficult to encompass all the documentary evidence connected with it in just a few pages. The only previous article concerning the Bulgarian presence on Mount Athos pertained exactly to the late Ottoman period and was published in 1973.[1]

Early Bulgarian Monks on Athos

The first information about an Athonite monk of Bulgarian origin can be dated to the last decades of the tenth century. In 982 a person named 'Paul Stogoretsi' signed a document issued by the inhabitants of the tiny town of Ierissos, which is situated 16 kilometres to the north of what is today the official border of the Athonite monastic peninsula. This document is now kept in the archive of the monastery of Iviron.[2] Identifying Paul as a person of

---

1 G. Nešev, 'Les monastères bulgares du Mont Athos', *Études historiques*, 6 (Sofia, 1973).

2 Archives de l'Athos XIV. *Actes d'Iviron I*, ed. J. Lefort, N. Oikonomidès, and D. Papachrysanthou (with the collaboration of Hélène Métrévéli) (Paris, 1985), pp. 117–29, no. 4, l. 6.

Bulgarian origin is a sort of a puzzle. Essentially, everything we know about him derives from his surname, or, more probably, his nickname *Stogoretsi* (Στογόρετζι). At first glance this name even does not seem to be Slavic at all. Actually, it includes one very basic medieval Cyrillic abbreviation which, quite unexpectedly, is rendered with Greek letters. It is the abbreviation of the Slavonic term for saint, which in the late tenth century was pronounced as *sve^{n}tyj*.[3] However, this basic Slavic religious term is almost always written in its abbreviated variant *stiy*. In such a philological context Paul's surname or nickname should be read as *S(ve^n)togoretsi*. It is a normal and also very common Slavic translation of the Greek term *hagioreites* – 'the Athonite'.[4] Paul's signature of 982 offers us two very important pieces of information: (1) he must have been a monk on Mount Athos, otherwise his nickname *S(ve^n)togoretsi* would make no sense at all; (2) he was not an illiterate person, since he knew how to write his name in both Slavic and Greek. His knowledge of the written tradition connected with the Slavic translation of Holy Scripture had even compelled him to transliterate with Greek letters the most basic medieval Slavonic abbreviation – that of the term 'saint'. The abundant data concerning the demographic situation in the vicinity of the Athonite peninsula during the second half of the tenth century indicate that Paul must have been Bulgarian-speaking. As F. Dölger,[5] G. Soulis,[6]

3   Following common practice in Byzantine studies, Slavic bibliography will be given transliterated with the Latin alphabet, while Greek titles will remain written with Greek letters. In our transliteration of the Cyrillic alphabet *y* stands for ы, j for й, ŭ for ъ, ć for ħ, č for ч, š for ш, and ž for ж.

4   *Actes d'Iviron I*, p. 122. Cf. also P. Schreiner, 'Slavisches in den griechischen Athosurkunden', *Tgoli chole Mêstro, Gedenkschrift für Reinhold Olesch* (Köln-Wien, 1990), p. 309; K. Pavlikianov, Σλάβοι μοναχοί στὸ Ἅγιον Ὄρος ἀπὸ τὸν Ι´ ὡς τὸν ΙΖ´ αἰῶνα (Thessaloniki, 2002), pp. 1–2.

5   F. Dölger, 'Ein Fall slavischer Einsiedlung im Hinterland von Thessalonike im 10. Jahrhundert', *Sitzungsberichten der Bayerischen Academie der Wissenschaften, Philosophisch-historische Klasse*, 1952/1 (München, 1952), pp. 1–28.

6   G. Soulis, 'On the Slavic Settlement in Ierissos in the Tenth Century', *Byzantion*, 23 (1953), 67–72.

V. Tŭpkova-Zaimova,[7] I. Dujčev,[8] P. Schreiner,[9] and I. Božilov[10] have already argued, by the late tenth century the Slavs inhabiting the outskirts of Mount Athos were exclusively connected with the Bulgarian literary tradition. A perfect proof of this statement can be found, once again, in the archive of the monastery of Iviron: the earliest firmly dated example of usage of the Bulgarian Glagolitic alphabet is the signature of a priest named George who is attested as an inhabitant of the town of Ierissos during the year 982.[11]

According to the prevailing view, the first Slavic monastery on the Holy Mountain was the Russian monastery of Xylourgou, an inventory list of which, drawn up in 1142, mentions the existence of forty-nine 'Russian books' in its depository.[12] The second monastery which accepted monks of Slavic origin was surely the Bulgarian monastery of Zographou, whose abbot in 1163 signed a document of the Russian monastery of St Panteleimon using a Slavic vernacular of Bulgarian type.[13] The monastery of Hilandar was taken over by the Serbs thirty-five years later, in 1198, when

7   V. Tŭpkova-Zaimova, 'Svedenija za bŭlgari v žitieto na sv. Atanasij', *Izsledvanija v čest na akad. Dimitŭr Dečev po slučaj 80-godishninata mu* (Sofia, 1958), pp. 759–62.

8   I. Dujčev, 'Le Mont Athos et les Slaves au Moyen Âge', *Le Millénaire du Mont Athos 963–1963, Études et Mélanges* II (Venezia-Chevetogne, 1964), pp. 125–7.

9   Schreiner, 'Slavisches in den griechischen Athosurkunden', pp. 308–9.

10 I. Božilov, *Bŭlgarite vŭv Vizantijskata imperija* (Sofia, 1995), p. 81.

11 Cf. *Actes d'Iviron I*, pp. 117–29, no. 4, l. 1–18; I. Sreznevskij, 'Iz obozrenija glagoličeskih pamjatnikov', *Izvestija imperatorskago arheologičeskago obščestva*, 3 (1861), 1–8; P. Uspenskij, 'Suždenie ob Afono-iverskom akte 982 goda i o glagoličeskoj podpisi na nem popa Giorgija', *Izvestija imperatorskago arheologičeskago obshchestva*, 5 (1865), 13–18; J. Ivanov, *Bŭlgarski starini iz Makedonija* (Sofia, 1931; repr. 1970), pp. 21–3.

12 *Akty russkago na svjatom Afone monastyrja svjatago velikomučenika i celitelja Panteleimona*, ed. F. Ternovskij (Kiev, 1873), pp. 50–4, no. 6; Archives de l'Athos XII, *Actes de Saint-Pantéléèmôn*, ed. P. Lemerle, G. Dagron, and S. Ćirković (Paris, 1982), pp. 3–12, 65–76, no. 7, l. 25–7. Cf. also V. Mošin, 'Russkie na Afone i russko-vizantijskie otnošenija v XI–XII vv.', *Byzantinoslavica*, 9 (1947–8), 55–85; I. Smolitsch, 'Le Mont Athos et la Russie', *Le Millénaire du Mont Athos 963–1963. Études et Mélanges* I (Chevetogne, 1963), pp. 279–318; D. Nastase, 'Les débuts de la communauté œcuménique du Mont Athos', Σύμμεικτα, 6 (Athens, 1985), 284–99.

13 D. Papachrysanthou, Ὁ ἀθωνικὸς μοναχισμός. Ἀρχὲς καὶ ὀργάνωση (Athens, 1992), pp. 239–41 (notes 267–80); I. Božilov, *Bŭlgarite vŭv Vizantijskata imperija*, pp. 80–4,

St Sava and his father Stefan Nemanja received it officially from the Byzantine Emperor Alexios III Angelos and the Protos of the Holy Mountain Gerasimos.[14] However, we must point out that the first Athonite monastery directly connected with a person of Slavic origin was founded almost a century earlier.

The Monastery of Zelianos

During the eleventh century several Athonite documents mention the existence of a minor monastic house named 'the monastery of Zelianos'.[15] The name of its founder, Zelianos, seems to be purely Slavic and must have been pronounced as Željan. An act of sale dated 1033–4 makes it clear that by that time the minor Athonite monastery of Katzari possessed a terrain which was denoted as belonging to a certain Zelianos.[16] The act offers no

352 (no. 443); idem, 'Osnovavane na svetata atonska bŭlgarska obitel Zograf. Legendi i fakti', *Svetogorska obitel Zograf*, 1 (Sofia, 1995), p. 18 (notes 46–9).

14   Archives de l'Athos XX. *Actes de Chilandar I*, ed. Mirjana Živojinović, Vassiliki Kravari, and Christophe Giros (Paris, 1998), pp. 3–32; Archives de l'Athos V. *Actes de Chilandar I. Actes grecs*, ed. L. Petit and B. Korablev, *Vizantijskij Vremennik*, Priloženie (Appendix) 1 to vol. XVII (St Petersburg, 1911; repr. Amsterdam, 1975), pp. 6–15, nos. 3–5; T. Burković, *Hilandar u doba Nemanjicha* (Belgrade, 1925); D. Dimitrievich, 'L'importance du monachisme serbe et ses origines au monastère athonite de Chilandar', *Le Millénaire du Mont Athos 963–1963. Études et Mélanges* I (Chevetogne, 1963), pp. 265–78; F. Barisić, 'Hronološki problemi oko godine Nemanjine smrti', *Hilandarski zbornik*, 2 (1971), 31–57; M. Živojinović, 'Hilandar in the Middle Ages (origins and an outline of its history)', *Hilandarski zbornik*, 7 (1989), 7–25.

15   Cf. K. Pavlikianov, 'Manastirŭt na Željan – pŭrvoto slavjansko monašesko učreždenie na Aton', *Svetogorska obitel Zograf*, 2 (Sofia, 1996), 17–23; idem, 'The Monastery of Zelianos – The First Slavic Monastic Institution on Athos', Σύμμεικτα, 11 (Athens, 1997), 37–48; Pavlikianov, Σλάβοι μοναχοί στὸ Ἅγιον Ὄρος, pp. 23–31.

16   *Akty russkago na svjatom Afone monastyrja*, pp. 10–17, no. 2; *Actes de Saint-Pantéléêmôn*, pp. 31–5, no. 2, l. 2–3 and 23–5.

evidence that in 1033–4 Zelianos's terrain enjoyed the status of a monastery. Zelianos was definitely the name of a person who was involved in the sale described in the document, but it remains uncertain if he was a solitary hermit or an abbot of a monastery. Half a century later, in 1089, the name Zelianos is mentioned once again, in a document which is now kept in the monastery of Xenophontos. In this case it denoted a small monastic house, its monastic group, and its residence.[17] However, it is also clear that by 1089 the monastic institution founded by Zelianos in the beginning of the eleventh century was no longer independent, so the term 'monastery' which was used for describing it contained only a reminiscence of its former status. According to D. Papachryssanthou, it was the Russian monastery of St Panteleimon that finally annexed the territory once controlled by Zelianos.[18] Nevertheless, the document of 1089 makes it clear that the monastery of St Panteleimon was not a direct heir to Zelianos's domain, since in the late eleventh century the monastery of Zelianos was already absorbed by the neighbouring monastery of Katzari. The latter remained autonomous till 1363, when the Serbian Protos Dorotheos finally granted it to the Russian monastery of St Panteleimon. In 1363 the name of Zelianos is mentioned once again – in Dorotheos's act arranging the donation of Katzari to the Russians.[19] However, in this case it was just a toponym in the vicinity of Katzari. It was referred to for a last time in 1612, in a Slavic act of the Xenophontos monastery, where it was transliterated exactly as it had been written in the Greek prototype of the document. This detail clearly indicates that the Serbian-speaking scribe of Xenophontos's act was unaware of the Slavic origin of the place-name Zelianos.[20] The document of 1612 contains no data about any further development of Zelianos's foundation, so we must

17 Archives de l'Athos XV, *Actes de Xénophon*, ed. by D. Papachryssanthou (Paris, 1986), pp. 59–75, no. 1, l. 126–7.
18 *Actes de Xénophon*, pp. 7–9.
19 *Actes de Saint-Pantéléèmôn*, p. 111, no. 13, l. 12 (in the text of the interpolated copy B).
20 K. Pavlikianov, 'The Athonite Monastery of Xenophontos and its Slavic Archive – An Unknown Slavic Description of the Monastery's Land on Athos', *Palaeobulgarica*, 36/2 (Sofia, 2002), pp. 102–11.

acknowledge that all the evidence about its existence disappears before the year 1100. The Athonite archives contain no direct indications as to where the monasteries of Katzari and Zelianos were built, but an early modern Russian description of the monastery of St Panteleimon tells us that the so-called skete of Xenophontos, which was founded in 1766, was erected on the land of Katzari.[21] G. Smyrnakis identifies the monastery of Katzari with some ruins near the stream of Chrysorrares, not far away from the monastery of Pantokrator on the east coast of the Athonite peninsula.[22] On the contrary, D. Papachryssanthou states that the place-name Katzari still exists at a distance of about 1.5 kilometres to the north-east of the medieval site of the Russian monastery – the so-called Palaion Rossikon, which can be found high above the west coast of Mount Athos.[23] A. Papazotos, who is the author of the only detailed study on Athonite topography, shares the same view.[24] Thus the monastery of Zelianos must have been built on the western slope of the Athonite peninsula, in the vicinity of the monasteries of Palaion Rossikon and Xenophontos.

The monastery of Zelianos was a Slavic monastic institution from its very inception, while all the other monasteries which gradually took on a Slavic character were originally established as Greek monastic houses. Zelianos was probably not an eminent person, but he may have been connected with the Bulgarian population of the Halkidiki peninsula, which we have already discussed above. What is clear is that the other Athonite monks never paid any attention to his mother tongue, and always regarded him not as a foreigner but as an integral member of their society. In view of this detail, the existence of his monastery indicates that the Bulgarian population of the regions adjacent to the Athonite peninsula probably participated, though on a limited scale, in the life of the Athonite monastic community during the early eleventh century.

21   *Russkij monastyr svjatago velikomučenika i celitelja Panteleimona na Svjatoj gore Afonskoj* (Moskva, 1886⁷), p. 31.

22   G. Smyrnakis, *Tὸ Ἅγιον Ὄρος* (Athens, 1903; repr. Karyai, 1988), p. 678.

23   *Actes de Xénophon*, p. 9.

24   A. Papazôtos, 'Recherches topographiques au Mont Athos', *Géographie historique du monde méditerranéen* (Paris, 1988), pp. 154–5, 162–3 (fig. 2).

The Bulgarian Monastery of Zographou

The monastery of Zographou is surely one of the most ancient Athonite monastic houses as in 972 its founder, a painter (in Greek *zographos*) named George, signed the *typikon* of John I Tzimiskes.[25] The monastery was obviously named after the profession of its founder, who presumably earned his living by painting icons and frescos. Yet we know virtually nothing about how his foundation came into being. The first document preserved in Zographou's archive dates from 980 and is an act of sale.[26] Its text makes it clear that an Athonite abbot named Thomas had then sold to one Onesiphoros a terrain labelled 'of the Holy Apostles', which was also known as Xerokastron.[27] The text of 980 is only indirectly connected with the monastery of Zographou, because it states that the terrain of Xerokastron shared a common border with some land belonging to Zographou.[28] This means that by 980 the foundation of George the Painter already possessed some property on Mount Athos, i.e. it must have had the status of an autonomous monastery.

The second copy of the act of 980 contains an additional confirmative note,[29] which N. Oikonomides has convincingly dated to 1311.[30] It was written in the monastery of Zographou whose Slavic-speaking abbot,

25 Archives de l'Athos VII, *Actes du Prôtaton*, ed. D. Papachrysanthou (Paris, 1975), p. 167, no. 7; Papachrysanthou, Ὁ ἀθωνικὸς μοναχισμός, pp. 240–1 (notes 276–7); K. Pavlikianov, 'Οἱ Σλάβοι στὴν ἀθωνικὴ μονὴ Ζωγράφου', Σύμμεικτα, 12 (Athens, 1998), 109; idem, Σλάβοι μοναχοὶ στὸ Ἅγιον Ὄρος, pp. 32–7; idem, *Istorija na bŭlgarskija svetogorski manastir Zograf ot 980 do 1804 g.* (Sofia, 2005), pp. 17–23.

26 Actes de l'Athos IV, *Actes de Zographou*, ed. W. Regel, E. Kurtz, and B. Korablev, *Vizantijskij Vremennik*, 13 (1907), Priloženie (Appendix) 1 to vol. 13 (repr. Amsterdam, 1969), no. 1; Ivanov, *Bŭlgarski starini*, pp. 526–35, no. 63.

27 *Actes de Zographou*, no. 1, l. 1–6; Ivanov, *Bŭlgarski starini*, p. 528.

28 *Actes de Zographou*, no. 1, l. 23; Ivanov, *Bŭlgarski starini*, pp. 528–9.

29 *Actes de Zographou*, no. 1, l. 49–54; Ivanov, *Bŭlgarski starini*, p. 529.

30 Archives de l'Athos IX, *Actes de Kastamonitou*, ed. N. Oikonomidès (Paris, 1978), p. 3 (note 14). See also *Actes du Prôtaton*, 93 (note 336); Archives de l'Athos II2, *Actes de Kutlumus*, ed. P. Lemerle (Paris, 19882), p. 4.

Makarios, had signed it as a witness. According to I. Božilov, the eminent
Bulgarian scholar J. Ivanov has made an error in imposing on the Bulgarian
scholarly community the opinion that Makarios's signature was added to
the main text as early as 980.[31] What is very important for our study of the
Bulgarian monastic presence on Mount Athos is that Makarios's signature
appears not in 980, but as late as 1311.[32]

The period from 980 to 1311 offers us only four signatures of Zographite
monks. The first one, which we have already commented on, is that of its
founder, the painter George.[33] It dates from 972. The second one belongs
to an abbot of Zographou named John, who is attested as active in about
1037–51. According to J. Lefort, this person must have been the prototype
of the semi-mythical Zographite abbot John Selina, who is mentioned in
the famous sixteenth-century composite legend about the monastery's early
years. This text is known among Bulgarian scholars as *Svodna gramota*,
that is a compiled charter.[34] His name seems to be also mentioned in a false
chrysobull attributed to Andronikos II Palaiologos with a date 1286–7.[35]

31   Cf. Ivanov, *Bŭlgarski starini*, pp. 527, 533–5; Božilov, *Bŭlgarite vŭv Vizantijskata
     imperija*, p. 82.

32   See also Pavlikianov, Σλάβοι μοναχοί στὸ Ἅγιον Ὄρος, pp. 32–3; idem, *Istorija na
     bŭlgarskija svetogorski manastir Zograf*, pp. 17–18.

33   *Actes du Prôtaton*, no. 7, l. 167; Papachrysanthou, Ὁ ἀθωνικὸς μοναχισμός, pp. 240–1
     (notes 276–7); Pavlikianov, Οἱ Σλάβοι στὴν ἀθωνικὴ μονὴ Ζωγράφου, 109; idem, 'Ἡ
     ἔνταξη τῶν Βουλγάρων στὴν μοναστηριακὴ κοινότητα τοῦ Ἁγίου Ὄρους – οἱ περιπτώσεις
     τῶν μονῶν Ζωγράφου καὶ Ζελιάνου', *Göttinger Beiträge zur byzantinischen und neu-
     griechischen Philologie*, 2 (2002), 64.

34   *Actes de Zographou*, pp. 150–7, no. 66, 169–74, Slavic act no. 5; See also A. Stoilov,
     'Svoden hrisovul za istorijata na Zografskija manastir', *Sbornik v čest na V. Zlatarski*
     (Sofia, 1925), pp. 452–4; Ivanov, *Bŭlgarski starini*, pp. 537–40.

35   This act is preserved in a Greek and Slavic version. For the Greek text cf. *Actes de
     Zographou*, no. 67, l. 27–8; F. Dölger, *Aus den Schatzkammern des Heiligen Berges*
     (Munich, 1948), no. 48, l. 21–2; idem, *Regesten der Kaiserurkunden des oströmischen
     Reiches von 565–1453. 4. Teil: Regesten von 1282–1341* (Munich-Berlin, 1960), no.
     2119. For the Slavic text see *Actes de Zographou*, pp. 163–5, Slavic act no. 2, l. 24–5;
     K. Tchérémissinoff, 'Les archives slaves médiévales du monastère de Zographou au
     Mont-Athos', *Byzantinische Zeitschrift*, 76 (1983), 18, no. 5.

The next two signatures of abbots of Zographou are already Slavic ones and belong to the superiors Symeon (1169)[36] and Makarios (1311).[37] During the second half of the thirteenth century three more Zographou abbots are attested – Ephraim in 1270,[38] Poimen in 1274,[39] and Arkadios in 1299.[40] Unfortunately, nothing is known about their mother tongue or ethnic origin. The infiltration of Bulgarian-speaking monks in the monastery of Zographou must have become rather intense during the first half of the fourteenth century, since it was then that numerous Slavic signatures of monks connected with Zographou began to appear in the Athonite acts.[41] Within this context, our most important conclusion is that we lack the necessary evidence that could tell us exactly when the foundation was taken over by the Bulgarians. However, this must have occurred prior to the year 1169, when Zographou's earliest Bulgarian-speaking abbot, Symeon, is attested to have signed in Bulgarian an act of the monastery of

36 *Actes de Saint-Pantéléèmôn*, no. 8, l. 59; Božilov, *Bŭlgarite vŭv Vizantijskata imperija*, no. 443; Pavlikianov, *Οἱ Σλάβοι στὴν ἀθωνικὴ μονὴ Ζωγράφου*, pp. 111–12, 117; idem, *Ἡ ἔνταξη τῶν Βουλγάρων στὴν μοναστηριακὴ κοινότητα τοῦ Ἁγίου Ὄρους*, p. 64.

37 *Actes de Zographou*, no. 1, l. 59; Dujčev, *Le Mont Athos et les slaves au Moyen Âge*, p. 128; Papachrysanthou, *Ὁ ἀθωνικὸς μοναχισμός*, p. 241 (notes 279–80); Božilov, *Bŭlgarite vŭv Vizantijskata imperija*, no. 398; Pavlikianov, *Οἱ Σλάβοι στὴν ἀθωνικὴ μονὴ Ζωγράφου*, p. 118; idem, *Ἡ ἔνταξη τῶν Βουλγάρων στὴν μοναστηριακὴ κοινότητα τοῦ Ἁγίου Ὄρους*, p. 64.

38 *Actes de Zographou*, no. 9, l. 25–7; Pavlikianov, *Οἱ Σλάβοι στὴν ἀθωνικὴ μονὴ Ζωγράφου*, p. 117; idem, *Ἡ ἔνταξη τῶν Βουλγάρων στὴν μοναστηριακὴ κοινότητα τοῦ Ἁγίου Ὄρους*, p. 64.

39 Archives de l'Athos XX. *Actes de Chilandar I*, no. 9, l. 53–4 (= Archives de l'Athos V. *Actes de Chilandar I. Actes grecs*, no. 19, l. 60–1. In this edition the document is erroneously dated to 1304). Cf. also Pavlikianov, *Οἱ Σλάβοι στὴν ἀθωνικὴ μονὴ Ζωγράφου*, pp. 117–18; idem, *Ἡ ἔνταξη τῶν Βουλγάρων στὴν μοναστηριακὴ κοινότητα τοῦ Ἁγίου Ὄρους*, p. 64.

40 *Actes de Zographou*, no. 14, l. 2–6; Pavlikianov, *Οἱ Σλάβοι στὴν ἀθωνικὴ μονὴ Ζωγράφου*, p. 118; idem, *Ἡ ἔνταξη τῶν Βουλγάρων στὴν μοναστηριακὴ κοινότητα τοῦ Ἁγίου Ὄρους*, p. 64.

41 Pavlikianov, *Οἱ Σλάβοι στὴν ἀθωνικὴ μονὴ Ζωγράφου*, pp. 117–38; idem, *Σλάβοι μοναχοὶ στὸ Ἅγιον Ὄρος*, pp. 32–7; idem, *Ἡ ἔνταξη τῶν Βουλγάρων στὴν μοναστηριακὴ κοινότητα τοῦ Ἁγίου Ὄρους*, pp. 64–5.

St Panteleimon. On the other hand, the only Zographou act dated to the period 1052–1266 is a false one, dated 1142.[42] It mentions as abbot a certain Joachim and relates to an estate the monastery possessed near Ierissos. The donor who had bequeathed it to Zographou was one Maria Tzousmene, a person claiming to be an 'offspring of the pious emperors'.[43] In 1910 P. Bezobrazov explicitly proved that her document in favour of Zographou was a poor-quality fake.[44] However, he was unaware of the fact that in about 1200 the same noblewoman was mentioned as a donor of the monastery of Xeropotamou in a charter issued by her grandson, the *sebastokrator* Nikephoros Komnenos Petraleiphas. In 1964 J. Bompaire assumed that her donation to the Bulgarian monastery was probably not just an invention of the person who had forged the document 'of 1142'.[45] Two acts of 1266–7 kept in Zographou's archives make it clear that the charter of '1142' must actually have been compiled in the second half of the thirteenth century, when the monks of Zographou were desperately trying to replace some recently destroyed documents concerning their property.[46]

   Prior to the year 1266–7 there was a serious conflict between the monasteries of Zographou and Megiste Lavra. It concerned the estate at Ierissos which Maria Tzousmene had donated to the Bulgarian monastic house in the mid-twelfth century. The conflict was triggered by some new territorial acquisitions which the Lavriote monks made in the same region in 1259, when the brother of Michael VIII Palaiologos, John Komnenos Palaiologos, granted to Megiste Lavra the villages of Sellada, Metallin, and Gradista.

---

42   In the obsolete edition *Actes de Zographou* (1907) the earliest Zographite act after
      1051 dates from the year 1267. However, in 1948 F. Dölger published one unknown
      Zographite act dated 1266. Cf. Dölger, *Aus den Schatzkammern des Heiligen Berges*,
      no. 34.

43   *Actes de Zographou*, no. 5, l. 8–9.

44   P. Bezobrazov, 'Ob aktah Zografskago monastyrja', *Vizantijskij Vremennik*, 17 (1910),
      403–5.

45   Archives de l'Athos III, *Actes de Xéropotamou*, ed. J. Bompaire (Paris, 1964), pp. 16,
      67–71, no. 8, l. 1, 5, 11. See also S. Binon, *Les origines légendaires et l'histoire de
      Xéropotamou et de Saint-Paul de l'Athos* (Louvain, 1942), pp. 103–8, 205–6.

46   *Actes de Zographou*, nos. 6 and 7. See also Bezobrazov, *Ob aktah Zografskago monastyrja*, pp. 403–5.

All these settlements were situated within a short range to the north of Ierissos. In 1263 the emperor confirmed his brother's donations by issuing a chrysobull in favour of the Lavra of St Athanasios.[47] At a certain moment the conflict was transferred to the imperial court in Constantinople. It appears from a document of 1267, issued by the Byzantine tax officials Basil Eparchos or Aparchon and Nikephoros Malleas, that the governor of Thessaloniki, Constantine Tornikios, had initially settled the dispute in favour of Zographou,[48] but the Lavriote monks immediately appealed to the Byzantine emperor.[49] The whole affair concerned two agricultural terrains situated in the localities of Armenon and Loustra near Ierissos. The witnesses who were summoned to testify stated that Armenon belonged to Zographou, but the monks of Megiste Lavra were claiming it because it was situated very close to their own property in the same region.[50] Tornikios was ready to hand over the terrain in question to the monastery of Zographou, but the statement of the Lavriote monks that Zographou's testimonies were fraudulent compelled him to send both parties to the imperial court at Constantinople.[51] The emperor settled the case in favour of Zographou. Nevertheless, when the representatives of the two monasteries left the Byzantine capital, a monk of Megiste Lavra named Theodoulos broke the law by forging a false imperial *horismos*, which he presented to Tornikios. This document ordered the governor of Thessaloniki to give the terrains in question to Megiste Lavra and to destroy all Zographou's documents connected with the affair.[52] The same situation is also described in a document which the *sebastokrator* Constantine Tornikios issued for the monastery of

---

47 Archives de l'Athos VIII, *Actes de Lavra II. De 1204 à 1328*, ed. P. Lemerle, A. Guillou, N. Svoronos, and D. Papachrysanthou (Paris, 1977), pp. 12–16, no. 72.

48 Dölger, *Aus den Schatzkammern des Heiligen Berges*, pp. 93–4, no. 34, l. 7; idem, *Regesten der Kaiserurkunden des oströmischen Reiches von 565–1453. 3. Teil: Regesten von 1204–1282* (Munich-Berlin, 1932), 1939b.

49 *Actes de Zographou*, no. 7, l. 86–8; Dölger, *Aus den Schatzkammern des Heiligen Berges*, pp. 93–5, no. 34.

50 Actes de Zographou, no. 7, l. 64–7.

51 Actes de Zographou, no. 7, l. 89–94.

52 Actes de Zographou, no. 7, l. 103–7; Pavlikianov, Ἡ ἔνταξη τῶν Βουλγάρων στὴν μοναστηριακὴ κοινότητα τοῦ Ἁγίου Ὄρους, pp. 65–8.

Zographou when he finally restored to it the terrains at Loustra and Armenon. In this last act the governor of Thessaloniki clearly stated that he had
destroyed two Zographite documents – one of Nikephoros Petraleiphas
and another one of his grandmother, Maria Tzousmene.[53]

What is important in this case is the fact that Constantine Tornikios
refers to a dependency of Zographou near Ierissos. This was the administrative centre of all the property the Bulgarian monastery possessed in
that region.[54] What emerges from the documents of 1266–7 is that it must
have been founded several decades before the conflict with the monastery of Megiste Lavra. If we take it for granted that it was established on
the land bequeathed to Zographou by Maria Tzousmene in about 1142,
it is self-evident that this date is quite close to the appearance of the first
Bulgarian-speaking abbot of Zographou in 1169.[55] Maria Tzousmene, as
we have argued elsewhere, was probably of Cuman origin.[56] Was there any
connection between her donation and the gradual infiltration of Bulgarian
monks into the monastery of George the Painter? Due to the lack of direct
documentary evidence we shall probably never know for sure.

At this point we must also comment on the legend of the twenty-
six martyrs of Zographou, whose martyrdom, presumably incited by the
Constantinopolitan Patriarch John Bekkos, is traditionally dated to the
reign of Michael VIII. As A. Rigo has already shown, the whole story
derives from a literary work written not earlier than the sixteenth century
or maybe even later.[57] It forms part of a whole network of texts which are

53   *Actes de Zographou*, no. 6, l. 25–33; Bezobrazov, *Ob aktah Zografskago monastyrja*,
     pp. 403–5; Pavlikianov, Ἡ ἔνταξη τῶν Βουλγάρων στὴν μοναστηριακὴ κοινότητα τοῦ
     Ἁγίου Ὄρους, pp. 65–8.
54   Actes de Zographou, no. 6, l., 69.
55   See *Actes de Saint-Pantéléèmôn*, no. 8, l. 59; Božilov, *Bŭlgarite vŭv Vizantijskata imper-
     ija*, no. 443; Pavlikianov, Οἱ Σλάβοι στὴν ἀθωνικὴ μονὴ Ζωγράφου, pp. 111–12, 117.
56   See Pavlikianov, Ἡ ἔνταξη τῶν Βουλγάρων στὴν μοναστηριακὴ κοινότητα τοῦ Ἁγίου
     Ὄρους, pp. 65–8.
57   A. Rigo, 'La Διήγησις sui monaci athoniti martirizzati dai latinofroni (BHG 2333) e
     le tradizioni athonite successive: alcune osservazioni', *Studi Veneziani*, 15 NS (1988),
     71–106.

known as the *Patria* of Mount Athos.[58] As a literary topos, the legend of the twenty-six Zographite martyrs is very similar to the well-known legend about the early years of the monastery of Konstamonitou.[59] Though it was composed several centuries after the events of 1267, we cannot exclude the possibility that its basic plot – the semi-mythical story of the destruction of a Zographite defensive tower where the twenty-six martyrs had taken refuge – could contain a vague reminiscence of the act of injustice committed against the monastery of Zographou by the Lavriote monk Theodoulos, who pretended that he was executing orders of the Byzantine Emperor Michael VIII Palaiologos, and thereby inflicting serious damage on the archive of the Bulgarian monastery and its property. However, we must stress that this is only a conjecture. It cannot be proved for sure.

An imperial order (*prostagma*) of Andronikos II Palaiologos, which in 1907 the Russian scholars W. Regel, E. Kurtz, and B. Korablev dated to 1291, makes it clear that by that date a dependency dedicated to Our Lady Kraniotissa and situated near the river Strymon already belonged to the monastery of Zographou.[60] However, the dating proposed by the Russian scholars in 1907 could be contested. F. Dölger has reasonably argued that this document could have been issued either in May 1291 or in May 1276.[61] Looking at the history of the Bulgarian Athonite foundation, in 2005 we supported the earlier date as more plausible.[62] However, what is of paramount importance in this imperial charter is that this is the first Athonite document which mentions Zographou as 'monastery of the Bulgarians': ἐπεὶ οἱ μοναχοὶ τῆς ἐν τῷ Ἁγίῳ Ὄρει τοῦ Ἄθω διακειμένης σεβασμίας μονῆς τῶν Βουλγάρων, τῆς εἰς ὄνομα τιμωμένης τοῦ ἁγίου μου μεγαλομάρτυρος Γεωργίου καὶ ἐπικεκλημένης τοῦ Ζωγράφου ('because the monks from the monastery of the Bulgarians, which is situated on Mount Athos and being dedicated

58 S. Lampros, 'Τὰ Πάτρια τοῦ Ἁγίου Ὄρους', *Νέος Ἑλληνομνήμων*, 9 (1912), 116–61, 209–44.
59 *Actes de Kastamonitou*, pp. 10–11, 97–101.
60 *Actes de Zographou*, no. 13.
61 Dölger, *Regesten der Kaiserurkunden des oströmischen Reiches von 565–1453. 3. Teil: Regesten von 1204–1282*, no. 2024.
62 Pavlikianov, *Istorija na bŭlgarskija svetogorski manastir Zograf*, pp. 28–9.

to the holy martyr St George is called Zographou').[63] One may, therefore, reasonably conclude that by 1276 the Athonite monks must have already been accustomed to using this term in their everyday contacts.

Zographou's archive also contains a composite delimitation of several terrains (in Greek *praktikon*), which is dated to January of the 7th *indiction* (the Latin term *indictio* is used in medieval Greek to denote a recurring fifteen-year period of time).[64] In 1907 the editors of the already obsolete edition *Actes de Zographou*, W. Regel, E. Kurtz, and B. Korablev, assumed that it dated from the late fourteenth century. However, as J. Lefort established in 1973, the persons who had issued it, Alexios Amnon and Constantine Tzympanos or Tzympeas, were tax officials in the region of Thessaloniki in about 1279–83.[65] Based on the *indiction* and on the fact that Tzympeas must have died before June 1283,[66] Lefort dated the *praktikon* in question to 1279. What is very important for us is that this is the second Athonite document offering direct evidence that Zographou was then currently labelled 'the monastery of the Bulgarians': τὴν ἐν τῷ Ἁγίῳ Ὄρει τοῦ Ἄθω διακειμένην σεβασμίαν βασιλικὴν μονὴν τοῦ ἁγίου καὶ ἐνδόξου μεγαλομάρτυρος καὶ τροπαιοφόρου Γεωργίου, τὴν καὶ τοῦ Ζωγράφου ἤτοι τῶν Βουλγάρων ἐπονομαζομένην ('the revered Athonite royal monastery of the holy and glorious martyr George, which is also called Zographou or the monastery of the Bulgarians').[67] The appearance in 1276 and 1279 of two official Byzantine acts describing Zographou as a Bulgarian monastic foundation indicates that this must have been common practice on Athos in the late thirteenth century.

63 *Actes de Zographou*, no. 13, l. 1–3. Cf. also Božilov, *Bŭlgarite vŭv Vizantijskata imperija*, 82–3; Pavlikianov, *Οἱ Σλάβοι στὴν ἀθωνικὴ μονὴ Ζωγράφου*, pp. 115–16.

64 *Actes de Zographou*, no. 52. Cf. also V. Mošin, 'Zografskie praktiki', *Sbornik v pamet na P. Nikov. Izvestija na Bŭlgarskoto istoričesko družestvo*, 16–18 (Sofia, 1940), 292–3.

65 Cf. *Archives de l'Athos VI, Actes d'Esphigménou*, ed. J. Lefort (Paris, 1973), p. 78.

66 See *Archives de l'Athos XVIII, Actes d'Iviron III*, ed. J. Lefort, N. Oikonomidès, D. Papachrysanthou, and Vassiliki Kravari with the collaboration of Hélène Métrévéli (Paris, 1994), pp. 113–15, no. 62, l. 10–11: διὰ πρακτικοῦ τοῦ Τζιμπέα ἐκείνου [i.e. the deceased] καὶ τοῦ Ἀμνὼν κυροῦ Ἀλεξίου ('with a delivery protocol of the late Tzimpeas and Sir Alexios Amnon').

67 *Actes de Zographou*, no. 53, l. 6–9. See also Božilov, *Bŭlgarite vŭv Vizantijskata imperija*, pp. 82–3; Pavlikianov, *Οἱ Σλάβοι στὴν ἀθωνικὴ μονὴ Ζωγράφου*, pp. 115–16.

Slavic-Speaking Benefactors of the Zographou Monastery

At this point we shall summarize the information we have about Zographou's sponsors during the fourteenth century. In 1342 the Bulgarian Tsar John Alexander (1331–71) issued the only medieval Bulgarian royal charter in favour of Zographou which has survived. It is written according to the Bulgarian orthographic style of the late medieval Slavic language.[68] Being one of the very few Bulgarian royal charters to have survived, John Alexander's chrysobull contains three basic points: (1) it states that the monastery of Zographou had been placed under the auspices of the Bulgarian tsars ever since the time of John Alexander's grandfather;[69] (2) it makes it clear that John Alexander had asked his relative, the Byzantine Emperor John V Palaiologos, to bequeath to Zographou the village of Chandax which was situated near the river Strymon;[70] (3) the charter also sanctions a tax exemption of 50 golden coins (*hyperpyra*) which John Alexander had asked his Byzantine cousin, John V, to grant to Zographou.[71] In truth, quite a modest donation for a person of royal rank.

Another Bulgarian benefactor of the Bulgarian monastery was one Stracimir, a *pinkernes* or high civil official of the Bulgarian Tsar John Alexander. In 1344 he bequeathed to the monastery the village of Marmarion on the coast of the Strymonic gulf.[72]

---

68 I. Sreznevskij, 'Svedenija i zametki o maloizvestnyh i neizvestnyh pamjatnikah', *Zapiski Imperatorskoj akademii nauk* (Appendix to vol. 34) (St Petersburg, 1879), pp. 24–8; *Actes de Zographou*, pp. 165–8, Slavic act no. 3; G. Ilinskij, *Gramoty bolgarskih carej* (Moscow, 1911; repr. London, 1970), pp. 21–33, no. 3; Ivanov, *Bŭlgarski starini*, pp. 587–90; A. Daskalova-M. Rajkova, *Gramoti na bŭlgarskite care* (Sofia, 2005), pp. 37–40.

69 Ilinskij, *Gramoty bolgarskih carej*, p. 22, no. 3, l. 18–21; *Actes de Zographou*, p. 166, Slavic act no. 3, l. 25–9; Daskalova-Rajkova, *Gramoti na bŭlgarskite care*, pp. 37–8.

70 Ilinskij, *Gramoty bolgarskih carej*, pp. 22–3, no. 3, l. 38–48; *Actes de Zographou*, pp. 166–7, Slavic act no. 3, l. 50–65; Daskalova-Rajkova, *Gramoti na bŭlgarskite care*, pp. 38–9.

71 Ilinskij, *Gramoty bolgarskih carej*, p. 23, no. 3, l. 48–60; *Actes de Zographou*, p. 167, Slavic act no. 3, l. 65–80; Daskalova-Rajkova, *Gramoti na bŭlgarskite care*, pp. 39–40.

72 Cf. *Actes de Zographou*, no. 36, l. 12–16. Cf. also Ph. Malingoudis, *Die mittelalterlichen Inschriften der Hämus-Halbinsel. I. Die bulgarischen Inschriften* (Thessaloniki,

In July 1372 the Patriarch of Constantinople, Philotheos Kokkinos,[73] issued a special charter in favour of Zographou. According to this document, there was a church dedicated to St Demetrios in the Bulgarian Athonite monastery. It was erected by a certain Branislav who was Philotheos's spiritual son. The church of St Demetrios is said to have been directly under the jurisdiction of the Constantinopolitan patriarch.[74] Branislav was surely the second eminent aristocrat of Slavic (presumably Bulgarian) origin, who had acted as Zographou's major benefactor. Branislav is not mentioned in any other source,[75] but Philotheos's act makes it clear that he must have been an eminent person. His social background and ethnic origin remain uncertain, but it is clear that it was he who had asked the patriarch to issue a confirmative charter in favour of the Bulgarian monastery of Zographou.[76] On the other hand, the tax exemption granted by Philotheos Kokkinos in July 1372 concerned only Branislav's church of St Demetrios and did not apply to the whole monastery, which was promoted to the rank of a stavropegic (dependent on the Patriarchate) foundation by the Patriarch Theoleptos I in 1521.[77]

1979), p. 87; V. Gjuzelev, *Bulgarien zwischen Orient und Okzident. Die Grundlagen seiner geistigen Kultur vom 13. bis zum 15. Jahnhundert* (Vienna-Köln-Weimar, 1993), p. 107; K. Pavlikianov, *The Medieval Aristocracy on Mount Athos* (Sofia, 2001), p. 164; *Prosopographisches Lexikon der Palaiologenzeit*, I–XII, ed. E. Trapp (Vienna, 1976–95) (hereafter *PLP*), no. 26861.

73 For Philotheos, see *PLP*, no. 11917; Pavlikianov, *The Medieval Aristocracy on Mount Athos*, pp. 95–6.

74 *Actes de Zographou*, no. 46; H. Gelzer, 'Sechs Urkunden des Georgsklosters Zografu', *Byzantinische Zeitschrift*, 12 (1903), 499–500 and 507–8, no. 1.

75 For Branislav cf. G. Moravcsik, *Byzantinoturcica*, 2 (Berlin, 1958), 206; *PLP*, no. 19811.

76 *Actes de Zographou*, no. 46, l. 19–22; Gelzer, *Sechs Urkunden des Georgsklosters Zografu*, pp. 499–500, 507, no. 1, l. 14–16 (verses 21–4). Cf. also J. Darrouzès, *Les regestes des actes du Patriarchat de Constantinople. I. Les actes des patriarches. Fascicle 5. Les regestes de 1310–1376* (Paris, 1977), pp. 546–7, no. 2653.

77 *Actes de Zographou*, no. 57; D. Papachryssanthou, 'Histoire d'un évêché byzantin: Hiérissos en Chalcidique', *Travaux et Mémoires*, 8 (1981), 378–9 (notes 50–3).

Prior to 1393 a certain Theodore Vladimiriou donated to Zographou an agricultural terrain named Skorivitza. Actually, it was not exactly a donation but a payment for an *adelphaton* which Vladimiriou was entitled to use in the monastery of Zographou. In late Byzantium *adelphaton* meant a sort of a prepaid lifelong annuity or social insurance provided by a religious foundation in exchange for a financial contribution.[78] Based on Vladimiriou's *adelphaton* contract, which is kept in Zographou's archive, Vladimiriou even acknowledged that Skorivitza was an ancient property of Zographou, which he had acquired without knowing that detail. The same statement is repeated in an *adelphaton* contract signed by the eminent Byzantine state official Bryennios Laskaris. According to this document, Laskaris had bequeathed to Zographou an agricultural terrain near the castle of Serres in exchange for an *adelphaton*. The text of his donation precedes Vladimiriou's contract on the same piece of paper. Neither act bears a date but, fortunately for us, Bryennios's name appears in other sources. In 1355 he is named in a *praktikon* or property description issued for the monastery of Megiste Lavra.[79] In 1361, in another *praktikon* signed by George Synadenos Astras,[80] Bryennios Laskaris is mentioned as a receiver of an imperial order (*prostagma*) dated 1354.[81] In his history John VI Kantakouzenos states that in 1327 a person with the same name was ordered by the Emperor Andronikos II Palaiologos to transfer 2,000 Cumans from Thrace to the islands of Lemnos, Thasos, and Lesbos.[82] If Bryennios was active as early as 1327, by 1354–5 he must have already been at least in his fifties. For a person of that age the purchase of an Athonite *adelphaton* should have been exactly what he needed for his approaching old age.

78   For the term *adelphaton*, see E. Herman, 'Die Regelung der Armut in den byzantinischen Klöstern', *Orientalia Christiana Periodica*, 7 (1941), 444–9; M. Živojinović, 'Adelfati u Vizantiji i srednjevekonoj Srbiji', *Zbornik radova Vizantološkog institute*, 11 (Belgrade, 1968), pp. 241–70.

79   Archives de l'Athos X, *Actes de Lavra III. De 1329 à 1500*, ed. P. Lemerle, A. Guillou, N. Svoronos, and D. Papachrysanthou (Paris, 1980), no. 136, l. 160–1.

80   *PLP*, no. 1598.

81   *Actes de Lavra III*, no. 139, l. 67–8.

82   Ioannes Cantacuzeni imperatoris Historiarum libri IV, *CSHB*, ed. L. Schopen, I (Bonn, 1828), p. 259. Cf. also *Actes de Lavra III*, 60.

The *adelphaton* contracts of Bryennios Laskaris and Theodore Vladimiriou refer to Zographou's Abbot Paul and several other monks, of whom only one, Kallistos, appears in both acts. It is, therefore, quite probable that the two documents were issued at about the same time. Based on the data discussed above, Laskaris's document could be dated to about 1350–60. Vladimiriou's act must have been composed a decade or two later, but in all events prior to the year 1393, since by that date the land of Skorivitza was already the property of Zographou.

Theodore Vladimiriou seems to have been Slavic-speaking. But his Slavic surname is not quite typical for a person of Slavic origin born in Halkidiki, since in that region the prevailing variant of the name Vladimir is usually Vlado.[83] Our conclusion, therefore, is that Vladimiriou could have been a military officer of the Serbian Tsar Stefan Dušan, whose property in the vicinity of Mount Athos was probably acquired during the Serbian military expansion in eastern Macedonia in 1345–55.

Eminent Bulgarian Churchmen on Athos during the Fourteenth Century

In 1348 the Patriarch of Bulgaria, Theodosios of Tŭrnovo, donated to the monastery of Zographou two books, which are currently kept in Russian collections. A note he had added to one of them reveals that he was a former monk of Zographou.[84] The identity of the Bulgarian Patriarch Theodosios, however, is problematic. During the last decades of the nineteenth century the prevailing opinion was that of the Russian scholar P. Syrku, who

---

83   For an example cf. Archives de l'Athos XI, *Actes de Lavra IV*, ed. P. Lemerle, A. Guillou, N. Svoronos, and D. Papachrysanthou with the collaboration of S. Ćirković (Paris, 1982), p. 236.

84   Cf. P. Syrku, *K istorii ispravlenija knig v Bolgarii v XIV veke. I. Vremja i žizn patriarha Evtimija Ternovskago* (St Petersburg, 1898; repr. London, 1972), p. 355; Ivanov, *Bŭlgarski starini*, pp. 234–5, no. 4.

considered that in the mid-fourteenth century there was only one eminent Bulgarian churchman and patriarch named Theodosios who had ruled the Bulgarian Church from 1337 to about 1360–2. This Theodosios was a supporter of the hesychast movement and founder of the famous Kilifarevo monastery near the Bulgarian capital of Tŭrnovo.[85] In 1948 A. Burmov, on the basis of the medieval *Synodikon* of the Bulgarian Church[86] and the *Introduction* to the Law Code of Stefan Dušan,[87] argued that from 1346 to 1348 the patriarch of Bulgaria was a certain Symeon, who took part in Dušan's coronation as a tsar in Skopje at Easter, 16 April 1346. Burmov's final conclusion was that the Theodosios of the aforesaid note was not the Bulgarian hesychast leader, but another, little-known, and rather obscure person with the same name, whom he labelled Theodosios II.[88] Burmov's interpretation was accepted by V. Gjuzelev,[89] but was rejected by E. Trapp and I. Božilov who spoke of only one Theodosios.[90] Burmov's arguments against the conjecture that Theodosios might have been appointed to the Bulgarian patriarchal throne twice are not very convincing: he simply stated that there was no evidence of such a practice in the Bulgarian Church. At this point special attention must be given to a text written by the Constantinopolitan Patriarch Kallistos I. This text reveals that in his youth Theodosios of Tŭrnovo had spent some time on Athos, but was finally compelled to return to Bulgaria because of the Turkish incursions on Athos.[91]

85 Syrku, *K istorii ispravlenija knig v Bolgarii v XIV veke*, pp. 141–411.

86 M. Popruzenko, *Sinodik carja Borila* (Sofia, 1928), p. 91.

87 S. Novaković, *Zakonik Stefana Dušana cara srpskog* (Belgrade, 1898), p. 4.

88 A. Burmov, 'Hronologični beležki za tŭrnovskite patriarsi Teodosij I i Teodosij II', *Izvestija na Bŭlgarskoto istoričesko družestvo*, 22–4 (Sofia, 1948), 6–11.

89 V. Gjuzelev, *Tri etjuda vŭrhu bŭlgarskija XIV vek* (Sofia, 2009), pp. 82, 96.

90 *PLP*, no. 7182; I. Bozilov, *Bulgarite vuv vizantijskata imperija* (Sofia, 1995), pp. 137, 354, no. 446.

91 V. Zlatarski, 'Žitie i žizn prepodobnago otca našego Theodosija iže v Trŭnove postničŭstvovavšago, sŭpisano svetejšim patriarhom Konstantina grada kir Kalistom', *Sbornik za narodni umotvorenija, nauka i knižnina*, 20/2 (Sofia, 1904), no. 5, 1–41, chapter 10; V. Kiselkov, *Žitieto na sv. Teodosij Tŭrnovski kato istoričeski pametnik* (Sofia, 1926), pp. XXI–XXII, 10–11. See also D. Gonis, *Tὸ συγγραφικὸν ἔργο τοῦ οἰκουμενικοῦ πατριάρχου Καλλίστου Α΄* (Athens, 1980), p. 84.

The appearance between 1337 and 1360 of two ex-Athonite Bulgarian patriarchs with the same name and the same pro-hesychast theological orientation cannot but be highly suspicious. Our opinion is that there was only one
patriarch named Theodosios and he was a former monk of Zographou.

The second eminent Bulgarian churchman attested on Athos in about
1365–70 was the famous Euthymios, the last patriarch of medieval Bulgaria
(1375–93). From Euthymios's *enkomion* by Gregory Camblak, it appears that
in about 1365 the future Bulgarian patriarch arrived on the Holy Mountain as a companion of the Constantinopolitan Patriarch Kallistos I who
was then travelling to Serbia. On Athos Euthymios joined for a while the
monks of Megiste Lavra.[92] Euthymios's monastic experience in the Lavra
of St Athanasios is also confirmed by one of his literary works, the Life of
St Paraskeve of Epivata or St Petka Epivatska, in which he tells us that the
Bulgarian Tsar John II Asen had conquered all the territory around Thessaloniki and Athos and had appointed new bishops there. Euthymios states
that he knew this from the Bulgarian imperial chrysobulls he had seen in
the monastery of Megiste Lavra and in the Protaton.[93] After several months
in the Lavra of St Athanasios he finally established himself in the vicinity of
the Bulgarian monastery of Zographou where his residence was the tower
of Selina.[94] Even today the place-name Selina is connected with a locality
between the monasteries of Zographou and Esphigmenou. The medieval
monastic settlement of Selina must have been situated somewhere in the
long valley of Vagenokamara which runs from the monastery of Esphigmenou in the north to Zographou in the south.[95] According to Camblak's

92   Syrku, *K istorii ispravlenija knig v Bolgarii v XIV veke*, pp. 553–5.
93   E. Kalužniacki, *Werke des Patriarchen von Bulgaren Euthymius (1375–1393)* (Vienna,
     1901), p. 70; Ivanov, *Bulgarski starini*, p. 432; Pavlikianov, Ἡ παρουσία Σλάβων
     μοναχῶν στὴ Μεγίστη Λαύρα κατὰ τὸ ΙΔ΄ καὶ τὸ ΙΕ΄ αἰῶνα, Ὁ Ἄθως στοὺς *140–160
     αἰῶνες* (Ἀθωνικὰ Σύμμεικτα, 4) (Athens, 1997), pp. 78–81.
94   Syrku, *K istorii ispravlenija knig v Bolgarii v XIV veke*, pp. 555–6; V. Kiselkov, *Mitropolit
     Grigorij Camblak* (Sofia, 1943), pp. 38–41.
95   *Actes d'Esphigménou*, pp. 13–14 (map) and 18. The same locality is also mentioned
     in Archives de l'Athos XX, *Actes de Chilandar I*, p. 93, no. 1 (1018), l. 7–8 and no. 14
     (1294), l. 18–19, 44.

enkomion, in 1370–1 Euthymios had a very unpleasant confrontation with a Byzantine emperor, presumably John V Palaiologos, who exiled him to Lemnos. The historical accuracy of Euthymios's imprisonment on Lemnos is highly dubious because no other sources refer to this event. Thus the only certain fact is that Euthymios must have left Athos prior to 1371.

Bulgarian Saints on Mount Athos

1. St Romylos of Vidin

St Romylos of Vidin is a well-known saint of Bulgarian origin. He was born in the Danubian town of Vidin and died in the Serbian monastery of Ravanica in about 1385.[96] The Greek and Slavic versions of his Life refer to the period he spent on Mount Athos, combining popular hagiographical clichés and offering no essential data about his participation in the philological activities of the monastic community. P. Syrku, the Russian scholar who first discovered and published St Romylos's Slavic Life in 1900, assumed that it was not a translation but an original text, composed directly in Slavic.[97] But in 1937 I. Dujčev identified a fragment of the saint's Greek Life and later a full copy of its text in the Athonite monastery of Dionysiou.[98] In 1961 F. Halkin finally published St Romylos's Greek Life, using a manuscript kept in another Athonite foundation – the monastery

96 Cf. K. Ivanova, 'Prostranno žitie na Romil Vidinski ot Grigorij Dobropisec', *Stara bulgarska literatura. IV. Žitiepisni tvorbi* (Sofia, 1986), pp. 656–8.

97 P. Syrku, 'Monaha Grigorija žitie prepodobnago Romila', *Pamjatniki drevnej pismennosti i iskusstva*, 136 (St Petersburg, 1900), pp. I–IV, XIV–XXXIII. Cf. also P. Devos, 'La version slave de la Vie de S. Romylos', *Byzantion*, 31 (1961), 149–87.

98 I. Dujčev, 'Un manuscrit grec de la Vie de St. Romile', *Byzantinoslavica*, 7 (1937–8), 124–7; idem, 'Un manuscrit grec de la Vie de St. Romile', *Studia historico-philologica Serdicensia*, 2 (Sofia, 1940), 88–92; idem, 'Romano (Romilo, Romolo) anacoreta in Bulgaria, santo', *Bibliotheca Sanctorum*, 11 (1969), 312–16.

of Docheiariou.[99] What must be immediately underscored is that the Greek tradition connected with St Romylos's life seems to be exclusively dependent upon Mount Athos and its libraries.[100]

St Romylos was neither a very popular nor a widely venerated saint. According to K. Ivanova, his cult is well attested only on Mount Athos and in the region adjacent to the monastery of Ravanica in Serbia, where he had passed away.[101] Being one of the founders of a major monastic centre at Paroria in eastern Thrace, he was compelled to escape to Athos shortly after the first Turkish assaults struck this monastic desert in the early 1350s.[102] Both versions of his Life state that when arriving on Mount Athos he encountered monks of his own nationality.[103] What we have to determine in this case is the meaning of the phrase ἐκ τοῦ ἰδίου γένους / отъ своего рода (= from his own nation). The two versions of St Romylos's Life make it clear that his lay name – Raiko in the Greek and Rusko in the Slavic text – was typically Bulgarian. Moreover, the Slavic text explicitly emphasizes that he was half-Greek and half-Bulgarian.[104] Within this framework F. Halkin considered that the passage καὶ μάλιστα ἐκ τοῦ ἰδίου γένους might well refer to the Bulgarian monks of Zographou.[105] However, neither the Greek nor the Slavic Life offers any evidence of such a connection. On the contrary, both texts state that, after a long wandering across the most desolate parts of the Holy Mountain, Romylos finally took up residence in the vicinity of Megiste Lavra, at a locality called Melana.[106] The two versions of the saint's Life offer a lot of information about his activity

99   F. Halkin, 'Un ermite des Balkans au XIVe siècle. La Vie grecque inédite de St. Romylos', *Byzantion*, 31 (1961), 111–47.

100   Cf. Pavlikianov, 'The Athonite Period in the Life of Saint Romylos of Vidin', *Σύμμεικτα*, 15 (Athens, 2002), 247–55.

101   Ivanova, *Prostranno žitie na Romil Vidinski*, p. 657.

102   Cf. *Oxford Dictionary of Byzantium*, 3 (New York – Oxford, 1991), p. 1812.

103   Halkin, *Un ermite des Balkans au XIVe siècle*, p. 131, chapter 12, l. 29–33; Syrku, *Monaha Grigorija žitie prepodobnago Romila*, p. 20, chapter 19.

104   Syrku, *Monaha Grigorija žitie prepodobnago Romila*, p. 3, chapter 2.

105   Halkin, *Un ermite des Balkans au XIVe siècle*, p. 131, note 1.

106   Halkin, *Un ermite des Balkans au XIVe siècle*, p. 132, chapter 12, l. 41–4; Syrku, *Monaha Grigorija žitie prepodobnago Romila*, p. 21, chapter 20.

there.[107] It would, therefore, be quite unlikely that Romylos's disciple and biographer, Gregory the Calligrapher, had deliberately paid no attention to the contacts that his spiritual instructor had with the monastery of Zographou, if there were any.

In the early twentieth century the Serbian scholar L. Stojanović discovered in a Slavic manuscript kept in the Bibliothèque Nationale in Paris an additional note revealing that the codex had been copied in the district Kakiplak beneath the peak of Mount Athos by a certain Dionysios, who was residing there with his spiritual father, Theoktistos, and the monks Simon and Thomas. The most intriguing element in this note is that Dionysios states that he was working at the instigation of a person he describes as 'our father and master *kyr* [sir] Romylos, the spiritual instructor'.[108] The note bears no date. Nevertheless, it is clear that Theoktistos, Dionysios, Simon, and Thomas were living somewhere at the desolate southern end of the Athonite peninsula, and were under the spiritual jurisdiction of one Romylos, who had commissioned them to copy a Slavic manuscript. To commission the reproduction of a Slavic manuscript the spiritual superintendent of this small monastic group must have been Slavic-speaking. But was he to be identified with St Romylos of Vidin, the hesychast anchorite residing at the locality Melana near the monastery of Megiste Lavra?

L. Stojanović was the first scholar to suggest, as early as 1903, that the text of the note referred to St Romylos of Vidin.[109] A strong argument supporting his suggestion derives from the text of St Romylos's Life. Being frequently disturbed by many monks who wished to benefit from his spiritual instruction, shortly before leaving Athos for good in 1371, the saint requested his spiritual son and biographer, Gregory, to find a place at the

---

107 Halkin, *Un ermite des Balkans au XIVe siècle*, pp. 131–43, chapters 12–22; Syrku, *Monaha Grigorija žitie prepodobnago Romil.*, pp. 20–32, chapters 19–32; Devos, *La version slave de la Vie de S. Romylos*, pp. 160–87.

108 L. Stojanović, *Stari srpski zapisi i natpisi*, 2 (Belgrade, 1903), p. 408, no. 4205. For a photographic reproduction of the note cf. T. Jovanović, 'Inventar srpskih ćirilskih rukopisa Narodne biblioteke u Parizu', *Arheografski prilozi*, 3 (Belgrade, 1981), pp. 306–8, no. 8 (f. 231r), p. 325 (plate 6).

109 Stojanović, *Stari srpski zapisi i natpisi*, p. 408.

northern foot of Mount Athos, sufficiently lonely and solitary to become his next, more secluded abode.[110] Analysing the expression describing the location of St Romylos's new hermitage – εἰς τὰ πρόποδα τοῦ Ἄθωνος / въ подгориа аѳонскаа – one must acknowledge that it is essentially identical with the phrase под аѳономъ used by the aforesaid scribe Dionysios. However, the evidence provided by this coincidence is not conclusive, so we must look for more arguments.

The location where the four Slavic-speaking disciples of *kyr* Romylos resided is known by a purely Greek name – Κακὴ πλάξ / на Какиплацѣ. This place-name appears in no other Athonite Greek sources. However, in 1560 a Slavic text composed by the abbot of the monastery of St Panteleimon, Joachim, offers us an unexpected solution to the problem: it states that Kakiplak was the name of a torrential stream in the vicinity of the monastery of St Paul.[111]

It is evident that, despite his intention to live in seclusion, St Romylos acted as spiritual instructor to a small, probably Bulgarian-speaking group of anchorites, led by a certain Theoktistos and including at least three other monks – Dionysios, Simon, and Thomas. Their residence was a small hermitage at the northern foot of the highest peak of Mount Athos, not far from the monastery of St Paul.

At this point we must also discuss the recent (1993) discovery of an Athonite text written by St Romylos. Its title can be rendered in English as *Rules Recommended for Proper Monastic Behaviour* (= Κανόνες τοῦ τυπικοῦ τῆς σκήτης or Правила скитскаго устава).[112] The most important detail concerning this compilation of spiritual instructions is that it is preserved in a single copy kept in the monastery of Hilandar. The dating of the *Rules*, as proposed by the editors K. Ivanova and P. Matejić, is not

---

110   Halkin, *Un ermite des Balkans au XIVe siècle*, p. 142, chapter 21, l. 6–8; Syrku, *Monaha Grigorija žitie prepodobnago Romila*, p. 31, chapter 31.

111   Arhimandrit Leonid (L. Kavelin), *Skazanie o svjatoj Afonskoj gore igumena russkago Pantelejmonova monastyrja Joakima i inyh svjatogorskih starcev* (St Petersburg, 1882), pp. 26–7.

112   K. Ivanova – P. Matejić, 'An Unknown Work of St Romil of Vidin (Ravanica)', *Palaeobulgarica*, 17/4 (1993), 3–15.

very certain – 'prior to the year 1385 (possibly 1376)'.[113] On the basis of the data discussed above, one could reasonably conclude that St Romylos's only known literary work must have been composed during his stay at Melana near the Lavra of St Athanasios before 1371, since by that date the Turkish incursions compelled him to leave Mount Athos for ever.[114] St Romylos's activity on Mount Athos seems to have been mostly connected with spiritual instruction and literary work, and the same is true of the activity of several other Bulgarian monks attested in Megiste Lavra.

Two Slavic manuscripts kept in the monastery of St Catherine on Mount Sinai – a *Triodion* and *Pentekostarion* (nos. 23 and 24) – make it clear that in about 1335–60 two Bulgarians – an elder named Joseph and one Zakchaios Zagorenin known as 'the Philosopher' – had worked as copyists and translators in the monastery of Megiste Lavra. The additional note revealing their names stresses that they were translating from Greek into Bulgarian, which was their mother tongue. The chronological framework of their activity we proposed above is based on two facts. (1) The *Triodion* contains texts written by Nikephoros Kallistos Xanthopoulos who died in 1335.[115] Logically, it must have been translated into Bulgarian after that date. (2) The two manuscripts were sent to Sinai by the Serbian metropolitan of Serres Jacob in 1360, so they must have been translated and copied before this date.[116] However, in 1355 or 1359 the Constantinopolitan Patriarch Kallistos I recommended that the monks of Megiste Lavra expel from their

113   Cf. ibid., p. 8.

114   Cf. Pavlikianov, 'Saint Romylos of Vidin and his Activity as the Spiritual Instructor of an Unknown Slavic Monastic Settlement on Mount Athos', *Annuaire de l'Université de Sofia 'St Kliment Ohridski', Centre de Recherches Slavo-Byzantines 'Ivan Dujčev'*, 91/10 (Sofia, 2002), 147–54.

115   Cf. A. Papadopoulos-Kerameus, 'Νικηφόρος Κάλλιστος Ξανθόπουλος', *Byzantinische Zeitschrift*, 11 (1902), 38–49; M. Jugie, 'Poésies rhythmiques de Nicéphore Calliste Xanthopoulos', *Byzantion*, 5 (1929–30), 357–90; F. Winkelmann, *Die Kirchengeschichte des Nicephorus Callistus Xanthopulus und ihre Quellen* (Berlin, 1966).

116   See V. Rozov, 'Bolgarskie rukopisi Jerusalima i Sinaja', *Minalo*, 5 (Sofia, 1914), 17–19; P. Uspenskij, *Pervoe putešestvie v Sinajskij monastyr v 1845 godu arhimandrita Porfirija Uspenskago* (St Petersburg, 1856), p. 219; G. Popov, 'Novootkrito svedenie za prevodačeska dejnost na bŭlgarski knižovnitsi ot Sveta gora prez pŭrvata polovina na

monastery several persons, whose theological orientation was considered erroneous and rather harmful. One of them was Gennadios the Bulgarian. The motives for Gennadios's expulsion were unrelated to his nationality, since one Albanian and a monk of 'Isaurian' origin (whatever this might mean!) had to be expelled together with him.[117]

2. St Kosmas the Zographite

St Kosmas is the only Bulgarian saint of the Byzantine period who is known to have been a monk in the monastery of Zographou. His activity in the Bulgarian Athonite foundation is traditionally dated to the end of the fourteenth and the beginning of the fifteenth century. According to his Life, the date of his death was 22 September 1422. The Greek and Slavic texts of his Life were published by I. Dujčev in 1971.[118] He used an earlier Venetian edition of St Kosmas's Greek Life published in 1803 by St Niko-dimos the Athonite,[119] the text referring to St Kosmas included in the *Megas Synaxaristes* of K. Doukakis,[120] and Codex Suppl. Gr. 1182 in the Biblio-thèque Nationale in Paris (sixteenth century, ff. 5–15v).[121] For the Slavic text of the saint's Life Dujčev also resorted to a little-known Bulgarian variant of St Kosmas's Life published by the monastery of Zographou for liturgical purposes in 1911.[122] According to Dujčev, the Zographite monks

XIV vek', *Bŭlgarski ezik*, 28/ 5 (Sofia, 1978), 402–4; Pavlikianov, Ἡ παρουσία Σλάβων μοναχῶν στὴ Μεγίστη Λαύρα, pp. 75–87.

117 *Actes de Lavra III*, no. 135, l. 19–21.

118 I. Dujčev, 'La Vie de Kozma de Zographou', *Hilandarski Zbornik*, 2 (Belgrade, 1971), 59–67; F. Halkin, *Bibliotheca Hagiographica Graeca*, I (Brussels, 1957³), p. 136, no. 393, 393b.

119 Cf. *Νέον Ἐκλόγιον*, ed. Nikodemos Hagioreites (Venice, 1803), pp. 324–6 (2nd edn, Constantinople, 1863, pp. 289–91).

120 K. Doukakis, *Μέγας Συναξαριστὴς πάντων τῶν ἁγίων*, I (September) (Athens, 1889), pp. 282–6.

121 Dujčev, 'La Vie de Kozma de Zographou', p. 60 (notes 5–8).

122 *Služba i žitie otca našego Kosmy zografskago čudotvorca* (Thessaloniki, 1911), pp. 1–21 (the religious service in honour of the saint), 23–44 (the life of the saint).

had compiled their Bulgarian version of St Kosmas's Life by translating and enriching his Greek Life as it was published by St Nikodimos the Athonite in 1803.[123]

From a literary point of view the content of St Kosmas's Life is rather trivial.[124] Its Greek version contains no references at all to miracles performed by the saint. Undoubtedly, the most important section of the Life is that which discusses how the saint had received from God the gift to foresee the future.[125] There are also two other passages which are connected with the monastery of Hilandar – one involving an anonymous abbot of Hilandar, whose death Kosmas had foreseen, and another concerning two monks of Hilandar whom Kosmas had saved from a snake attack. However, all these episodes are nothing but hagiographic commonplaces. They offer us no names, and so no cross-references can be established. One might conclude that the so-called 'Hilandar section' of St Kosmas's Life is only a compilation of banalities and clichés typical of the Athonite hagiographic tradition and mentality. Yet, there are two distinctive names that appear in St Kosmas's Life – Christophoros and Damianos. Christophoros is said to have been a hermit and St Kosmas's neighbour.[126] Unfortunately, there are no other clues to his real identity. The case of Damianos, however, is quite different. He is said to have been a resident of Samareia, a locality near the monastery of Esphigmenou.[127] Even today this is the name of a steep hill to the north-west of that monastery. St Kosmas's Greek Life makes it clear that Damianos had taken a vow never to spend even a single night outside his monastic abode. This information offers us the clue we need in order to identify him. According to J. Lefort, Damianos – 'un moine à

---

123 Dujčev, 'La Vie de Kozma de Zographou', p. 59 (note 4).

124 Pavlikianov, 'Cosma e il monastero athonita bulgaro di Zographou', *Atanasio e il monachesimo del Monte Athos*, Atti del XII Convegno ecumenico internazionale di spiritualità ortodossa, sezione bizantina, Qiqajon Publishing House (Comunità di Bose) (Torino, 2005), pp. 141–51.

125 Dujčev, 'La Vie de Kozma de Zographou', pp. 62–5.

126 Dujčev, 'La Vie de Kozma de Zographou', pp. 64–7.

127 Dujčev, 'La Vie de Kozma de Zographou', pp. 64–5. For Samareia cf. Smyrnakis, *Tò Ἅγιον Ὄρος*, pp. 635–6; *Actes d'Esphigménou*, pp. 1–7.

la limite de la légende et de l'histoire' – was a saint of Esphigmenou who died in 1281. His Life reveals that he had given to the Lord exactly the same promise – never to spend even a single night outside his cave.[128] According to the Life of St Kosmas, Damianos was visiting a friend when a heavy storm almost compelled him to break his vow. Nevertheless, his prayers were fervent enough to save his soul. He was miraculously transferred to his secluded dwelling, and on the next morning he ran to the abode of his friend Kosmas, eager to tell him about the miracle. What is important for us in this case is that St Damianos's Greek Life, which presumably refers to events before the year 1281, describes exactly the same episode. Moreover, according to the Esphigmenou text of St Damianos's Life, Damianos was visiting a friend of his named Kosmas when he was surprised by a storm. There can be very little doubt that the Lives of St Kosmas the Zographite and St Damianos the Esphigmenite essentially refer to the same event. Having studied Dujčev's publication of St Kosmas's Life, J. Lefort concluded in 1973 that its chronological framework had not been altered by subsequent editorial interventions.[129] According to him, the date of Kosmas's death – 22 September 1422 – must be the correct one. In other words, Kosmas and Damianos must have been contemporaries. Given that the date of St Damianos's death is based largely on Athonite oral tradititon, one might conclude that he must have been active during the late fourteenth century, and not during the seventh and eighth decades of the thirteenth century.[130] Yet this conclusion is of absolutely no importance as far as the monastery of Zographou is concerned. Consequently, for the time being, St Kosmas's role in the spiritual life of the Bulgarian Athonite foundation cannot be fully understood.[131]

---

128   Cf. Doukakis, *Μέγας Συναξαριστής πάντων τῶν ἁγίων*, I (February), pp. 368–71; *Actes d'Esphigménou*, p. 21.

129   *Actes d'Esphigménou*, p. 21 (note 71); Pavlikianov, *Οἱ Σλάβοι στὴν ἀθωνικὴ μονὴ Ζωγράφου*, p. 124; idem, *Istorija na bŭlgarskija svetogorski manastir Zograf*, p. 110.

130   *Actes d'Esphigménou*, p. 21 (note 69).

131   Pavlikianov, 'Saint Kosmas the Zographite and his Place in the History of the Bulgarian Athonite Monastery of Zographou', *Göttinger Beiträge zur byzantinischen und neugriechischen Philologie*, 4/5 (Gottingen, 2004/2005), 151–9.

The Bulgarian Presence in the Monastery of Koutloumousiou

At the beginning of the sixteenth century the monastery of Koutloumousiou was abandoned by its Greek tenants and was taken over by a group of foreign monks. The Constantinopolitan Patriarch, Joachim I, was officially asked to legalize the new situation.[132] A document he issued in May 1501 makes it clear that the new monastic group had immediately embarked on restoring the damaged monastery buildings, but it tells us nothing about the origin of the foreigners. Fortunately, a document issued in February 1541 by Patriarch Jeremiah I clearly refers to a Bulgarian monastic group established in the monastery. Jeremiah's main concern was the destruction of the monastery caused by the indifference of the Bulgarians who inhabited it. According to him, Koutloumousiou was then experiencing a rapid decline due to the activity of some Bulgarian monks, whose most distinctive feature was their addiction to alcohol. However, by 1541 they had already been replaced by Greeks. The patriarch underscores that, after the establishment of a new, Greek monastic group in Koutloumousiou, a serious attempt was made to restore the monastery:

καθὰ γὲ δὴ συνέβη γενέσθαι ἐν τῇ τοῦ Κωτλωμουσίου σεβασμίᾳ καὶ ἱερᾷ μονῇ. Ἕως μὲν ἦν ἐν ταῖς τῶν Βουλγάρων χερσὶν ἡ κατ᾽ αὐτοὺς μονή, μικροῦ δὴ καὶ ταύτην ἂν ταῖς οἰνοφλυγίαις καὶ ἀδιαφορίαις κατηδαφίσαντο καὶ εἰς παντελῆ ἐρήμωσιν ἤγαγον. Ἀφ᾽ οὗ δὲ ταύτην διεδέξαντο οἱ ἐκ τοῦ ἡμετέρου γένους μοναχοὶ καὶ προσεποιήσαντο, ἀνέθαλλέ τε καί, ὡς εἰπεῖν, ἀνέθορε καὶ ἀνεζωοποιήθη τὰ κάλλιστα

[As it happened in the holy monastery of Koutloumousiou: as long as it was in the hands of the Bulgarians it was quite close to total destruction because of their addiction to alcohol and complete abstinence from active engagement in the monastery's affairs. When these Bulgarians were replaced by monks from our nation, the monastery once again began to flourish.].[133]

---

132 *Actes de Kutlumus*, no. 48, l. 15–19.
133 *Actes de Kutlumus*, pp. 19–21, 173–4, 416, no. 54, l. 3–9.

The presence of Bulgarian monks in Koutloumousiou, however, had initially led to positive results. A massive donjon was constructed in 1508[134] and the main church was covered with lead in 1514.[135] These works were sponsored by the Wallachian rulers John Radul and Neagoe Basarab, but their financial support must have followed a request from the monks who were then residing in the monastery. We may therefore conclude that, after a positive development during the first two decades of the sixteenth century, the number of the Bulgarian monks in Koutloumousiou must have decreased and some parts of the monastery consequently been abandoned. The central Athonite authorities must have been seriously disturbed by this, so they would have had no objections when a Greek-speaking monastic group with significant financial potential settled in Koutloumousiou in about 1540.[136]

A year later, in March 1542, Patriarch Jeremiah I signed another document connected with the presence of Bulgarian monks in the monastic capital of Karyes. The act is kept in the monastery of Vatopedi and makes it clear that by that date some Bulgarian monks had occupied a property owned by the monastery of St Nicholas of Chouliara, despite the protests of its legal tenants.[137] The monastery of Chouliara was situated in Karyes, not far from Koutloumousiou and quite close to the site of the present-day skete of St Andrew. It would be difficult to prove that the Bulgarians who attacked the monastery of Chouliara were the monks expelled from Koutloumousiou. On the other hand, it seems unlikely that there were two separate groups of Bulgarian monks generating unrest in Karyes at the same time. Most probably there was only one group, and it was the group expelled from Koutloumousiou before February 1541.[138]

---

134   *Actes de Kutlumus*, pp. 20–1, 260–1, Appendix VII, no. 1.
135   See P. Mylonas, 'Le catholicon de Koutloumousiou (Athos). La dernière étape de la formation du catholicon athonite: l'apparition des *typicaria*', *Cahiers Archéologiques*, 42 (1994), 78–85.
136   Cf. Pavlikianov, 'The Slavs in the Monastery of Kutlumus and the Post-Byzantine Murals of its *Catholicon*', *Problemi na izkustvoto (Art Studies Quarterly)* (Sofia, 2000/4), 29–32.
137   Pavlikianov, Σλάβοι μοναχοί στὸ Ἅγιον Ὄρος, pp. 58–72.
138   Cf. Pavlikianov, *The Athonite Monastery of Vatopedi from 1462 to 1707. The Archive Evidence* (Sofia, 2008), pp. 65–7, 163, no.22.

Conclusions

The Bulgarian monastic presence on Mount Athos has always maintained a relatively low profile. It featured no impressive spiritual figures, no spectacular royal donations, and, above all, no organized interest on the part of the medieval Bulgarian Church and state, as was common practice in the case of the Serbian monastery of Hilandar. The Bulgarian infiltration of the Athonite monasteries and hermitages was always the result of a humble personal initiative, most probably because the majority of the Bulgarians attested on Mount Athos seem to have been connected with the regions adjacent to the Holy Mountain.

Bibliography

I. *Primary Sources*

A. Series Actes de l'Athos (1900–1915)

Actes de l'Athos IV: *Actes de Zographou*, ed. W. Regel, E. Kurtz, and B. Korablev, *Vizantijskij Vremennik* 13 (1907), priloženie 1 (repr. Amsterdam, 1969).

——V: *Actes de Chilandar, I, Actes grecs*, ed. L. Petit, *Vizantijskij Vremennik* 17 (1911), priloženie 1 (repr. Amsterdam, 1975).

——VI: *Actes de Philothée*, ed. W. Regel, E. Kurtz, and B. Korablev, *Vizantijskij Vremennik* 20 (1913), priloženie 1 (repr. Amsterdam, 1975).

——VII: *Actes de Chilandar, II, Actes slaves*, ed. L. Petit and B. Korablev, *Vizantijskij Vremennik* 19 (1915), priloženie 1 (repr. Amsterdam, 1975).

B. Series Archives de l'Athos (1945–)

Archives de l'Athos III: *Actes de Xéropotamou*, ed. J. Bompaire (Paris, 1964).

——IV: *Actes de Dionysiou*, ed. N. Oikonomidès (Paris, 1968).

——VI: *Actes d'Esphigménou*, ed. J. Lefort (Paris, 1973).

——VII: *Actes du Prôtaton*, ed. D. Papachrysanthou (Paris, 1975).

——IX: *Actes de Kastamonitou*, ed. N. Oikonomidès (Paris, 1978).

——V, VIII, X, XI: *Actes de Lavra I–IV*, ed. P. Lemerle, A. Guillou, N. Svoronos, and D. Papachrysanthou with the collaboration of S. Ćirković (Paris, 1970–82).

——XII: *Actes de Saint-Pantéléèmôn*, ed. P. Lemerle, G. Dagron, and S. Ćirković (Paris, 1982).

——XIII: *Actes de Docheiariou*, ed. N. Oikonomidès (Paris, 1984).

——XV: *Actes de Xénophon*, ed. D. Papachrysanthou (Paris, 1986).

——II²: *Actes de Kutlumus*, ed. P. Lemerle (Paris, 1988).

——XVII: *Actes du Pantocrator*, ed. V. Kravari (Paris, 1991).

——XIV, XVI, XVIII, XIX: *Actes d'Iviron I–IV*, ed. J. Lefort, N. Oikonomidès, D. Papachrysanthou, and V. Kravari with the collaboration of H. Métrévéli (Paris, 1985–95).

——XX: *Actes de Chilandar I*, ed. M. Živojinović, V. Kravari, and Ch. Giros (Paris, 1998).

——XXI, XXII: *Actes de Vatopédi I–II*, ed. J. Bompaire, J. Lefort, V. Kravari, Ch. Giros, and K. Smyrlis (Paris, 2001–6).

C. Other Editions of Athonite Documents

[Ternovskij, F.] *Akty russkago na svjatom Afone monastyrja sv. velikomučenika i celitelja Panteleimona (Acta praesertim Graeca, Rossici in monte Athos monasterii)* (Kiev, 1873).

Mošin, V., and A. Sovre, *Dodatki h grškim listinam Hilandarja (Supplementa ad acta graeca Chilandarii)* (Ljubljana, 1948).

Kravari, V., 'Nouveaux documents du monastère de Philothéou', *Travaux et mémoires*, 10 (1987).

II. Studies, Monographs and Articles

Bezobrazov, P., 'Ob aktah Zografskago monastyrja', *Vizantijskij Vremennik*, 17 (1910).

Bolutov, D., *Bŭlgarski istoričeski pametnici na Aton* (Sofia, 1961).

Bompaire, J., and L. Mavromatis, 'La querelle des deux Andronic et le Mont Athos en 1322', *Revue des études byzantines*, 32 (1974).

Božilov, I., *Bŭlgarite vŭv vizantijskata imperija* (Sofia, 1995).

——, 'Osnovavane na svetata atonska bŭlgarska obitel Zograf. Legendi i fakti', *Svetogorska obitel Zograf*, 1 (1995).

Božkov, A., and A. Vasiliev, *Hudožestvenoto nasledstvo na manastira Zograf* (Sofia, 1981).

Christou, P., *Τὸ Ἅγιον Ὄρος. Ἀθωνικὴ πολιτεία – ἱστορία, τέχνη, ζωή* (Athens, 1987).

Dölger, F., *Aus den Schatzkammern des Heiligen Berges* (Munich, 1948).

——, 'Die Mühle von Chandax. Untersuchung über vier unechte Kaiserurkunden', *Εἰς μνήμην Σπυρίδωνος Λάμπρου* (Athens, 1935).

Dujčev, I., 'Le Mont Athos et les slaves au Moyen âge', *Le millénaire du Mont Athos 963–1963. Études et mélanges II* (Venezia-Chevetogne, 1964).

Gelzer, H., 'Sechs Urkunden des Georgsklosters Zografu', *Byzantinische Zeitschrift*, 12 (1903).

Il'inskij, G., *Gramoty bolgarskih carej* (Moscow, 1911; Variorum Reprints, 1970).

——, 'Rukopisi Zografskago monastyrja na Afone', *Izvestija Russkago arheologičeskago instituta v Konstantinopole*, 13 (Sofia, 1908).

Ivanov, J., *Bŭlgarski starini iz Makedonija* (Sofia, 1931²; repr. Sofia, 1970).

Kodov, H., B. Rajkov, and S. Kožuharov, *Opis na slavjanskite rŭkopisi v bibliotekata na Zografskija manastir v Sveta gora*, I (Sofia, 1985).

Kovačev, M., *Bŭlgarski ktitori v Sveta gora. Istoričeski očerk, izsledvanija i dokumenti* (Sofia, 1943).

——, *Bŭlgarsko monašestvo v Aton* (Sofia, 1967).

——, *Zograf. Izsledvanija i dokumenti*, I (Sofia, 1942).

Mavrommatis, L., 'Andronikos II Palaiologos and the Monastery of Zographou (1318)', *Byzance et ses voisins. Mélanges à la mémoire de Gyula Moravcsik à l'occasion du centième anniversaire de sa naissance* (Szeged, 1994).

——, 'Le chrysobulle de Dušan pour Zographou', *Byzantion*, 52 (1982).

——, 'Ἡ πρόνοια τοῦ Μονομάχου καὶ ἡ διαμάχη γιὰ τὸν Χάντακα (1333–1378)', *Σύμμεικτα*, 14 (2001).

——, 'Μεσαιωνικὸ ἀρχεῖο μονῆς Ζωγράφου. Ἔγγραφο πρώτου Δωροθέου', *Ἀφιέρωμα στὸν Νίκο Σβορῶνο*, I (Rethymnon, 1986).

——, 'La pronoia d'Alexis Comnène Raoul à Prévista', *Σύμμεικτα*, 13 (1999).

Mošin, V., 'Akti iz svetogorskih arhiva', *Spomenik Srpske kraljevske akademie*, 91 (1939).

——, 'Zografskie praktiki', *Sbornik v pamet na P. Nikov. Izvestija na Bŭlgarskoto istoričesko družestvo*, 16–18 (Sofia, 1940).

Nešev, G., 'Les monastères bulgares du Mont Athos', *Études historiques*, 6 (1973).

Oikonomides, N., 'Theodora δέσποινα τῶν Βουλγάρων in a prostagma of Michael IX (September 1318)', *Byzantine Studies/Études byzantines*, 5, parts 1–2 (1978).

Ostrogorskij, G., 'Vizantijskie piscovye knigi', *Byzantinoslavica*. 9 (1947–8).

Papachryssanthou, D., *Ὁ ἀθωνικὸς μοναχισμός. Ἀρχὲς καὶ ὀργάνωση* (Athens, 1992).

Pavlikianov, C., *The Medieval Aristocracy on Mount Athos* (Sofia, 2001).

Pavlikianov, K., Ἡ ἔνταξη τῶν Βουλγάρων στὴν μοναστηριακὴ κοινότητα τοῦ Ἁγίου
    Ὄρους – οἱ περιπτώσεις τῶν μονῶν Ζωγράφου καὶ Ζελιάνου', *Göttinger Beiträge
    zur byzantinischen und neugriechischen Philologie*, 2 (2002).

——, 'Οἱ Σλάβοι στὴν ἀθωνικὴ μονὴ Ζωγράφου', *Σύμμεικτα*, 12 (1998).

——, *Σλάβοι μοναχοὶ στὸ Ἅγιον Ὄρος ἀπὸ τὸν Ι' ὧς τὸν ΙΖ' αἰῶνα* (Thessaloniki,
    2002).

Popov, G., 'Novootkrito svedenie za prevodačeska dejnost na bŭlgarski knižovnici ot
    Sveta gora prez pŭrvata polovina na XIV vek', *Bŭlgarski ezik*, 28/5 (1978).

Smyrnakis, G., *Τὸ Ἅγιον Ὄρος* (Athens, 1903; repr. Karyai, 1988).

Solovjev, A., and V. Mošin, *Grčke povelje srpskih vladara* (Belgrade, 1936).

Stoilov, A., 'Pregled na slavjanskite rŭkopisi v zografskata manastirska biblioteka',
    Cŭrkoven vestnik, 3/7–9 (1903), priloženie 1.

——, 'Svoden hrisovul za istorijata na Zografskija monastir', *Sbornik v čest na V. Zla-
    tarski* (Sofia, 1925).

Syrku, P., *K istorii ispravlenija knig v Bolgarii v XIV veke. I. Vremja i žizn' patriarha
    Evtimija Ternovskago* (Sankt Petersburg, 1898; repr. London, 1972).

Tchérémissinoff, K., 'Les archives slaves médiévales du monastère de Zographou au
    Mont-Athos', *Byzantinische Zeitschrift*, 76 (1983).

VLADETA JANKOVIC

The Serbian Tradition on Mount Athos

'The Holy Mountain has, from its earliest emergence as a monastic community in the ninth and tenth centuries, played an important role not only as a place where Byzantine asceticism was cherished but also as the centre of a cultural mission', wrote the late Dimitrije Bogdanović, Serbian literary historian, scholar, and authority on the Athonite tradition.[1] In his view, the Christianization of the Slav peoples was accomplished with the active involvement and participation of the Holy Mountain's monastics who were steeped in authentic Byzantine spirituality. These monks of the Slav peoples – Russians, Bulgarians, Serbs – were adopting the traditions of one state culture and transporting them back to their own countries of origin. It proved in subsequent ages to have been, in one form or another, a two-way process: the debt which the Slavs owed to the Byzantine and Athonite traditions was variously repaid and reciprocated. The monastery of Hilandar is a good example to support this theory.

The existence of the Serbian tradition on the Holy Mountain is inseparably linked to that of the monastery of Hilandar. There are no data regarding the presence of any Serbian monks on the Holy Mountain before the middle of the twelfth century, although there were probably a small number of individuals such as hermits or members of already established brotherhoods similar to those in Lavra, Vatopedi, Esphigmenou, or Iviron, and certainly some travelling pilgrims. Even so, one can say that Serbian history on the Holy Mountain begins properly in 1191 with the arrival of Prince Rastko Nemanjić (the future St Sava), while the official date can be taken to be 1198 when the main church of the restored Hilandar was completed and consecrated.

---

1   D. Bogdanović, 'Svetogorska književnost kod Srba u XIV veku', *Naučni sastanak u Vukove dane*, 8 (Beograd, 1980), 291.

The original, pre-Serbian Hilandar was situated in the same location as the present one and was founded almost certainly by the monk Grigorios Hilandaris, who by all accounts was a well-known and much-respected personality on the Holy Mountain. His name suggests that he had some connection with shipping and freight ships which were known as *helandion*, hence the name of the monastery itself (Helandariou in Greek), which could be translated as 'the boatman's'. Hilandaris, who in 976 and 979–80 intervened between the Athonite community and Emperor Basil II,[2] in April 982 sold his habitat, together with the surrounding land, to the monks of the neighbouring monastery of Iviron 'in order to live nearer the sea',[3] evidently on the very site of the present Hilandar. It is equally clear that his new premises evolved into a monastery which now carries the name of its founder and was dedicated then, as it is now, to the Presentation of the Holy Virgin. In the Holy Mountain's archives there is mention of the three abbots of Hilandar before it became a Serbian monastery;[4] the last of these was noted in 1169, from which one concludes that it must have been around the same time that the monastery was ransacked by pirates who often made raids in that part of the Holy Mountain, known as Milea. When the Serbs took it over, at the very end of the twelfth century, Hilandar was deserted and in ruins, under the jurisdiction of the Protos in Karyes.

It would be appropriate here to remind ourselves of the story, well known and reliably documented,[5] about the arrival on Athos of the man who was to resurrect Hilandar. Rastko Nemanjić was the third and young-est son of Stefan Nemanja, the founder of the medieval Serbian state and of the dynasty that ruled Serbia from the twelfth until almost the end of the fourteenth century. His early youth was spent at the court with his parents where he was especially well loved, being a late and unexpected child. Having received the best education that was on offer and befitting

2   Archives de l'Athos XIV, XVI, XVIII, *Actes d'Iviron I–III*, éd. par J. Lefort, N. Oikono-mides, D. Papachrysanthou, V. Kravari, avec la collaboration d'H. Métrévéli (Paris, 1985, 1990, 1994); *Iviron I*, no 7, l. 18–19.

3   *Iviron I*, no 8.

4   M. Živojinović, *Istorija Hilandara I* (Beograd, 1998), pp. 54, 98.

5   All sources for the early period of Hilandar's history are in M. Živojinović, *Istorija Hilandara I* (Beograd, 1998), pp. 47–53, 96.

a medieval prince, the young Rastko was particularly drawn to spiritual values and deeply impressed by tales of the austere ascetic life of the Holy Mountain, which were related to him by a Russian monk from Athos, probably a wayfaring mendicant friar, who had stopped for respite at the Serbian court. Contemporary sources[6] would have it that the youth, who was only seventeen at the time, left the court without his parents' knowledge and followed the monk to the Holy Mountain, where he initially found refuge in the monastery of St Panteleimon. The anxious father sent a posse after his favourite son and when the military contingent reached the Russian monastery, which was then situated about 3 kilometres inland from its present location, the young man hurled his princely robes and his shorn hair down from a *pyrgos* to the soldiers below, bidding them tell his father that he had become a monk and that his name was no longer Rastko, but Sava. This same tower from the eleventh century still stands in what is known as the Old Roussikon, while Sava, who was later to become a saint, remains the most deserving and revered son of the Serbian nation in its entire history.

Not long after, Sava moved from Roussikon to Vatopedi from where he proceeded to visit all of the Mountain's monasteries, but also spent extensive periods in total isolation as a recluse in the desert. In 1196 his father, Stefan Nemanja, relinquished his throne in favour of his son Stefan, who became known as 'the First Crowned' – the first Serbian ruler to become a king – while he himself 'took the cowl', entering the monastery of Studenica in Serbia as monk Simeon. From there, at Sava's summons, he joined his son on the Holy Mountain. Chronicles record in a vivid description the emotional reunion of the two men in the Vatopedi *arsanas* in November 1197.[7] Father and son then undertook a tour of all the monasteries, lavishing on them generous gifts but especially richly rewarding their hosts in Vatopedi. They also lost no time in systematically pressing for the establishment of a

6   Domentijan, *Život svetoga Simeuna i svetoga Save*, izd. Dj. Daničić (Beograd, 1865), pp. 122–7; Teodosije Hilandarac, *Život svetoga Save*, izd. Dj. Daničić (Beograd, 1860), pp. 9–21.

7   Sveti Sava, *Život svetoga Simeona* (Beograd-Sremski Karlovci, 1928), pp. 162–3; Domentijan, op.cit., pp. 154–5; Teodosije Hilandarac, op.cit., pp. 40–3.

Serbian monastic order on Athos. At the beginning of 1198, Sava obtained from Emperor Alexios III Angelos in Constantinople the chrysobull by which the monastery of Hilandar no longer belonged to the governance of the Protos in Karyes, but came under the jurisdiction of Vatopedi 'for the purposes of restoration'. The *sigillion* was accompanied by the appropriate deeds and land registry documents regarding the boundaries of the property.[8]

Almost immediately work commenced on the rebuilding of Hilandar, liberally financed by the new king of Serbia, Nemanja's son and Sava's brother, Stefan. (In truth, money for Hilandar was not a problem, either then or during the following two centuries.) The Vatopedi brotherhood was, in the beginning, reluctant to cede the monastery altogether to the Serbs, but Nemanja and Sava overcame their recalcitrance with the help of the Protos and the Holy Community in Karyes. All of them together approached Emperor Alexios with a petition appealing for Hilandar to be granted the status of an independent monastery, citing as examples the Georgian monastery of Iviron and the Italian one of Amalfitans (then in existence). The emperor granted the request in June 1198 and issued a charter with the Golden Seal whereby Hilandar, together with 'all holy ground in Milea', was to be subjected to the rule and governance of Simeon Nemanja and Sava and was henceforth to be considered 'a gift to the Serbs in perpetuity'. The original of this charter is still kept in the treasury of Hilandar.[9]

It is necessary to emphasize the significance of the fact that Hilandar, from the beginning of the twelfth century, enjoyed the status of an 'imperial *lavra*'. In the Byzantine world, monasteries were divided into episcopal, metropolitical, patriarchal, and imperial. The first three categories were bound by certain obligations to the bishops, the metropolitans, and patriarchs respectively, while the imperial ones, those under the emperor's protection, were exempt from all dues and independent of church authorities in all administrative matters (although not in matters of ecclesiastical jurisdiction).[10]

---

8   Archives de l'Athos XX, *Actes de Chilandar I, des origines à 1319*, éd. par M. Živojinović, V. Kravari (Paris, 1998), no. 4, 24–5.
9   *Chilandar I*, no. 4.
10   B. Ferjančić, 'Hilandar i Vizantija', *Manastir Hilandar* (Beograd, 1998), p. 51.

In addition to the chrysobull regarding its self-governance, Hilandar was also presented with nine villages in the environs of Prizren (in what is now Kosovo), two vineyards, four bee-keeping farms, one mountain, and 170 peasants. Together with the wealth of properties donated by King Stefan the First Crowned, the material base for the existence of Hilandar was secured.[11] Of equal importance was the fact that the first brotherhood consisted of men of the highest quality. Its core was made up of prominent nobles devoted to Stefan Nemanja, who had come with him from Serbia. They put an aristocratic stamp on the monastery, so that wealth and a certain elegance remained a characteristic of the place, well into the period of Ottoman occupation.

The renewal of Hilandar was not quite finished when, on 13 February 1199, Simeon Nemanja died. He was of a venerable age and died most probably from pneumonia. The main church must have been completed by then because sources confirm that Nemanja died in its narthex and was buried in the temple itself.[12] The remainder of the works must have been completed in the following few months because it is known that, in June of the same year, Sava had been again to Constantinople to receive from Alexios III confirmation of all the rights and privileges which had been granted to Hilandar in 1198, as well as the gift of yet another abandoned monastery, Zygou, the remains of which are not far from Ouranoupolis.[13] On his return, Sava wrote Hilandar's *typikon*, which remains in use to this day.

Hilandar's constitution was modelled on that of the Virgin Evergetis monastery in Constantinople, that is to say, a closely knit cenobitic community, working together, sharing their meal-times, all under the guidance of an abbot, with priority always given to matters spiritual. Hilandar, as the *typikon* emphasized, was independent of the Protos in Karyes and even of the emperor in the sense that it had the freedom to elect its own abbot without the need of the emperor's approval. It is also of interest that, since earliest times, the Hilandar hospital was in operation, where treatment was administered according to what were then the most up-to-date standards of western medicine, based on the teachings of Hippocrates and Galen.

11   M. Živojinović, *Istorija Hilandara I*, pp. 60–1.
12   D. Bogdanović, V. Djurić, D. Medaković, *Hilandar* (Beograd, 1985), p. 365.
13   Teodosije Hilandarac, op.cit., p. 53; Domentijan, op.cit., pp. 65, 69.

In 1199 St Sava had a cell (*hesychasterion*) built in Karyes, where he himself first lived alone and for which he wrote a specific *typikon*. In it the rules prescribe very strict norms for a hermit's life which are still adhered to. This cell in Karyes was only one of many properties belonging to Hilandar which comprised churches, fortresses, and cells, scattered all over the Holy Mountain. The most notable of these are St Basil, a very picturesque fortress and church in the harbour of Hilandar, built by King Milutin towards the end of the thirteenth century, and the *pyrgos* of the Transfiguration, in the hills an hour's walk from the monastery. All these buildings were built in locations which were strategically important for security but also, incidentally, in settings that were aesthetically pleasing. From the Karyes hermitage a magnificent view opens out to the mountain range of Athos and the open sea looking towards Thasos, while the *pyrgos* of St Basil is situated on a rocky promontory directly above the sea, and the *pyrgos* of the Transfiguration in woodland, atop a cliff from which the sea can be seen in the distance. From its beginnings Hilandar cultivated Orthodox spirituality and asceticism in various degrees, from the humble communal life accessible to all and attainable by many, to the elitist separatism and isolationism, where two or three monks would retreat for purposes of deep spiritual contemplation, hesychastic prayer, and also, very often, literary work. Indeed, some of the most notable Serbian medieval hagiographies, biographies, and hymns were written by Hilandar monks (such as Domenthian or Theodosios) in the *pyrgos* of the Transfiguration.

The economic bedrock for Hilandar's survival was the great number of estates donated to the monastery by Serbian rulers and landed gentry, from the beginning of the thirteenth right through to the fifteenth century. These holdings were situated not only in Halkidiki but scattered all over present-day Macedonia, central Serbia, and especially Kosovo. At the beginning of the fifteenth century, according to reliable sources,[14] Hilandar owned thirty *metochia* with about 360 villages, over which it excercised feudal rights. These produced so much revenue, while at the same time

---

14   R. Grujić, 'Topografija hilandarskih metohija u Solunskoj i Strumskoj oblasti od XII do XIV veka', *Zbornik radova posvećen Jovanu Cvijiću* (Beograd, 1924), pp. 517–34.

enjoying legal and administrative tax exemptions, that Hilandar was at that time virtually a state within a state. On the Holy Mountain alone it owned around 60 square kilometres, that is, effectively a fifth of the entire peninsula.[15]

There is no doubt that the thirteenth and fourteenth centuries, while the Nemanjić dynasty ruled Serbia (and right up to the battles on the river Marica and in Kosovo, which opened the way for the Turkish invasion of the Balkans), were Hilandar's 'golden age'. Apart from being one of the biggest and most influential of the Holy Mountain's monasteries, Hilandar also represented the centre of the spiritual life of medieval Serbia. At the same time it was a vital factor in matters of foreign policy, as a representative and intermediary in relations between Serbia and Byzantium. In the eyes of Byzantium, Hilandar was a lasting and inalienable testament of legitimacy, because it bore the golden seal of the emperor. With the status of an imperial lavra, Hilandar – independent and wealthy – was Serbia's best diplomatic 'envoy' in Byzantium. Moreover, without the mediating agency of Hilandar, medieval Serbia would not have embraced Byzantine culture and civilization and adopted its ancient heritage so comprehensively. Everything that was best in Serbia, its ecclesiastical, political, and cultural elite, all passed through Hilandar, whose radiance cast its light and marked out the country – economically, politically, and culturally – as one of the great powers of medieval Europe.

Deserving of mention is the turbulent period after the Fourth Crusade, when the Latin prelates, stationed on Byzantine territory by the Roman Curia, were putting great pressure on the inhabitants of the Holy Mountain to acknowledge the supremacy of the Pope, to mention his name in their church services, and to adopt the dogmas and rituals of the Roman Church. Sources confirm[16] that all the non-Greek monasteries, with the exception of Iviron, vigorously resisted, remaining loyal to Orthodoxy and loyal in their affiliation to the Byzantine state and cultural tradition. But let us return to the Serbian tradition on medieval Athos.

---

15 D. Bogdanović, V. Djurić, D. Medaković, op.cit., p. 40.
16 Cf. B. Ferjančić, op.cit., p. 51.

After Sts Sava and Simeon, its founders, the man to whom Hilandar owed most for its progress and development was King Milutin of Serbia (1286–1321). It was he who was responsible for the way Hilandar more or less looks today. The monastery's katholikon was completed in 1293 and is believed to have been the work of the master-builder Georgios Marmara of Thessaloniki. Milutin also erected sizeable ramparts and fortifications at all approaches to the monastery, such as the already mentioned *pyrgos* of St Basil by the sea and a fortified tower on the road linking the monastery to the harbour. The katholikon of Hilandar is considered to be an excellent example of Byzantine architecture, with its use of space akin to the older churches on the Holy Mountain (those of Lavra, Vatopedi, and Iviron), but with structural details taken from the so-called Palaiologan renaissance. About 100 years later, during the reign of Prince Lazar Hrebeljanović, one more narthex was added. So spontaneously and elegantly did it blend in with the whole, that the difference is hardly perceptible even to the expert eye.

By the autumn of 1321, the interior decoration of the church was also completed. For this work King Milutin had engaged some of the best artisans and craftsmen of the time. Their names unfortunately cannot be definitively verified, although, in the literature, one does come across efforts at identification. According to some conjectures, the frescos were painted by Manuel Panselinos, the great master to whom the painting in the Protaton in Karyes is attributed. Another, more likely hypothesis points to Georgios Kaliergis from Thessaloniki, who used to sign himself as 'the best painter in all Thessaly' and who is known to have been in contact with the Hilandar brotherhood in 1320.[17] Whatever the truth regarding their authorship, the Hilandar frescos are deemed to be among the most beautiful of all on the Holy Mountain. Accumulations of soot and dust had, in the course of time, darkened them to the extent that they had become almost invisible, so in 1803–4 the Hilandar monks engaged the renowned painters, Benjamin and Zachariah from Galatista, to reinvigorate the frescos

17   The issue is discussed by M. Marković, 'Prvobitni živopis glavne manastirske crkve', *Manastir Hilandar*, pp. 221–42.

by applying a fresh coat of paint. That the appearance of the frescos today is identical to the originals has been proved by probing in several parts of the church and lifting small sections of the newer layers of paint. To do this throughout would be a complicated and expensive undertaking, but with today's modern techniques it would certainly be possible, and then the Hilandar paintings would be revealed in all their original glory.

The Serbian presence on the Holy Mountain was at its peak in the second half of the fourteenth century, or more precisely, between the years 1345 and 1371, during the reign of Stefan Dušan and his immediate successors.[18] The civil war in Byzantium between John V Palaiologos and John VI Kantakouzenos, following the death of Andronikos III in 1341, opened the way for the conquests of the Nemanjić dynasty's fourth ruler. To the Serbian state, which at one time stretched from the Danube to the Peloponnese, he added Halkidiki, crowning himself in Skopje as the 'tsar of the Serbs and Greeks' – the first time in history that the Holy Mountain had accepted the reign of a ruler not crowned by the Ecumenical Patriarch; indeed, it accepted it amicably, by mutual agreement, and in a spirit of tolerance. Dušan, after all, was an Orthodox ruler, who sought to bring the Serbian empire into line with the Byzantine model and who respected and scrupulously adhered to the traditions of the Holy Mountain. In November 1345 agreement was reached that the Holy Mountain would not sever links with the emperors of Byzantium and the Ecumenical Patriarch but would, in all monasteries and during all liturgies, commemorate the name of Dušan, the new ruler, immediately after the names of the emperor and the patriarch. Dušan had magnanimously acknowledged all the privileges that the Holy Mountain had hitherto enjoyed, while the Athonites for their part, headed by the Protos, attended his coronation. The monks received chrysobulls reaffirming their privileges – something that had always been done when any change occurred on the Byzantine throne. Tsar Dušan became particularly closely involved in the affairs of the Holy Mountain between August 1347 and April 1348, when he stayed on Athos uninterruptedly,

18 This period is extensively covered in D. Korać, 'Sveta Gora pod srpskom vlašću (1345–1371)', *Zbornik radova Vizantološkog instituta*, 31 (Beograd, 1992), 9–199.

taking refuge from the plague with his whole family, including his wife
Tsarina Jelena – a rare documented case of a female presence on the Holy
Mountain. On that occasion he traversed the whole peninsula, distributing generous gifts to the monasteries, but always scrupulously avoiding any
interference in the workings of the Karyes administration. The considerable rise in influence that the Serbian monks had on the life of the Holy
Mountain can be explained by the simple fact that through them it was
easier to conduct business with the ruling administration. Also, it was the
first time in history that a number of Serbs held positions at the head of
the Protaton in Karyes. Perhaps it was because it fell between the two low
points of the recent civil war and the imminent Turkish occupation that
this particular period was to be remembered as a time of prosperity and
wellbeing. Many stories attest to this, but also documents in which the
Athonites refer to Dušan as 'our mighty lord and emperor'.[19]

When Dušan died, on 20 December 1355, he was succeeded on the
throne by his only son, Stefan Uroš V, known as 'Uroš the Weak'. The Holy
Mountain then found itself part of the so-called state of Serres, first ruled
by Jelena, Dušan's widow, and then by Prince Ioannis Uglješa. After the
defeat by the Turks in the battle on the river Marica in 1371, the state of
Serres disintegrated and the Holy Mountain temporarily (until it finally
fell to the Turks) reverted to the rule of Byzantium. Although at this point
the period of Serbian state domination on Athos was over, the presence
and influence of the Serbian noblemen continued to the end of the fourteenth century and beyond.

With the death of Uroš the Weak in 1371 the Nemanjić dynasty was
extinguished. Through the rivalries of two other prominent aristocratic families, two new names came to the fore, those of Prince Lazar Hrebeljanović
and his son-in-law, Vuk Branković. Prince Lazar (in Serbia mostly called
'Tsar' Lazar) was the leader who took his troops into the fateful battle
of Kosovo against the Turks in 1389 in which both he and Sultan Murat
were killed, spelling the final defeat of the Serbs. And although nearly 100
years were to pass before the fall of Smederevo, the last remaining free
town in Serbia, the relationship between the Serbs and Hilandar and the

19   D. Korać, op.cit., p. 122.

Holy Mountain did undergo a fundamental change. The ruling families of Lazarević and Branković still continued to support the monasteries, but now, in a situation of permanent retreat from the insurgent Turks, the relationship took on the shape of a kind of contract – *adelphaton* – whereby, in return for their deeds of charity, they could count on the Holy Mountain as a place of refuge. In time this resulted in a growing number of Serbian monks, mostly men of high birth, living not only in Hilandar but also in some of the other monasteries. The economic power of the Serbian nobility was such that they continued to fund building projects and finance literary activities, as well as donating objects of the greatest artistic value, and in this way they left an indelible mark on the Holy Mountain, until the first half of the sixteenth century.

A good example is the monastery of St Paul's[20] which, after the Catalan attacks, had practically disappeared and was reduced to the rank of a cell. In the last quarter of the fourteenth century two Serbian noblemen who had opted for the monastic life, Gerasimos Radonja and Arsenios Pagasi, built a church there, together with a lodge and a *pyrgos*. In the following decades, under the patronage of the powerful Branković family, St Paul's was as Serbian a monastery as Hilandar. A prominent role was played by Mara Branković, daughter of the despot Georgios, who was married to the Sultan Murat and later became the much-loved step-mother of Mehmet the Conqueror. She used her considerable influence to help the monasteries on the Holy Mountain and took particular care of St Paul's. There is a beautiful legend that tells of how, after the fall of Constantinople, she found in the imperial treasure house some of the gifts borne by the Three Wise Men to the new-born Christ Child. She set off with these, intending to give them to the monastery, when a voice from Heaven warned her that women were forbidden to tread on the Virgin's hallowed ground. She stopped in her tracks and handed the gifts over to the monks. On that spot a chapel was later built, which visitors can still see today on the slope between St Paul's and the sea-shore.

---

20 G. Subotić, 'Obnova manastira Svetog Pavla u XIV veku', *Zbornik radova Vizantološkog instituta*, 22 (Beograd, 1983), 207–58; see also M. Spremić, 'Brankovići i Sveta Gora', *Druga kazivanja o Svetoj Gori* (Beograd, 1997), pp. 81–100.

There is another reliably documented[21] story, which attests to the close links between St Paul's monastery and Serbia. In 1333 Tsar Dušan ceded the conquered town of Ston on the Adriatic coast to the city of Dubrovnik in exchange for an annual payment of 500 *perpera*, which was to provide a regular income for Hilandar. Later, the sultan's widow Mara, when renewing the contract with Dubrovnik, allotted half of that sum to the monastery of St Paul's. When the monks came to collect the rent, they always proved their identity with a segment of a gold piece, broken up into three parts. One bit of the coin was kept by Dubrovnik, one by the monks of Hilandar, and the third by the monks of St Paul's. Only when these three pieces were brought together and found to fit was the payment (the 'Ston stipend') disbursed. It is to the great credit of the Republic of Ragusa that this payment continued to be honoured until as recently as 1792.

In a paper of this scope and remit one can include only the most significant examples of Serbia's contributions to the monasteries on the Holy Mountain to illustrate its tradition on Athos. As already mentioned, St Paul's was one such example, where the Serbian grandees of the fourteenth century held the status of second *ktetores* (founders). Even older and more convincing is the case of Vatopedi. During the first few years of St Sava's sojourn on the Holy Mountain, he built in Vatopedi a church dedicated to the birth of the Virgin, a smaller church of St John Chrysostom, and, on top of the *pyrgos* of the Transfiguration, a *paraklesis* of the same name. He also had the roof of the monastery recovered, replacing the stone slabs with lead. After the arrival of Simeon Nemanja, father and son renovated the neighbouring little monastery of St Simeon in Prosphora and gave it as a gift to Vatopedi. They built several lodges within the monastery complex, enlarged the refectory, and had the extension adorned with frescos. It is no wonder that, after so many obvious benefits which Vatopedi received from its royal guests, there was some 'disenchantment' when Sava and Simeon left to take possession of Hilandar, no longer under Vatopedi's control. This caused some tension in the relationship for a while, but a compromise was

---

21   M. Živojinović, 'Svetogorci i stonski dohodak', *Zbornik radova Vizantološkog instituta*, 23 (Beograd, 1983), 179–88.

soon found: Vatopedi and Hilandar were to be regarded as one monastery and 'the holy *kyrios* Sava as father to both'.[22]

This 'special relationship' between Vatopedi and Hilandar still holds good today: it is not, for instance, generally known that the festive Liturgy on the day of the Presentation of the Virgin in Hilandar has for centuries been conducted by the abbot of Vatopedi, while the abbot of Hilandar does the same in Vatopedi on the day of the Annunciation. In the courtyard of Vatopedi, to the right as one enters the gate, there is a church dedicated to the Holy Anargyroi, built by Despot Ioannis Uglješa in the fourteenth century. Not long ago, some wonderfully preserved frescos were discovered there, beneath the top nineteenth-century layer, including a portrait of the despot himself as a *ktetor*. The church, dedicated to the Holy Healers, was doubtless built around 1363–4, when the plague was raging in Serres. It had killed the sister and the only son of Despot Uglješa. In the treasury at Vatopedi numerous precious objects are to be found which were gifts from Serbian noblemen. Among the relics there is a much-venerated garment of the Virgin, donated by Prince Lazar, and, in the archives, there are documents and covenants relating to estates and goods which the Serbs had given to the monastery. The cult of Sts Sava and Simeon has been preserved in Vatopedi from the Middle Ages to the present day, evidenced by depictions of them in the frescos situated immediately next to the famous mosaic in the narthex of the katholikon. Lastly, a few years ago in Vatopedi an icon was discovered depicting the face of St Sava, the oldest existing portrait of him, possibly painted from life.

Evidence of the Serbian presence on the Holy Mountain is also to be found in the chronicles of St Panteleimon, which was on the brink of extinction in 1348 when Tsar Dušan gave the monastery a gift of four villages in the hinterland of Halkidiki and, a year later, when he formally became second *ktetor*, another nine villages and a large donation of money.[23] The tsar's successors, especially the Lazarević family, continued to help the mon-

22   Domentijan, op.cit., p. 164.
23   R. Grujić, 'Svetogorski azili za srpske vladare i vlastelu posle kosovske bitke', *Glasnik Skopskog naučnog društva*, 1 (Skopje, 1932), 69.

astery, for which the Serbs were richly rewarded in later centuries, during the Turkish occupation, when Hilandar monks travelling through Russia received support from the Russian nobility and their rulers, among whom particular generosity was shown by Ivan the Terrible.[24]

In the second half of the fourteenth century the monastery of Simonopetra had become completely deserted. The Serbian Despot Ioannis Uglješa, with the permission of the Holy Community, rebuilt the whole monastery on the same cliff where it had stood before. All those buildings were destroyed in the disastrous fire of December 1580, when many of the monks also lost their lives. Today, all that is left of the despot's benefactions is one icon of the Virgin, but the brotherhood, generation after generation, still reveres the memory of their second *ktetor*.

All sources with references to St Sava, including two early biographies (one contemporary),[25] speak of the important role he played in renovating and revitalizing the monasteries of Xeropotamou, Karakalou, Konstamonitou, and Philotheou. In Xeropotamou he built the church of the Forty Martyrs. He paid off Karakalou's debts, which had caused the monastery at one point to be 'repossessed' and to become a *metochion* of Great Lavra. Apart from stories and legends Esphigmenou has no records from the time of Sts Sava and Simeon, but this monastery had a close connection with the Serbian nobility in the period between the second half of the fourteenth and the beginning of the fifteenth century. Despot Uglješa, for example, built a hospital in the south-western corner of the monastery's complex, which was known as his endowment, until it was burnt down in the fire of 1770. And Despot Georgios Branković accepted the brotherhood's invitation to become their new *ktetor* and granted the monastery an income of 50 litres of silver, to be paid annually from the silver mines in Novo Brdo in Kosovo. There is a charter, kept in Esphigmenou, relating to this arrangement which is a masterpiece of the calligraphic art and contains exquisite illustrations, among them a depiction of the ruler's family.[26]

---

24   S. Radojčić, 'Umetnički spomenici manastira Hilandara', *Zbornik radova Vizantološkog instituta*, 3 (Beograd, 1955), 175–6. See also S. Petković, 'Hilandar i Rusija u XVI i XVII veku', *Kazivanja o Svetoj Gori* (Beograd, 1995), pp. 143–70.

25   Domenthian was St. Sava's contemporary, while Theodosios lived a generation later.

26   *Esfigmenska povelja despota Djurdja*, ed. P. Ivić, V. Djurić, S. Ćirković (Beograd, 1989).

What is superbly documented is the role played by the Serbian noble-man, Radič Postupović, in the annals of the monastery of Konstamonitou. There, a document from 1430 has been preserved[27] which attests that he totally renovated an impoverished and mostly dilapidated monastery, equipped it with all necessities, and, in addition, introduced a *typikon* which sets out, in very precise detail, the way of life the monks should pursue and the strict cenobitic discipline they should follow. In all likelihood Radič himself retreated into monastic life and spent his old age in Konstamonitou and this is why his memory is very much revered at the monastery, which still operates according to the rules laid down by him.

Naturally, the greatest single contribution to the Serbian tradition on the Holy Mountain is the Hilandar monastery itself with its theological and liturgical heritage and priceless art treasures. The history of Hilandar is an organic part of the Holy Mountain's history. Hilandar enjoys the privilege of being the only non-Greek monastic community which heads one of the five *tetrades* (groups of four monasteries) on the Mountain. Hilandar also is officially ranked fourth in the Athonite hierarchy. So much has now been said about the influence exerted on the Holy Mountain by Serbian rulers, aristocracy, and clergy that too little space is left to take a look at the influence that Hilandar and the Holy Mountain had on the ecclesiastical and cultural development of Serbia. Such a glance would reveal, among other things, a seemingly paradoxical situation that arose when the influence of western art on the Orthodox Slav Balkans came, not directly, but in a roundabout way via the Holy Mountain, particularly during the period of the fall of Byzantium. The monks then increasingly adopted the icons and frescos of the Italo-Cretan masters, as well as the influences of late Gothic workmanship. These western achievements were more readily accepted by the Orthodox hinterland because they came to them 'sanctioned', as it were, from the Holy Mountain, whose Orthodoxy was above reproach and could be trusted.

I would like to mention one other, less well-known story, especially interesting in the light of the present inter-ethnic relations in the Balkans. An Albanian chieftain by the name of Ivan Kastriot, fleeing from the Turks, sought refuge and was granted asylum, in the manner of *adelphaton*, for

27   R. Grujić, 'Svetogorski azili', pp. 83–7.

himself and his four sons. For a certain sum of money (60 florins) they
were offered hospitality and given accommodation in a *pyrgos* for life.
Before he died, Ivan Kastriot most probably became a monk in Hilandar,
where he is buried, as is his son Repoš. Repoš's grave is in the north wall
of the Hilandar church and bears the inscription 'Here lies the slave of
God, Illyrian duke.' The youngest of Ivan Kastriot's sons, however, later
adopted Islam and became the national hero of all Albanians, celebrated
and universally known as Skenderbeg.[28]

Let me conclude this paper on a somewhat personal note. I wish to
state, from direct personal experience, what an uplifting and soul-enhancing
experience it is for a Serb, in our time, to make a pilgrimage to the Holy
Mountain. The reason for this is that, on Athos, memory is incomparably
longer and history more vividly present, than anywhere else in the modern
world. Remembrance of the ties with a Serbia of the past – a noble, generous, brave, and magnanimous Serbia – is passed on from generation to
generation of monks, and is as vivid as if the events of that glorious past
took place only yesterday. For one who belongs to a nation whose reputation, particularly in the last decade of the last century, has been systematically eroded by the media and dragged through the mud more than at
any time in its history, to be welcomed with open arms, with warmth and
respect, just because one is from Serbia, has a priceless, unparalleled value.
When you are offered lodgings for the night in a remote skete, where they
are normally unable to provide accommodation for visitors, it is because
they have not forgotten that 700 years ago a certain Serbian nobleman had
paid for repairing the roof of their church or had given the brotherhood a
gift of the book of the four Gospels, which they still treasure today. When
they invite you in a venerable ancient monastery to take part in their festive
Liturgy by reading the Symbol of Faith in your own language, the honour
is bestowed because the monks remember that it was your great ancestor
who built their *paraklesis* and their hospital. Such experiences are not only
personally rewarding but are the strongest possible proof of how deeply
rooted and alive is the Serbian tradition on the Holy Mountain.

28   Ibid., p. 81.

Bibliography

Bogdanović, D., V. Djurić, and D. Medaković, *Hilandar* (Beograd, 1978).

Christou, P., *Mount Athos* (Thessaloniki, 1990).

Ćorović, V., *Sveta Gora i Hilandar do XVI veka* (Beograd, 1985).

Deroko, A., *Sveta Gora* (Beograd, 1966).

Djurić, I., 'Podatak iz 1444. o svetogorskom manastiru Karakalu', *Zbornik Filozofskog fakulteta* (Beograd, 1979).

Grujić, R., 'Svetogorski azili za srpske vladare i vlastelu posle kosovske bitke', *Glasnik Skopskog naučnog društva*, 11 (Skopje, 1932).

Korać, D., 'Sveta Gora pod srpskom vlašću (1345–1371)', *Zbornik radova Vizantološkog instituta*, 31 (Beograd, 1992).

Lake, K., *The Early Days of Monasticism on Mount Athos* (Oxford, 1909).

Millet, G., *L'ancien art serbe, Les églises* (Paris, 1919).

Nasturel, P. S., *Le Mont Athos et les Roumains* (Roma, 1986).

Naumov, A., and D. Gil, 'Poljsko-litvansko pravoslavlje i Sveta Gora – Atos', *Zbornik radova sa skupa Osam vekova Hilandara* (Beograd, 2000).

Nenadović, S., 'Gradjenje i gradjevine', *Osam vekova Hilandara* (Beograd, 1987).

Ostrogorsky, G., *History of the Byzantine State* (New Brunswick, 1997).

Papahrisantu, D., *Atonsko monaštvo* (Beograd, 2005).

Petković, S., *Hilandar* (Beograd, 1989).

——, 'Hilandar i Rusija u XVI i XVII veku', *Kazivanja o Svetoj Gori* (Beograd, 1995).

Radojčić, S., *Srpske ikone od XII veka do 1459. godine* (Beograd, 1960).

——, 'Umetnički spomenici manastira Hilandara', *Zbornik radova Vizantološkog instituta*, 3 (Beograd, 1955).

Spremić, M., 'Brankovići i Sveta Gora', *Druga kazivanja o Svetoj Gori* (Beograd, 1997).

Subotić, G. 'Obnova manastira Sv. Pavla u XIV veku', *Zbornik radova Vizantološkog instituta*, 22 (Beograd, 1983).

Subotić, G. (ed.), *Manastir Hilandar* (Beograd, 1998).

Tachiaos, A. E., 'Le monachisme serbe de Saint Sava et la tradition hesychaste athonite', *Hilandarski zbornik* (Beograd, 1966).

Živojinović, M., 'Le domaine de Chilandar sur le territoire byzantine de 1345 a 1371', *Mount Athos in the 14th-16th Centuries* (Athens, 1997).

——, *Istorija Hilandara I* (Beograd, 1998).

——, *Svetogorski pirgovi i kelije u srednjem veku* (Beograd, 1972).

MARCUS PLESTED

Latin Monasticism on Mount Athos

Evocations of the universality of the monastic witness of Mount Athos tend, naturally, to focus on its pan-Orthodox character within the world of the Christian East, as the other contributions to this volume amply and ably illustrate. But it comes as a surprise to many to discover the existence for some centuries of a flourishing Latin and Benedictine monastery on the Holy Mountain. St Benedict himself remains deeply reverenced on the Mountain: his icon adorns many a katholikon and monks bearing his name are not unusual. It has even been suggested that the well-known Athonite greeting and response – '*Eulogeite*! *ho Kurios*' (Bless! The Lord [bless]) – is closely related to an almost identical Benedictine usage.[1] But while Benedict's name remains blessed on the Mountain, and few houses lack a monk of western provenance, the idea of a house celebrating the Latin rite and following the Benedictine rule can be contemplated today only with a very great imaginative leap. Indeed, the very existence of a Latin Athonite house is something some monks would prefer to forget. I have some personal experience of this: on a visit in 1993 I recall being hurried past the site of this monastery by an Athonite companion unwilling to linger at or dwell upon what is certainly one of most intriguing spots on the Mountain.

It is one of the tragedies of the schism between Greek East and Latin West that genuine and profound theological and ecclesiastical differences

---

1   See J. Leroy, 'Saint Benoît dans le monde byzantin' in idem, *Études sur le monachisme byzantin* (Bellefontaine, 2007), pp. 435–6 (originally published in P. Tamburrino (ed.), *San Benedetto e l'Oriente cristiano* (Novalesa, 1981), pp. 169–82). Leroy also notes that Byzantine liturgical texts sometimes present Benedict as a martyr or even as supreme pontiff: a sure sign of esteem, if not of historical accuracy.

have, on both sides, led too often to a blanket rejection of the whole tradition of the opposing party. Such a blanket rejection is, I fear, explicit in the recent declaration of the Holy Community in response to the papal visit to the Ecumenical Patriarch in November 2006 and the visit of the Archbishop of Athens to the Vatican in December of the same year. In this important statement, the Holy Community speaks of Athonite monasticism as the 'non-negotiable guardian of Sacred Tradition'. From that standpoint, the declaration criticizes various aspects of these visits that would seem to imply some sort of recognition of the legitimacy of the papacy and acceptance of common ground between Orthodoxy and the West. The declaration indeed asserts a fundamental *incompatibility* between the West and Orthodoxy.[2] Relations between Athos and the West have rarely, if ever, conformed to this black-and-white, dichotomous framework. There have been severe strains and great difficulties but, from the historical point of view, the situation that emerges is more complex and nuanced than the Holy Community appears to allow. The story of Latin Athonite monasticism is a shining and salutary reminder that East and West have met on the Mountain, and that both have been enriched in that encounter.

2   'It is important that all these [visits and discussions] do not give the impression that the West and Orthodoxy continue to have the same bases, or lead one into forgetting the distance that separates the Orthodox Tradition from that which is usually presented as the "European spirit". Europe is burdened with a series of anti-Christian institutions and acts, such as the Crusades, the "Holy" Inquisition, slave-trading and colonization. It is burdened with the tragic division which took on the form of the schism of Protestantism, the devastating World Wars, also man-centred humanism and its atheist view. *All of these are the consequence of Rome's theological deviations from Orthodoxy.* One after the other, the Papist and the Protestant heresies gradually removed the humble Christ of Orthodoxy and in His place, they enthroned haughty Man.' The Holy Community, Holy Mountain of Athos, Karyes, 30 December 2006. Protocol Number 2/7/2310. It is remarkable to note in this document the way in which the consequences of the Latin errors have been kept up to date, now encompassing slave-trading and the German wars. This practice of maintaining lists of errors was eagerly pursued by Latins and Greeks alike: Thomas Aquinas' *Contra errores graecorum* is perhaps the least edifying of that great doctor's works. Tia Kolbaba has produced an excellent study of the Byzantine part of this equation: *The Byzantine Lists. Errors of the Latins* (Urbana, IL, 2000).

Going back to the very beginnings of Athonite monasticism, we have a prime instance of Roman involvement in the career of St Peter the Athonite in the ninth century – one of the first Athonite hermits we know by name. According to his (semi-legendary) Life, it was to the Pope in Rome that St Peter went, at the instigation of St Nicolas, for his somewhat delayed monastic tonsure – perhaps around 839–40.[3] The fact that he should have gone to Rome is by no means improbable given that Rome was, at this time, a bastion of orthodoxy while the East had relapsed into iconoclasm.

In the tenth century, at the momentous time of the foundation of the cenobium of Great Lavra by St Athanasios, Latin monks had already begun beating a path to the *Monte santo*. The Life of St Athanasios speaks of Latin monks being among the many drawn to Athos because of his fame. Out of their great respect for him, certain western monks bring him a gift of caviar. This is a foodstuff too rich and fancy for the saint to eat, but he nonetheless accepts the gift so as not to offend them.[4] The *typikon* of St Athanasios contains several incontrovertible albeit minor borrowings from the rule of St Benedict.[5] The generous treatment of Latin monasticism by St Athanasios also intimated by the instruction in his statutes that a monk 'tonsured outside' (ξενόκουρος) be welcomed into the community and treated as an equal.[6] This injunction certainly does not apply only to Latin monks: the

3 The most widespread version of the Life is that of St Gregory Palamas (*PG* 150 996–1040). Kirsopp Lake gives an earlier version, on which Gregory's composition is dependent: *Early Days of Monasticism on Mount Athos* (Oxford, 1909), pp. 18–39. Gregory makes a point of mentioning the Pope's icon-veneration. See also E. Amand de Mendieta, *Mount Athos* (Berlin, 1972), pp. 56–7.

4 Ed. L. Petit, 'Vie de S. Athanase l'Athonite', *Analecta Bollandiana*, 25 (1906), 56. See also P. Lemerle, 'La vie ancienne de saint Athanase l'Athonite composée au début du XIe siècle par Athanase de Lavra', *Le millénaire du Mont Athos 963–1963* (Chevetogne, 1963), pp. 59–100.

5 See J. Leroy, 'Saint Benoît dans le monde byzantin', p. 449. The theme is also developed in the same author's 'S. Athanase et l'idéal cénobitique' (in *Le millénaire du Mont Athos*, pp. 101–20). Here he memorably describes the image built up in the Life as a conscious act of monastic synthesis: 'En [Athanase], Théodore le Studite et Benoît de Nursie se rejoignent, le byzantin et le romain, l'oriental et l'occidental'.

6 See P. Meyer, *Die Haupturkunde für die Geschichte der Athosklöster* (Leipzig, 1894), p. III lines 31–2.

distinction under censure is primarily that between those tonsured inside and outside the Lavra.[7] But this ruling, with the concomitant insistence that no one should be called a foreigner within the community, stands as a further sign of Athanasios's unswerving commitment to a truly catholic and universal vision of Athonite monasticism.

We are fortunate in possessing the names of some of the Latin monks within St Athanasios's orbit in a number of early Athonite documents. An act of Iviron dated December 984 (concerning a gift from the Lavra) bears the signatures in Latin of two monks – John and Arsenios – among the non-Lavriote witnesses to the donation.[8] These same names occur in a document of the following year, 985, with John now designated 'monachos ton Apothikon' and again serving as witness.[9] This toponym indicates an area at the northern limit of the territory of the Lavra as defined in the *typikon* of Athanasios, that is Cape Kosari, at the southern end of Morphonou bay, a region now best known as the location of the sacred spring of St Athanasios. These indications suggest that the establishment of a Latin house is to be dated before 984.

The place-name 'Morphonou' preserves the name of this house, which became the famous imperial monastery of the Amalfitans (variously referred to in the sources as ἡ μονὴ τῶν Ἀμαλφηνῶν or, later, ἡ τῶν Μολφηνῶν μονή).[10]

---

7   A comparison may be drawn here with *Catechesis* 18 of St Symeon the New Theologian. Here the term ξενοκουρίτης applies to monks tonsured in another monastery but seeking entry to a new community. Unlike Athanasios, Symeon disapproves of such wanderers and warns that they will always be in a position of inferiority. See H. J. M. Turner, "'A Carefree and Painless Existence'? Observations of St Symeon the New Theologian on the Monastic Life', in *Sobornost/ECR*, 12:1 (1990), 45n. Turner renders it 'alien monk'.

8   Iviron 6 in *Actes d'Iviron: I*, ed. J. Lefort et al. (Paris, 1985) (Archives de l'Athos XIV), pp. 135–40. The fact that these two are witnesses, and not members of the Lavra, is overlooked in a number of the secondary sources (Pertusi, Keller).

9   Iviron 7, op. cit., pp. 141–51. In this document, Arsenios is now Arsenius – not, I think, a significant shift. My geographical comments are dependent upon the notes accompanying the edition of the Acta.

10   On this foundation, see, in addition to the articles cited in note 16: L. Bonsall, 'The Benedictine Monastery of St Mary on Mount Athos', *ECR* 2 (1969), 262–7; O. Rousseau, 'L'ancien monastère bénédictin du Mont Athos', *Revue liturgique et*

All that remains now of this once thriving Latin and Benedictine house is its imposing tower, emblazoned with a single-headed eagle, together with a few lesser ruins. The house fell into disrepair in the thirteenth century, at which time Lavra assumed responsibility for the buildings and for the continuation of monastic life there, a responsibility it has done little to fulfil. There were, however, some significant restoration and rebuilding works at both the monastery and its maritime fortress in 1534–5 paid for by the Voyevod of Wallachia, Petru Rareş. These works give the ruins considerably more substance than they would otherwise have had.[11] But in its heyday this community provided an eloquent and living statement of the integrity of the Latin monastic and liturgical tradition at the heart of Athos. And, intriguingly, it did so well into the period conventionally dated as post-schism (i.e. after AD 1054).

Vivid details of the foundation are to be found in the Life of St John and St Euthymios, the Georgian founders of the monastery of Iviron.[12] In this Life, which is of considerable historical value, we have a record of the arrival of a certain monk Leo, brother of the Duke of Benevento, with six companions, on Mount Athos – perhaps around AD 980. It is quite conceivable that the John and Arsenius who signed the acts of 984 and 985 were among these companions. The two Georgian saints are recorded as having greeted Leo with great enthusiasm as fellow foreigners. They go on to offer their full support, material and spiritual, in establishing a Latin monastery. In response to this encouragement and to requests from fellow 'Romans' in Constantinople who wished to join him, Leo established a large community patterned on the rule and teachings of St Benedict and soon to enjoy an enviable reputation for piety and integrity, not to mention a delightful situation. The date of the foundation may be put between 980 and 984.

---

monastique (1929), 531–47; A. Keller, *Amalfion: Western Rite Monastery on Mount Athos* (Austin, TX, 1994–2002). More on the 'imperial' designation below.

11   Thanks to Archibald Dunn for drawing my attention to these later renovations.

12   Ed. B. Martin-Hisard, *REB* 49 (1991), 67–142. Chapter 27 (109–10) deals with this episode. Tamara Grdzelidze has recently produced a fine English translation, *Georgian Monks on Mount Athos: Two Eleventh-Century Lives of the Hegoumenoi of Iviron* (London, 2009).

Amalfi, in Campania, was the first of the Italian states to secure extensive trading privileges with the Byzantine empire, including the right to its own quarter in Constantinople.[13] According to Liutprand of Cremona, they were not (in 968) above flirtation with contraband.[14] Mercantile savvy coupled with good relations with the Arabs helped create a flourishing maritime power down to the time of its surrender to the Normans in 1073. Amalfi had a church and monastery in Constantinople from the early tenth century and, from 1020, a monastery that functioned as the chief hostel for western pilgrims in Jerusalem. The monasteries in all three places were dedicated to the Mother of God. We do hear of other Italian houses on Athos in this period, monasteries of Sicilians and Calabrians, but these were Greek-speaking communities and certainly lesser in importance than the great house of the Amalfitans.

The *Chronica monasterii Casinensis* of Leo of Ostia records a monastic tour made by John of Benevento which included, after six years on Sinai, a sojourn (around 986) on Mount Athos during which St Benedict himself appeared in a nocturnal vision urging his return. There are strong grounds for assuming that he lodged with his fellow Benedictine countrymen at this time.[15] Some further details of the history of the Athonite monastery of the Amalfitans may be gleaned from other Athonite documents of the period. Lavra §9 (991) is again witnessed in Latin script by a John now styled abbot (*higuminus*).[16] This appears to be the same John who

13   See M. Balard, 'Amalfi et Byzance (Xe–XIIe siècles)', in *Travaux et Mémoires*, 6 (1976), 85–95.

14   *Relatio de legatione*, 359, cited in Balard, op. cit., p. 89.

15   MGH 34, ed. H. Hoffman (Hanover 1980), p. 206.

16   Lavra 9, in *Actes de Lavra: I*, ed. P. Lemerle et al. (Paris, 1970), pp. 118–22. Further references to the Athonite *acta* concerning this monastery can be sourced in the following articles: A. Pertusi, 'Nuovi documenti sui Benedettini Amalfitani dell'Athos', *Aevum*, 27 (1953), 410–29; P. Lemerle, 'Les archives du monastère des Amalfitans au Mont Athos', *Epeteris Hetaireias Byzantinon Spoudon*, 23 (1953), 548–66; A. Pertusi, 'Monasteri et Monaci Italiani all'Athos nell' Alto Medioevo', in *Le millénaire du Mont Athos 963–1963* (Chevetogne, 1963), pp. 217–51. The Lemerle article offers an important critique of some of the interpretations, datings, and sources of Pertusi (1953), to which Pertusi (1963) offers a response.

had signed the acts of 984 and 985. Lavra §17 (1012) is signed by 'Johannes monachus', Lavra 19 (1016) by 'Johannes monachus et abbas', and Lavra §21 (1017) (in Greek) by 'John the Amalfitan'.[17] In all instances, this appears to be the same John, acting in an official and representative capacity, adding his weight to these important documents, whether issued by the Protos or some other authority. John often signs in a prominent position in the list, indicating something of the prestige of his monastery The variations in self-designation are not of great moment: there appears to be no great premium placed on consistency of titles in the Athonite *acta*.

Lavra §15 (1010) mentions the property of the Amalfion, while Lavra §23 (1018–19) finds in favour of the monastery in a dispute over property and associated rights with Lavra and Karakalou. The monastery of the Amalfitans is singled out for special privileges in the *typikon* of Emperor Constantine IX Monomachos (September 1045). One of the main points of the *typikon* was to restrict the mercantile activities of the monasteries, many of which had, it seems, taken to fitting out ships to trade wine and other commodities as far as the Queen of Cities and beyond. The *typikon* therefore forbids the monasteries to keep large boats, excepting cases where they had already secured permission to do so from a previous emperor – as Vatopedi had done. A further exception was made for the Amalfion:

> All agreed to a further dispensation whereby monastery of the Amalfitans was to be allowed to own a large boat since they were unable to survive by any other means. They were not to make use of this boat for commercial gain, but they were to travel with it to the Reigning City if they wanted to import anything they needed for their monastery or to be supplied from those who love Christ.[18]

The implication here is that the monastery's needs were to a certain extent supplied from the Amalfitan community in Constantinople – a definite point of vulnerability. Shortly after the surrender of Amalfi to the Normans we have, in 1081, two documents indicating that the Amalfion was

---

17   The 'Johannes humilis monachus Amalfitanus' of Lavra §29 (1035) is distinguished from the former John in the index to the *Actes de Lavra*, presumably on grounds of autograph.

18   Given in Meyer, *Die Haupturkunde*, p. 157 lines 22–7.

building up its landholdings – perhaps as a way of addressing the material problems caused by the decline in Amalfitan power and prestige. The
monks of Kosmidion in Constantinople confirm to Abbot Benedict of
the 'imperial monastery of the Amalfitans' the perpetual possession of an
estate by the river Strymon in Macedonia.[19] Note the 'imperial' status of
the monastery – the same rank as Lavra, Iviron, and Vatopedi. In the same
year, Alexios I Komnenos addresses a chrysobull to the 'imperial monastery
of the Amalfitans', again confirming their possession of certain lands.[20] The
crisis of 1054 evidently had no impact on the ability of the Amalfitans to
secure imperial patronage.

A glimpse of the spiritual labours of the Amalfion is given by some
of its literary products in this period. A certain Leo translated the miracle
of St Michael at Chonae into Latin at the instigation of the brethren of
the Latin cenobium of Mount Athos. There are other Latin translations
of saints' lives which may have an Amalfitan connection.[21]

Moving to the end of the eleventh and into the twelfth century, the
name of the abbot of the Amalfion continues to appear in a prominent
place on a series of Athonite documents, lending his authority to the Protos
as higoumenos of one of most senior monasteries. This abbot is named as
Vito in 1087[22] and 1108.[23] A certain 'M.' signs in fifth place a document of
1169 as abbot of 'the cenobium of St Mary of the Amalfitans', his signature
following that of the Protos and the representatives of Lavra, Iviron, and
Vatopedi.[24] At the end of the twelfth century, in 1198, the establishment
of Hilandar as a specifically Serbian monastery is justified by analogy with

---

19   Lavra §42.
20   Lavra §43.
21   Keller, op. cit., p. 13, gives a useful account albeit one that indulges a little too much
      speculation as to the specifically Athonite and Amalfitan connections of these
      texts.
22   Philotheou §1 (See Lemerle, 'Les archives', p. 553). Bito is named twice, second only
      to the abbot of Lavra, as one who assists the Protos.
23   In the last of these, Lavra §57, Abbot Bito signs in fifth place, after the Protos and
      the abbots of Iviron, Vatopedi, and Karakalou, granting possession of a ruin close
      to the *kellion* of Prophourni in Karyes to Lavra.
24   Acta Rossici Monasterii §7. See Lemerle, 'Les archives', p. 554.

the existence of other non-Hellenophone houses on the Mountain: those of the Georgians and of the Amalfitans. The Serbian house is also granted precisely the same autonomy and self-governing status as that enjoyed by those houses.[25] At that time the monastery was certainly a fully functioning community. But by 1287 the monastery is said to be in a ruinous and deserted state, hence its properties and rights were transferred to the Great Lavra on the basis that Lavra would undertake to restore and repopulate the monastery.[26] In succeeding centuries, the last references in the Athonite archives are to squabbles over formerly Amalfitan land between Karakalou and Lavra, with Lavra invariably maintaining the upper hand.

The reasons behind this fall from prosperity are unknown. Certainly there is never any indication in any of the sources of Athonite objections to the liturgy or theology of the Latin house. The Amalfitan house in Constantinople supported the papal claims and the superiority of the Latin liturgy in the 1054 crisis but there is no such indication with regard to the Athonite house.[27] No mention whatsoever is made of the house in the period of the Latin empire (1204–61), nor in connection with the Latinizing policy of Michael VIII Palaiologos (1259–82). While the general anti-Latin feeling aroused by the Fourth Crusade may well have made a Latin foundation – however Orthodox – unsustainable on Athos, I suspect that economic pressures may have had the final word. Amalfi itself declined to insignificance as a Mediterranean power in the twelfth century: in the 1130s alone it was sacked or captured three times. The massacre of Latins in Constantinople in 1186 will also have limited the capacity of the

---

25 Hilandar §3 contains the petition of the Protos and council to Emperor Alexios III Angelos. In Hilandar §4 the emperor graciously accedes to the request, expressly concurring with the analogy drawn with Iviron and the Amalfion. *Actes de Chilandar I* (Archives d'Athos XX) ed. M. Zivojinovic et al. (Paris, 1998), pp. 100–10.

26 Lavra 79 (*Actes de Lavra* II, ed. P. Lemerle et al. (Paris, 1977), pp. 46–50). The monastery is referred to as ἡ τῶν Μολφηνῶν μονή. Lavra §80–1 record the confirmation of the grant by the patriarch and emperor respectively.

27 See Balard, op. cit., and A. Michel, *Amalfi und Jerusalem in griechischen Kirchenstreit (1054–1090)* (OCA 121) (Rome, 1939). Peter Damian explicitly commends the Constantinopolitan brethren for their loyalty *a catholica Fide* at this time (*Ep.* 6.13: *PL* 144: 396C–397C).

Amalfion to secure revenue from the Latin faithful of the City. The ravages of the Crusaders in the lead-up to the sack of the City will certainly have decreased the revenues from the Amalfitan estates. Perhaps the Amalfion was already dying on its feet by 1204. Much of this, however, is conjecture. We simply do not know exactly what happened to this intriguing Orthodox *and* Latin house.

The Fourth Crusade – whether or not it caused the decline of the Amalfion – was certainly a low point in Athonite–Latin relations.[28] Shortly after the eternally shameful sack of Constantinople by the Crusaders in 1204, the Latin successor to the bishop of Sebaste, superintendent of Athos, set about a systematic pillage of the monasteries of the Holy Mountain. This rapacious prelate established a fortified base just outside the current land boundary of Athos, on the site of the former monastery of Zygou (itself a reminder that the Amalfion was not the only powerful monastery to come and go in the early years of Athonite history). This is the place known as Frangokastro today. Hearing of the vexatious activities of this bishop, Pope Innocent III, who had initially opposed the attack on Constantinople and who deplored the crimes committed at that time, relieved this bishop of his position in 1209[29] and in 1213 placed Athos directly under the protection of the Holy See.[30] In the bull of 1213, which was issued in response to a petition of the downtrodden monks, the Pope praised the Holy Mountain and its denizens in the highest possible terms and confirmed them in all their previous imperial privileges. But he makes no mention of the Amalfion. Athonite reaction to this mark of favour is not recorded, although by 1223 Pope Honorius III was complaining that the monks were, unsurprisingly, 'disobedient to the Apostolic see and rebellious'.[31] Again, the Amalfion is passed over in silence.

---

28   The relations between Athos and the West are expertly and helpfully discussed by
      C. Korolevskij in *DHGE* 5, 81–9.
29   *De custodia monasteriorum Montis Sancti* (*PL* 216: 229 BC).
30   The bull is given in G. Hofman, 'Athos e Roma', *Orientalia Christiana*, 5 (1925),
      148–50.
31   This letter, 'Priori et fratribus domus Cruciferorum Nigripotensibus', is cited in
      G. Hofman, 'Rom und Athosklöster', *Orientalia Christiana*, 8 (1926), 8.

Matters did not greatly improve with the restoration of Byzantine control of Constantinople in 1261. Michael VIII concluded a union with Rome in 1274 at the Council of Lyons, a union he and many of his successors thought essential to the survival of the empire (and which had some tangible short-term benefits: union was an essential precondition of the intricate diplomacy behind the Sicilian Vespers). The emperor and his patriarch John Bekkos naturally sought a measure of conformity to this policy across the restored empire. The monks of Athos were, after their dire experiences at the hands of the Latins, unlikely to welcome this policy. It is probably to this period, and not so much to the period of the Latin empire, that most of the tales of Latinizing persecution are to be dated. While our sources for this period are largely in the form of legends, and thus of only very limited historical value, they serve to indicate at least some measure of coercion. Certainly, this period remains the imaginative centre of Athonite anti-westernism (for all that much of the 'western' persecution was directed by a Byzantine emperor). Michael's son and successor Andronikos II repudiated his father's unionist policy; but, while he enthusiastically and lavishly supported the monks, he was also indirectly responsible for inflicting upon them the ravages of Catalan mercenaries in the early fourteenth century. Mendieta calls this 'the most dreadful experience that the Holy Mountain had to undergo in its thousand years of existence'.[32]

Perhaps the most evocative tale of the period is the grisly story of the Cave of the Wicked Dead. In this cave lie the blackened bodies of some monks of Lavra who at a certain time conformed to the Latin rite of the mass. As divine punishment for this enormity, the dead bodies of these unhappy monks were not given to decay in the normal way but rather remained intact – with their hair and nails still growing. These gross specimens are now hidden away in a cave (which Dawkins, who records the legend, locates between Prodromou and Lavra)[33] as a permanent warning against involvement with the wicked West. It seems most unlikely that such a tale could emerge except at a time and in a context when the very existence of a Latin-rite house on the Mountain had been all but forgotten – perhaps deliberately so.

---

32 *Mount Athos* (Berlin, 1972), p. 90.
33 R. M. Dawkins, *The Monks of Athos* (London, 1936), pp. 305–6.

It would be a great mistake to suppose that all Athonite monks of the Palaiologan period were implacably opposed to union with Rome. The greatest defender of the Athonites, St Gregory Palamas, was by no means opposed to union. Likewise, the profoundly Palamite Patriarch of Constantinople, Philotheos Kokkinos, actively pursued a scheme to convoke a new Ecumenical Council that would 'unite the Church'.[34] Indeed it was often the opponents of Palamas, such as Barlaam, Akindynos, and Gregoras, who were most strenuously anti-unionist.

It is therefore not entirely surprising to find senior Athonites supporting the reunion project that culminated in the Council of Ferrara-Florence in 1438–9 – shortly after Athos itself had submitted to the Turks in 1430. The declaration of union *Laetentur caeli* contains the signatures of representatives of Lavra, Vatopedi, Pantokrator, St Basil's, and St Paul's.[35] At this time, Pope Eugenius IV granted a substantial indulgence to those who visited and supported the monastery of Vatopedi.[36] An official policy of union seems to have prevailed at both Lavra and Vatopedi at least for a decade or so after Florence. Perhaps this is the period to which the 'wicked dead' belong. The unionist policy evidently did not last: in 1459 the then Pope, Pius II, complained that both these houses had lapsed from their obedience to the apostolic see.[37]

The fall of the last Byzantine possessions to the Ottomans had, by that time, put the question of reunion firmly out to grass. The fact that the monks of Athos had voluntarily submitted to Sultan Murat II in 1430 stood very much in their favour, although they were to find the tax burden imposed by the Ottomans extremely and increasingly burdensome. One of the solutions was to seek funds from Christian territories and this certainly included territories in the West. In 1593 Clement VIII granted two monks of Docheiariou permission to seek alms in Catholic lands. He did the same to a group of monks from Esphigmenou in 1604, even going so

34   John Meyendorff, 'Mount Athos in the Fourteenth Century', in *Dumbarton Oaks Papers*, 42 (1988), 161–2.
35   Given in Hofman, 'Athos e Roma', pp. 150–1.
36   Hofman, 'Rom und Athosklöster', pp. 9–10.
37   Ibid., p. 10.

far as to write them a letter of recommendation to King Philip II of Spain.[38] Such marks of favour generally required profession of the Catholic faith. This is something these monks do not appear to have found problematic, at least on a temporary basis.

It was in the seventeenth century that one of the most remarkable chapters in the history of Athos took place: the Jesuit connection.[39] The Jesuits, who were active in many areas of the Sultan's realm, certainly sought to encourage reunion with Rome. They were, it seems, also genuinely keen to provide spiritual and material succour, and more generally to help shore up the Eastern Church against the very real threat of Protestantism through education, preaching, and the administration of confession. Contacts between the Jesuits and Athos go back to at least the early seventeenth century when an Athonite monk was among the students at the Jesuit school in Constantinople (and is reported to have taken to practising the spiritual exercises of Ignatius Loyola). In 1628 the Jesuits were approached by a former abbot of Vatopedi who offered to negotiate the reunion of the Mountain with Rome (nothing came of the scheme). More tangibly, in 1635 a Jesuit school was founded, by invitation, at the Protaton. Much of the curriculum was based on the teaching of classical Greek, but it also involved lectures on the sacraments. The head of the school, Fr Nicolas Rossi, also spoke out against the degeneracy of the idiorrhythmic system. We have no evidence that the presence of the Jesuits on Athos was in any way resented by the monks. Quite to the contrary, we have from 1643 records of an offer by the Holy Community of a permanent residence for Italian monks on Athos, provided the Jesuits could produce in exchange a church in Rome, a *metochion* to be served by Athonite monks. The project foundered when the church offered by the Jesuits was turned down by the Holy Community on the grounds that it was in an unsatisfactory location.

---

38 Ibid., pp. 17–19.
39 The documents concerning Jesuit relations with Athos can be found in the above-mentioned collections of documents assembled by G. Hofman, 'Athos e Roma', *Orientalia Christiana*, 5 (1925), 137–83 and 'Rom und Athosklöster', *Orientalia Christiana*, 8 (1926), 4–39.

Athonite enthusiasm for the Jesuits is, at least in part, a testament to the Jesuits' own openness in dealing with the monks, and indeed with the Orthodox more generally. The Jesuits were careful to acknowledge the jurisdiction and prerogatives of Orthodox bishops and abbots. They recognized, at least implicitly, the validity of Orthodox orders and sacraments. They also valued similar texts to those of the fathers of the Mountain. To give just one example: both Jesuit and Athonite novices are recommended to read the *Macarian Homilies*.[40] To the more fundamentalist proponents of Roman Catholic dogma, all this amounted to 'going native' – and here we might see an analogy with the heavy Jesuit involvement with liberation theology in contemporary South and Central America. Competition over the holy places in Jerusalem had greatly worsened relations between Rome and Constantinople from the late seventeenth century onwards. In this atmosphere of worsening relations, pressure from the Inquisition led to the condemnation of the Jesuit policy of, in effect, accepting the continued existence of a partial communion between Rome and the Orthodox. After 1736 we no longer hear of any significant Jesuit activity on Athos.

One last example of a positive estimation of Latin ascetic traditions may be mentioned: St Nikodimos of the Holy Mountain. The co-editor of that incomparable work of Orthodox *ressourcement*, the *Philokalia*, Nikodimos wrote vigorously and vociferously against Latin theology but also genuinely esteemed certain examples of Counter-Reformation spirituality. He published lightly adapted translations of the *Spiritual Combat* of Lorenzo Scupoli and the *Exercises* of Ignatius Loyola, being careful in both cases to obscure the Catholic provenance of these works. So far as he was concerned, these sources might be freely employed in order to support and confirm the Orthodox tradition.

These examples, and the various others I have mentioned, should, I hope, have served to indicate that the story of 'Athos and the Latins' does not, after all, support the picture of unmitigated and eternal antagonism conjured up by the recent Karyes statement. Athos has often been ill-served by the West, it is true. But it has also been supported and defended by the

---

40   See my *The Macarian Legacy* (Oxford, 2004), p. 111.

West. The Latin rite and Benedictine rule have flourished on Athos. Even Jesuits have been welcomed and acclaimed at the very heart of the Mountain. In short, what I want to say is that the authentic and living Orthodox witness of Athonite monasticism is not best served by overly simplistic contrasts. The Latins have an honourable and eternal place in the Athonite *pleroma*. It is a legacy that must not be forgotten.

Bibliography

Amand de Mendieta, E., *Mount Athos* (Berlin 1972).

Bonsall, L., 'The Benedictine Monastery of St Mary on Mount Athos', *Eastern Churches Review* 2 (1969), 262–7.

Grdzelidze, T., *Georgian Monks on Mount Athos: Two Eleventh-Century Lives of the Hegoumenoi of Iviron* (London, 2009).

Hofman. G. (ed.), 'Athos e Roma', *Orientalia Christiana*, 5 (1925), 137–83.

——, 'Rom und Athosklöster', *Orientalia Christiana*, 8 (1926), 4–39.

Keller, A., *Amalfion: Western Rite Monastery on Mount Athos* (Austin, TX, 1994–2002).

Kolbaba, T., *The Byzantine Lists. Errors of the Latins* (Urbana, IL, 2000).

Lake, K., *Early Days of Monasticism on Mount Athos* (Oxford, 1909).

Lemerle, P., 'Les archives du monastère des Amalfitans au Mont Athos', *Epeteris Hetaireias Byzantinon Spoudon*, 23 (1953), 548–66.

Meyer, P., *Die Haupturkunde für die Geschichte der Athosklöster* (Leipzig, 1894).

Pertusi, A., 'Monasteri et Monaci Italiani all'Athos nell' Alto Medioevo' in *Le millénaire du Mont Athos 963–1963* (Chevetogne, 1963), pp. 217–51.

——, 'Nuovi documenti sui Benedettini Amalfitani dell'Athos', *Aevum*, 27 (1953), 410–29.

——, Rousseau, O., 'L'ancien monastère bénédictin du Mont Athos', *Revue liturgique et monastique* (1929), 531–47.

Speake, G., *Mount Athos: Renewal in Paradise* (New Haven, CT, 2002).

CONSTANTIN COMAN

Moldavians, Wallachians, and Romanians on Mount Athos

My presentation is structured on three levels: personal, historical, and an attempt to understand theologically the history of the relationship between Romanians and the Holy Mountain. I am not a historian. For this reason I have paid more attention to the other two components: personal testimony and the theological reading of history. For me, history makes sense only if assumed personally and evaluated theologically. For the historical part I have used two recent works.[1] I have long and rich experience of Mount Athos (this year makes three decades). Somehow it is indicative of a certain kind of approach Romanians have towards the Holy Mountain. I am attached to Athonite monasticism. I love the Holy Mountain. I find support in the Athonite monks' prayers for me, my family, and my work in teaching theology and in the Church. I find great comfort in the fact that certain Athonite monasteries and monks remember me, my family, and my community in their daily prayers. One of them is a young Romanian hermit whom I met last summer. Then we started a beautiful, intense spiritual relationship. I find support in the Athonite monastic experience in my theology too. I praise God for being alive during a strong renewal of Athonite monasticism.[2]

---

1 An almost complete anthology of articles published in Romanian in the last two centuries and recently edited by G. Vasilescu and I. Monahul, *Romanians and the Holy Mountain*, 2 vols [in Romanian] (Bucharest, 2007), and a doctoral thesis of one of my younger colleagues at the Faculty of Theology in Bucharest, Fr Ioan Moldoveanu, entitled 'Contributions to the History of the Relations between the Romanian Countries and Mount Athos' [in Romanian] (Bucharest, 2007).

2 It is an epoch of perceptible hesychast regeneration, similar to the ones that took place in the sixteenth and eighteenth centuries. The hesychast effervescence is sustained by the existence of several great spiritual personalities who have inspired the

I would identify two specific characteristics of Athonite monasticism: (1) the exclusive monastic character of the population of this region, which makes it a monastic republic, and (2) its multi-ethnic character. The special sanctity of the place is the result of its first specific trait, and Orthodox peoples' consequent approach to it. The second specific trait reveals the challenge addressed by God to the Orthodox peoples for leading the monastic life together.

From this perspective, I would describe the Holy Mountain as a multinational rather than a supranational structure, due to the fact that the former faithfully expresses the right perspective on the unification or unity that preserves the identity of those in union. Unity does not mean creating a superstructure, but fulfils the vocation of being together, of accepting each other the way we are. The beauty of the Holy Mountain lies in the fact that monks of all Orthodox nationalities should live there loving each other. Togetherness is a sort of marriage and it involves overcoming the borders that separate one from the other. As in the case of a mixed marriage, so in Athonite monasticism, there is one more border to cross without eliminating it, that of belonging to different nations.

The permanent coexistence, in different proportions, of all manner of weakness and the highest experiences of divinity, explains why the nationalist element can be transcended, but also manifested in a worldly manner, at the same time. I will use this hermeneutical framework to interpret the presence of Romanian monks on the Holy Mountain and its place in the Romanians' past and present self-conscience. For this reason, I will try to look at Romanians' specific gifts and weaknesses. That is the dowry with which they enter into the ecclesiastical and monastic marriage with other peoples.

---

current renewal of Athonite monasticism (St Silouan, Elder Joseph, Fr Sophrony, Fr Paisios, Fr Ephrem of Katounakia, etc.), of certain great communities dedicated to the practice of hesychasm, such as the monasteries of Simonopetra and Vatopedi, and the appearance of an abundant literature of spiritual testimonies.

Romanian Monks on the Holy Mountain

History records the continuous presence of Romanian monks on the Holy Mountain since the beginning. Romanians have had a special devotion and love for the Mountain and have always longed to live there, even though the Mountain has not always received them with the same love. Equally important is the Romanian people's special vocation for monasticism, consistently attested throughout history. Romania's territory has always been full of monasteries and sketes. Today there are 423 monasteries and 183 sketes housing more than 2,966 monks and 5,174 nuns.

The presence of a community of Vlachs on the Holy Mountain has been attested since the eighth century, when Athos had not yet become an exclusively monastic territory.[3] In the eleventh century we meet the Vlachs again as shepherds on Athos, simply living together with Athonite monks, helping them in many ways, but also causing them trouble.[4] Their memory has been kept alive until today. A Romanian historian discovered a baptismal font at the Protaton around 1930. The ecclesiarch told him that it dated back to the Vlachs' time.[5]

The first historical records of the presence of Romanian monks on the Holy Mountain date back to the fourteenth century. This is the century when the Romanian feudal states were established (1330, the Romanian Country or Wallachia; 1359, Moldavia) and also the first Romanian metropolitanates (Hungaro-Wallachia in 1359 and Moldavia in 1401). Mount Athos was to make an important contribution to the organization of church and monastic life in the newly formed Romanian states. Pious Nikodimos, a Serbian monk at Hilandar, set up the first monasteries in Muntenia (Vodita

---

3   In 885 Basil I the Macedonian and later on Leo the Wise stopped them coming into the Holy Mountain in order to protect the monks.

4   There are said to have been more than 400 families of Vlachs. Alexios I Komnenos had to expel them and forbid them access to Athos, as they were disturbing the monastic life.

5   Marcu Beza, 'The Vlachs at the Holy Mountain', in *Romanians and the Holy Mountain*, vol. 1, pp. 432f.

and Tismana) and established monastic rules. Some of the Greek Athonite monks became metropolitans of the Romanian principalities. This is also the time when the Romanians started helping the Holy Mountain.

The presence of a significant number of Romanians at Koutloumousiou is attested in the second half of the fourteenth century, from the evidence of supplies sent by the Romanian Voyevod Vladislav I. He had the Greeks grant the Romanians the right to follow the idiorrhythmic system, even though the Greek monks of the monastery lived a cenobitic life. Although Romanians flocked to this monastery, over which the Romanian Voyevod Vladislav I had obtained the title of 'owner and founder', the monastery remained under Greek jurisdiction. He had sworn that the Romanians would 'honour and obey the Greeks ... and not fall into the temptation of looking down upon the Greeks, on the grounds that the walls of the monastery, the refectory and the cells and even the properties that my lordship is going to buy are made for the Romanians ....'[6] That seems to have been the reason why the number of Romanians coming to Koutloumousiou decreased and the connections of the monastery with the Romanian principalities weakened by the end of the fourteenth century.[7]

This episode indicates a certain characteristic of Romanian monks, namely their preference for the idiorrhythmic life, unlike the Greek monks who prefer the cenobitic. It also illustrates an important aspect of the Romanian monks' presence on the Holy Mountain. Although Romanian rulers were to be the main supporters of the Athonite monasteries for five centuries, and the connections between the Holy Mountain and the Romanian principalities were very strong, the Romanian monks did not have a monastery of their own, but lived in monasteries mainly populated by other Orthodox nationalities or in the settlements dependent on them.

6   Alexandru Elian, 'Biserica Moldovei şi muntele Athos la începutul secolului al XIX-lea', in *Romanians and the Holy Mountain*, vol. 1, p. 483.

7   However, the number of the Romanian monks and the conditions that they had benefited from under Hariton were never repeated according to Byzantinist Al. Elian, who argues that the name 'Romanian Lavra' given to Koutloumousiou was inconsistent with the real state.

The beginning of Romanian establishments on the Holy Mountain can be dated back to the second half of the eighteenth century. Some Moldavian monks settled at Lakkou skete under the jurisdiction of St Paul's monastery in 1754. In 1760 the skete was renovated with the help of schema-monk Daniel, Paisios Velichkovsky's disciple. Lakkou skete became one of the most heavily populated Romanian establishments. In 1760 at New Skete, also on the territory of St Paul's monastery, there were sixteen cells and ten huts, all of them Romanian. At the time there were about twenty-four Romanian cells and almost a hundred Romanian hermits on the Holy Mountain.

The Esphigmenou 'Offer'

In May 1805 the monks at Esphigmenou, led by Abbot Theodoretos the Lavriote, suggested to the Metropolitan of Moldavia, Veniamin Costachi, that in exchange for yearly aid, which the monks desperately needed, it could become a Moldavian monastery.[8] The Greek monks resorted to this solution after a very difficult period in the life of the monastery. It seems that the idea was initiated by Metropolitan Daniel of Thessaloniki, who had saved Esphigmenou while he was its abbot. Seeing that 'the Moldavian monks who flock to the Holy Mountain wander about in vain and return to their own without any result', he thought that he could help both the monastery and the Moldavian monks by turning the monastery into a 'settlement of that nation'.[9]

The Byzantinist Alexandru Elian discovered the act in which this offer was made, unprecedented in the history of the relationship between Romanians and the Holy Mountain. The document has exceptional value for these relations and the question of a Romanian monastery on the Holy Mountain. In the eight chapters of the document it is stated, among other things, that,

8   Al. Elian, art. cit., pp. 484f.
9   Ibid., p. 486.

if the metropolitan of Moldavia and the Moldavians help the monastery survive, resist, and pay to the empire taxes of 4,000 grosz annually, then the monastery of Esphigmenou and all its fixed and current assets, many or few, wherever they are, will immediately and surely be considered the Moldavians' own property, which can never be alienated or taken away.[10]

It was also established in the same act that the metropolitan and the voyevod of Moldavia should be commemorated just as in Moldavia, that the abbot should be elected from the Moldavian monks, that the services should be sung in the Moldavian language, and the papers of the monastery 'should be drawn up in the Moldavian language and alphabet in the same way that Hilandar's and Zographou's papers are drawn up in Slavonic'.

The content of the last article of the document is relevant for the multinational character of Athonite monasticism:

> As it is customary that in the communities on the Holy Mountain there should also live monks of other nationalities (as in the case of the monasteries of the Greeks, Russians, Serbians, and Bulgarians), this should also happen in the sanctified Moldavian monastery of Esphigmenou, that the foreigners are to be treated just like the foreigners in the Greek monasteries and the monasteries of Hilandar and Zographou, and follow the customs, rules, and manners of the Moldavians, in all the affairs of the monastery.[11]

Stunningly, and almost inexplicably, the metropolitan rejected this offer,[12] though he did help the monastery by dedicating the monastery of Floresti to it.[13]

---

10   Ibid., p. 488.
11   Ibid., pp. 488–9.
12   The reason given by Metropolitan Veniamin Costachi is shortage of money: 'the great difficulties' that he had been confronted with when he became metropolitan (the absence of the voyevod's and the noblemen's support) 'stunned him into not accepting the offer that, in exchange for an annual amount, one of the great monasteries of Athos should become a Moldavian monastery, and the Romanians, like other Orthodox peoples, Russians, Serbians, Bulgarians, let alone the Greeks, should have a monastery of their own on the Holy Mountain'.
13   Metropolitan Veniamin's refusal is even more inexplicable when we learn that twenty-two years later the income from the Floresti monastery's lands in Barlad amounted to 21,020 piasters.

Metropolitan Veniamin's refusal is hard to explain in the light of his later initiative. In 1820 he asked the Great Lavra to give permission for the Romanians to establish a skete. This did happen, but only as a dependency of the Lavra, which was far less favourable to Romanians than the Esphigmenou offer.

The Romanian Skete Prodromou

The most important Romanian settlement on the Holy Mountain was to be the Prodromou skete. Originally a cell, its first known Romanian monks were from the brotherhood of the monastery of Neamț, Fr Justin and his disciples, Patapios and Gregory. Around 1810–16 they bought the Prodromou cell from the Lavra monastery. Following a request addressed by Metropolitan Veniamin Costachi of Moldavia to the Great Lavra, in 1820 the two disciples of Fr Justin obtained for the cell the status of 'cenobitic skete of the faithful people of the Moldavians', through an act which in thirteen sections defined the relation between the skete and the monastery. The Greek Revolution of 1821 saw the two monks banished from Prodromou. In 1840, when the community had reached thirty monks, the skete was devastated by an attack of the Turkish army.

In 1852 two other Romanian monks, Nifon and Nektarios, bought back the Prodromou skete from the Great Lavra for 7,000 grosz and reopened it. A new document was drawn up, adding four more sections to the existing thirteen. Prodromou was asked to pay 1,000 grosz annually to the Lavra and to limit the community to a maximum of twenty monks. The first prior and founder of the skete is thought to have been Hieroschemamonk Nifon Ionescu. In 1860 the construction of the church was finished.

This was when the state of Romania was formed by the unification of Moldavia and Wallachia in 1859. Romania acknowledged the Prodromou skete as a Romanian settlement and in 1863 the Romanian government decided to give the skete 1,000 ducats annually, which was later raised to 3,000 and then to 4,000 ducats. In 1871 King Charles acknowledged the skete as a Romanian community and changed the seal to 'the seal of the Romanian cenobitic skete of the Holy Mountain of Athos'. The maximum number of twenty admitted monks was exceeded. By then their number had reached 100.

The history of the skete was affected by events. The secularization of monastic estates in Romania nullified the Romanians' request addressed to the Holy Community in 1880 to obtain for the skete the status of a monastery. The liberation of the Holy Mountain from the Turks in 1912 and the transfer of its rule to the Greeks mark the beginning of a new stage, not only for Romanian monks, but for other nationalities as well - Russians, Serbians, Bulgarians, and Georgians.[14] The introduction of the new calendar in 1923 found the Romanian monks on the Holy Mountain in fierce opposition from their base in the Romanian skete. Consequently, starting in 1927, the Romanians' access to the Holy Mountain was practically blocked, being made conditional on the approval of one of the twenty monasteries, the Ecumenical Patriarchate, the Greek government, the archbishopric of Athens, and the renunciation of Romanian citizenship in favour of Greek.

Despite the vicissitudes of these times, monastic life at the Romanian skete of Prodromou has been kept alive to the present day. It was in serious decline by the 1970s, but it has since revived spectacularly together with all Athonite monasticism. Today the Romanian skete of Prodromou, considered by both Romanians at home and the Romanian Athonites to be 'the Romanian monastery', is completely restored and has a beautiful community of about forty monks gathered around two great spiritual fathers, Fr Petronios, the thirteenth prior of the skete, and Fr Julian.

14   Until then it was enough for monks to declare that they were Orthodox in order to benefit equally from all the rights and prerogatives granted to the Athonites by the Byzantine emperors and the Turkish sovereigns, irrespective of nationality. From now on, the Greek element of the Athonite population, subscribing to the current trend for national renewal, asserted itself by imposing severe measures against the monks of other nationalities who were regarded with reserve and considered undesirable. See Liviu Stan, 'Caracterul Interorthodox al Muntelui Athos', in *Romanians and the Holy Mountain*, vol. 1, p. 366.

The second most important Romanian establishment on the Holy Mountain is Lakkou skete, which belongs to St Paul's monastery. At the beginning of the nineteenth century, Lakkou had more than thirty cells where more than eighty monks lived in self-denial. Later in the nineteenth century 120 monks lived in the same number of cells. In 1975 the skete had only four monks left. There are currently thirteen cells and quite a few monks and brethren living the ascetic life there.

Today, about 200 Romanian monks live on Mount Athos.

Assistance Accorded to the Holy Mountain by Romanians[15]

For a period of about 500 years, from the fourteenth until the nineteenth century, the Romanians were the principal sustainers of the Holy Mountain. It was a unique historical and religious phenomenon which has not yet been fully studied and evaluated. It goes beyond the scope of my paper to cover this in depth, which is why I shall outline the beginnings and then try to offer some illuminating episodes.

The period when Romanians started sending aid to the Holy Mountain has been historically attested as the fourteenth century. In 1360 Ana, one of the daughters of the Romanian Voyevod Nicolas Alexander Basarab, married the Serbian Despot Stefan Uros.[16] It is possible that even during the wedding ceremony, which was attended by many Athonite abbots, or afterwards through Ana's intercessions, Abbot Hariton of Koutloumousiou contacted the Romanian voyevod in order to ask him for help.

15 See Teodor Bodogae, 'Historical Considerations Regarding the Relations between the Romanian Orthodox Church and Mount Athos', in *Romanians and Mount Athos*, vol. I, pp. 441–53.

16 See Petre Nasturel, 'The Links between the Romanian Countries and Mount Athos until the Middle of the Fifteenth Century', in *Romanians and Mount Athos*, vol. I. p. 456.

Nicolas Alexander died in 1364 and in 1369 his son, Vladislav I (Vlaicu Voda), committed himself to rebuilding the Koutloumousiou monastery:

> I will encircle the monastery with walls and a reinforcing tower and build a church, a refectory, cells; I will ransom lands and donate animals so that through this my lordship's parents and I should be commemorated [...] as the Serbian, Bulgarian, Russian, and Georgian rulers are commemorated on the Holy Mountain![17]

In 1372 Abbot Hariton became the second metropolitan of Hungaro-Wallachia. He was to play an important role in relations between the Romanian principalities and the Holy Mountain because he remained the abbot of Koutloumousiou and became the Protos of the Holy Mountain in 1376. The Romanian voyevod's title as founder was acknowledged along with his right to appoint the abbot.[18] Hariton imposed a categorical provision on the voyevod that he should sign a document in which Koutloumousiou was declared a Greek monastery, not Romanian, 'since threats and curses hang over him who dares upset the Greeks by claiming that the monastery ought to belong to the Romanians because of the lord's donations'.[19] The Romanian voyevod could have considered a Romanian monastery, just as the Serbian or Bulgarian rulers did. There were three big Serbian monasteries at the time, Hilandar, St Paul's, and Xenophontos, and two Bulgarian ones, Zographou and Philotheou.

This early episode was characteristic of the course of events over the next five centuries. It is a complex story in which the strengths and weaknesses of both the Romanians and the Athonites are revealed. But over all are seen God's hand and the Mother of God's protection. On the one hand, Romanian support steadily increased until it was stopped by the secularization of monastic estates under Cuza in 1863. On the other hand, Athonites were active in the Romanian principalities, making major contributions

---

17   Ioan Moldoveanu, 'Contributions to the History of the Relations between the Romanian Countries and the Holy Mountain' (PhD thesis, Bucharest, 2007), p. 15.
18   See Petre Nasturel, op. cit., p. 460.
19   Ibid., pp. 460–1.

to the Church, monastic organization, and cultural life. Meanwhile history records the Romanians' ceaseless presence on the Holy Mountain, their life and striving from their innate humility, and their aspirations for something more, stimulated by their protected status.

The help given by the Romanians to the Holy Mountain has been diverse: money, church objects, construction, renovation, and decoration of the churches and other Athonite monastic dependencies, the hospitality shown to the Athonite monks and their ecclesial and cultural activities, and lastly, the dedication of a great number of Romanian monasteries together with their estates.

We are dealing with a phenomenon which is unique in its dimensions[20] and hard to explain from a purely historical perspective. The voyevods of Wallachia and Moldavia, almost without exception, would regularly help all the Athonite monasteries. Their wives, the noblemen of the country, the Romanian hierarchs, and the people as well, all took part in this charitable activity both through the taxes that filled the state treasuries and directly. There were cases in which the voyevod 'asked all the inhabitants of the country to give money to the Xeropotamou monastery'.[21] Here are some examples.

St Stephan the Great of Moldavia was one of the principal Romanian benefactors of the Holy Mountain. He built the port tower, the cells, and the refectory of the Zographou monastery and towards the end of his reign he repaired the whole monastery and painted the main church at his own expense. In 1489 the monk Isaiah from Hilandar said the Zographou monastery was founded by Stephan the Great. In the archives it is described as 'my lordship's monastery'. He also completely rebuilt the Grigoriou monastery after it had been demolished by pirates. The belfry has been preserved from 1502 until today. He also helped the Vatopedi monastery, where he built the quay in 1496, and the Konstamonitou monastery as well.

20　Porfirios Uspensky, *Istorya Afona* (St Petersburg, 1877), vol. 3, p. 334: 'No other Orthodox people have done as much good to Athos as the Romanians have'.
21　Scarlat Ghica, ruler of Moldavia (1757–8). See Ioan Moldoveanu, op. cit., p. 298.

Stephan's successors continued to support these monasteries.[22] In 1651 Zographou received the Dobrovat monastery from Vasile Lupu with 14,000 hectares of land, and the Capriana monastery from Constantin Cantemir in 1698 with lands extending over 50,000 hectares. In 1769 Grigoriou received the Vizantea monastery with all its possessions. Ten years after he was appointed abbot of this monastery (1842–52), the Greek Visarion left 20,000,000 lei in his will (the equivalent of about 2,200 kg of gold) to the Grigoriou monastery, the Holy Community of Athos, the Athens hospital, and other Greek cultural and charitable settlements.[23]

In the sixteenth century five Athonite monasteries were revived by Romanian lords: Zographou, Grigoriou, and Konstamonitou by the Moldavian rulers, and the Lavra and Koutloumousiou by the rulers of Muntenia. Apart from two monasteries under Georgian patronage, Iviron and Philotheou, the others were in total decay: Pantokrator, Hilandar, Vatopedi, Xeropotamou, St Paul's, Dionysiou, Simonopetra, Stavronikita, Xenophontos, Docheiariou. All of them were waiting for their great sixteenth-century benefactors, Radu the Great and Neagoe Basarab from Muntenia, and Petru Rares and Alexander Lapusneanu from Moldavia.

Alexander Lapusneanu (1552–68) rebuilt and painted the church at Docheiariou (1566–8) and also at Karakalou, which had been begun by Petru Rares, from 1535 to 1563. The sultan's letter of permission made it clear that 'the buildings of the [Docheiariou] monastery were founded by the voyevods of Moldova-Wallachia, and the renovations made to the monasteries' ruins at various times were also the Romanian voyevods' work.'[24] Alexander Lapusneanu's charitable works were numerous: he repainted Xeropotamou, he bought a warehouse for Vatopedi for 65,000 aspers (Turkish currency, about 1,060 gold pieces) and granted it 300 gold coins per year in aid; he built the infirmary at Dionysiou and the southern wing of the monastery and he extended the refectory. His wife, Lady Ruxandra, bought

22   'What Stephan did here encouraged his successors to continue the sacrifices', wrote
      Nicolae Iorga. 'Romanian Voyevods and Boyars Who Were Founders at Athos' in
      Romanians and the Holy Mountain, vol. I, p. 582.
23   Ibid., p. 529.
24   Ibid., p. 522.

back the subsidiary monasteries belonging to Zographou from Macedonia in return for 52,000 aspers, and after her husband's death and in his memory donated 165,000 aspers (that is 2,700 gold pieces) to Docheiariou.

Neagoe Basarab, the voyevod of Wallachia (1512–21), was called 'the great benefactor of the whole Sveta Gora (Holy Mountain)'.[25] His systematic work of sustaining the Orthodoxy of the Balkans and the Middle East had an unparalleled scope and resonance.[26] At the consecration of his establishment of Curtea de Argeş on 15 August 1517, Neagoe Basarab invited the abbots of all the Athonite monasteries, along with a great number of Orthodox patriarchs and hierarchs. On this occasion he proclaimed the holiness of his spiritual mentor, Nifon, Patriarch of Constantinople and former Metropolitan of Hungaro-Wallachia.

Neagoe Basarab almost completely rebuilt the Lavra monastery and gave it financial support of 90,000 talers annually,[27] he completely rebuilt the Dionysiou monastery from 1512 to 1515, and in 1520 he also built the tower. At Koutloumousiou he built the church of St Nicolas, the cells, the refectory, the cellar, the quay, etc. He also helped the Vatopedi monastery (the Holy Belt of the Mother of God chapel, the great cellar, and a golden globe with precious stones for the icon of the Mother of God); Pantokrator (the high walls); Xeropotamou (a new refectory and a cellar); Zographou (3,000 aspers annually); St Paul's (a defence tower); and Iviron (an aqueduct).

Basil Lupu, voyevod of Moldavia (1634–53) had such a great influence in the east that he enthroned and dethroned the patriarchs of Constantinople, Alexandria, and Jerusalem. It was he who convened the pan-Orthodox Synod in Iasi in 1642. During his reign he repaid all the debts of the Holy Mountain. In 1641 he dedicated the monastery of the Three Hierarchs, one of the richest monasteries in Moldavia, to the entire Holy Mountain.

25 Gabriel the Protos in St Niphon's Life.
26 Nicolae Iorga, *Byzantium after Byzantium*, 2nd edn (Bucharest, 1972), pp. 129–30.
27 Gh. Moisescu, 'The Romanian Contribution to Sustaining Mount Athos throughout the Ages' in *Romanians and Mount Athos*, vol. I, p. 504.

The Simonopetra monastery was wholly rebuilt by Mihai Viteazul, who in 1599 dedicated to it his most important establishment, the Mihai Voda monastery in Bucharest. The income from this monastery made possible the reconstruction of Simonopetra after the fire of 1625. The monastery of Mihai Voda had been endowed with sixteen villages by its founder and his family. In 1850 its annual income was 1,000,000 lei, that is 110 kg of gold.

St Panteleimon monastery was rebuilt from its foundations by Scarlat Calimachi, the voyevod of Moldavia, from 1812 to 1819. One can still read the inscription: 'This beautiful church of the Holy, Venerated, Great Martyr and Healer Panteleimon was built from its foundations, just like this Holy Venerable Monastery, which is called Russian, by the very reverend Voyevod of Moldavia Scarlat Calimachi [...].'

I will stop here, thus doing injustice to Peter Rares, Radu the Great, Matthew Basarab,[28] Serban Cantacuzino,[29] Constantin Brancoveanu,[30] and all the others.

28   See Ioan Moldoveanu, op. cit., for a complete list of the Romanian voyevods' donations between 1650 and 1863. Matthew Basarab in 1634 confirms the dedication of Slobozia to the Docheiariou monastery, adding more estates; in 1636 11,000 aspers to Xenophontos; in 1637 confirms the dedication of the Roaba monastery to Xenophontos; in 1640 repairs the katholikon painting at Koutloumousiou; in 1640 4,000 aspers annually to Dionysiou; in 1641 two Gospels to the Lavra; buys St Michael of Sinada's relics for Amota; in 1646 confirms the dedication of the Clocociov monastery to Koutloumousiou; dedicates the monastery of the Dormition to Koutloumousiou; in 1637–41 renovates the western cells at Pantokrator; in 1642 4,000 aspers to Dionysiou; in 1643 an icon to Hilandar; in 1645 renovates the refectory at Hilandar; in 1644 a silver tabernacle to the Lavra; in 1648 dedicates the Holy Trinity monastery to Iviron; in 1650 donates a vineyard in Caciulesti to Dionysiou; in 1653 renovates the north-eastern wing at the Lavra, builds the chapel of St Michael of Sinada, and makes donations to Xenophontos.

29   In 1678 21,000 aspers annually to Vatopedi, renovates the chapel of Paramythia; in 1679 builds an aqueduct for Stavronikita; in 1680 builds the chapel of Portaitissa at Iviron; in 1681–2 dedicates the Budisteni skete to Protaton; 400 salt slabs annually; tax exemption; in 1684 dedicates the Valeni de Munte monastery; in 1686 dedicates the Calugareni skete to Stavronikita.

30   In 1689 dedicates the 'Maria Doamna' church in Bucharest; in 1691 6,000 aspers to the Lavra monastery and silver for the coffin containing St John Chrysostom's relics;

The Dedicated Monasteries

From the second half of the sixteenth century the most important component of this support was the dedicated monasteries. A dedicated monastery was no longer under the jurisdiction of the local hierarch, and was exclusively administered by the monastery to which it was dedicated. They were often exempt from taxes owed to the state. The incomes were used primarily for the maintenance of that monastery and secondly for the support of the monastery to which it was dedicated.

This kind of support has not yet been thoroughly evaluated. Most of the archives of the Athonite monasteries, which are said to include about 40,000 documents relating to Romanian–Athonite relations, remain closed to research. The most recent list of the Romanian monasteries, sketes, and churches dedicated to the Holy Mountain has 109 entries.[31] Most of them were dedicated as follows: to Vatopedi 23, to Esphigmenou 15, Iviron 13, Protaton 9, Zographou 7, Simonopetra 6, St Paul's 4. Only two monasteries, Philotheou and Pantokrator, are not listed. During Cuza's reign the dedicated monasteries and their properties owned between 700,000 and 1,000,000 hectares of land.[32]

---

in 1696 8,000 aspers to Dionysiou; in 1696 21,000 aspers annually to Vatopedi; in 1698 150 talers annually to St Paul's; in 1692 3,000 aspers annually to Pantokrator; in 1694 dedicated three villages to St Paul's; in 1703 exempts the Roaba monastery, dedicated to Xenophontos, from all taxes; dedicates the Caciulati monastery to Xenophontos; 11,000 aspers to Xenophontos; in 1704 dedicates the Baia de Arama monastery to Hilandar; in 1708 repairs the north-western cells at Vatopedi; in 1708 builds the west wing of cells, the refectory, two chapels, and general renovations at St Paul's; in 1709 a coffin/tabernacle for St Gregory the Theologian's relics at Vatopedi; in 1713 120 aspers to Dionysiou, supplies to Philotheou, and estates to Stavronikita.

31   See a complete table of the dedicated monasteries, sketes, and churches, mentioning the venue, the people who dedicated them, the date, and the monastery they were dedicated to in Ioan Moldoveanu, op. cit., pp. 301–4.

32   Through the secularization of the monastic possessions the Romanian state came into possession of 560,000 hectares of land.

Two of the greatest and richest royal monasteries, the Three Holy Hierarchs in Iasi and Cotroceni in Bucharest, were entirely dedicated to the Holy Mountain. The income went to the Protaton, and was further shared between the twenty monasteries.

As an illustration I will give details of the wealth of the two monasteries. The monastery of Cotroceni, which was built by Serban Cantacuzino, and in 1682 was the richest monastery dedicated to the Holy Mountain, had four subsidiary monasteries and numerous estates. In 1780 its annual income was 15 bags of gold coins. In 1828 its income had reached 300,000 lei and in 1860 it exceeded 1,000,000 lei.[33] What was that money worth? The value of the national currency against gold was 100 lei for 11g of gold. Therefore, the income of Cotroceni in 1828 was the equivalent of 33kg of gold, and in 1860 it was tantamount to 110kg.

The Three Hierarchs monastery, Basil Lupu's establishment, had numerous estates, forests, orchards, and vineyards, which around 1827 yielded an annual income of 50,000 piasters or 250,000 lei (the equivalent of 27kg of gold).[34] In Iasi alone the monastery owned an inn, 20 houses, 32 shops of its own, 150 leased shops, and 36 hectares of vineyards.[35]

The Secularization of the Monastic Estates

The relations between the Romanian principalities and Athos were radically transformed when the modern state of Romania was created under Alexandru Ioan Cuza and were severely shaken by the secularization of monastic estates. The main cause was the new vision of the Romanian political class, strongly influenced by secularism.

33   Gh. Moisescu, 'The Romanian Contribution to Sustaining Mount Athos throughout the Ages' in *Romanians and Mount Athos*, vol. I, p. 504.
34   Ibid.
35   Ioan Moldoveanu, op. cit., p. 80. Between 1831 and 1832 the Organic Statute established the following equivalents: 31.5 lei = 39.4g gold 990 % or 2.25 lei = 6.68g silver 583 % and 1 leu = 40 pence.

The Greek abbots, who administered and abused the dedicated monasteries, contributed much to this situation. Also, the conflicts and tensions between the local nobility and the vast Greek aristocracy that had settled in the principalities made the situation worse. There are many recorded examples of attempts to banish the Greeks and the rulers that supported them.[36] In the seventeenth century Matthew Basarab removed twenty-two dedicated monasteries from the jurisdiction of the holy places. With effect from the nineteenth century the dedication of monasteries was forbidden and every effort was made to increase the state's control over the dedicated monasteries.

The condition of the dedicated monasteries, left to rot, became a national problem for Romania. The taxes they owed to the state were huge.[37] The issue generated international concern. The Athonite monasteries appealed for support to the Sublime Porte, Russia, and the representatives of Western countries in Constantinople. On 16 December 1863 the Legislative Board voted on the law for the secularization of the monastic properties in Bucharest. Its first article read, 'All the monastic possessions in Romania are and will remain the Romanian state's property.' The Romanian authorities committed themselves to paying monetary compensation to the Athonite monasteries.[38] The Romanian state recovered between 25% and 27% of Wallachia's territory and 22% of Moldavia's territory.[39]

---

36 See Ioan Moldoveanu, op. cit., p. 23.

37 1,466,520 piasters in Moldavia and 19,920,124 piasters in Wallachia. The debts came from the fourth part of the incomes, which the monasteries were required to pay to the state at that time. By 1863 the debt amounted to 28,889,020 piasters.

38 The final sum they agreed on was 150,000,000 piasters, which was to be paid through a loan offered by a French bank in Constantinople, with the guarantee of the Porte, the Great Powers, and Romania.

39 Cf. Ioan Moldoveanu, op. cit., p. 72.

Rationale for Supporting the Holy Lands

Historians mention two main reasons for undertaking this campaign: political and missionary-religious. With regard to the political motive, Nicolae Iorga expressed his conviction that 'The Romanian rulers were renovators and protectors of most of the monasteries for centuries, as natural and entitled successors of the Byzantine emperors and the Serbian tsars.'[40] The missionary motivation seems to me to have been much stronger than the political. The support given to the Holy Mountain was part of a unique campaign for saving and maintaining all the holy lands and apostolic patriarchates. Jerusalem, Sinai, Constantinople, Alexandria, and Antioch benefited equally from Romania's support. It was a five-century crusade which is not discussed in church history books, although it appears to have achieved more than the better-known crusades. Perhaps silence is better. However, Iorga admitted that 'the Romanian voyevods' oblations to the Holy Mountain undoubtedly had religious meaning.'[41]

Stephan the Great endowed the Zographou monastery with an annual grant of 100 Hungarian gold coins,

> so that he, his wife, and their two children, Alexander and Helen, would be commemorated at the Prothesis; so that he should have a paraklisis sung on Saturday evenings and a Liturgy on Tuesdays as long as he was alive, and after he died he would be commemorated by tradition and then he would have a Panikhida sung in the evening and a Liturgy in the morning once a year.[42]

The same reason is invoked by Vladislav I and all the Romanian voyevods.

This concern of the voyevods that they should be commemorated as long as they were alive and especially after death reveals a profound faith in eternal life and resurrection. This faith is still to be found today in the

---

40   Nicolae Iorga, op. cit., p. 600: 'At a time when Byzantium no longer existed and Serbia had expired, our voyevods alone were responsible for helping the monasteries, which no longer had a patron'.

41   Ibid., p. 594.

42   Gh. Moisescu, art. cit., p. 519.

Romanians' spirituality, which has the most developed cult of the dead of all Orthodox peoples.[43] I am sure that this was the strongest reason behind the Romanian voyevods' and noblemen's endeavours – they invested their fortune in being commemorated on the Holy Mountain. They somehow tried to amass their wealth in heaven. They donated a quarter of Romania's territory so that after their death they would be commemorated every day at the holy services. The names of some of them can still be heard in the Athonite monasteries.

The Romanian voyevods invested not only in the holy places, but also in their own countries. Stephan the Great built forty-seven monasteries and churches, most of which have survived until today: Putna, Neamţ, Voroneţ, etc. Petru Rares, Alexandru Lapusneanu, Neagoe Basarab, Vasile Lupu, Matei Basarab, and the martyr Voyevod Constantin Brancoveanu followed suit.

The Romanians' Charismata

Apart from these historical motives, I believe that behind this sustained effort, which was made for centuries, there were some charismata with which God endowed the Romanians' nature. From among these I would mention two: a deep sense of holiness combined with a humble, modest character that makes them trust their fellows more than they trust themselves. I apologize for talking about Romanians' humility while I myself am Romanian.

---

43 Even people who have not entered a church before their parents died will come from that moment on to hold all the due memorial services, at three days, six days, nine days, three weeks, forty days, three months, six months, nine months, one year, and then every year after death until the seventh, all this in addition to the two occasions when the dead are jointly remembered during the church year.

To illustrate the Romanians' thirst for holiness I will mention their piety for the holy places, objects, and relics, and an extraordinary desire to take part in the building of churches and monasteries which still characterizes them. Since 1990 almost 2,000 monasteries and churches have been built or are still under construction. And since the fall of communism Romanians have resumed pilgrimage to the Holy Land and Mount Athos.

To illustrate their humility, I would cite their hospitality to foreigners. This humility can easily be traced in Romanian monasticism too. Everything about the Romanian monks is truly modest: the chants, clothes, vestments, church adornments, cells, guest houses, and food. Romanian monks do not have the eschatological daring that, for example, the Greeks and Russians have. Romanian monks take Holy Communion much less frequently. Their services are far less ceremonious. While the Greeks inhabit an atmosphere of eschatological joy, created by a heavenly liturgical environment, the Romanians dwell in the realm of asceticism and repentance, with an evident awareness of their unworthiness.

Seen from a competitive perspective, this condition of Romanian monasticism is unfavourable to them and can create problems. From a spiritual perspective, however, the situation can turn out differently.

The two sides of Athonite monasticism, eschatological daring and asceticism, can complement each other, preserving the tension between the human and the divine, between this world and the world to come. Overestimating the eschatological perspective without the support of humility, repentance, and asceticism risks falling into the trap of a kind of spiritual docetism, while remaining in the realm of asceticism and repentance risks a spiritual arianism.

It is the most eloquent example of the fact that 'there are varieties of gifts', according to St Paul's theology (I Cor. 12), and only when people are together can gifts complete each other; hence the need for coming together and sharing spiritual gifts. As I have spent much time on the Holy Mountain, I consider that it would be a great benefit for all if specific spiritual gifts were shared.

Epilogue

From a worldly perspective, the Romanians have turned out to be losers in their relationship with the Holy Mountain, which is not to ignore the contribution of Athos to the organization of ecclesial life and the cultural development of the Romanian principalities. They made so many donations, they supported the Holy Mountain for centuries on end with their wealth and their sacrifices, and yet they have almost always had a humble status in the monastic republic of Athos.

From the same perspective, the Romanians' sense of frustration seems justified. They do not have a monastery of their own, their gifts are kept out of sight, the condition of their monks is sometimes hard to bear and even humiliating, if only for the simple fact that they have no representatives in the Holy Community, the governing body, and they depend completely on the other monasteries.

From the spiritual point of view, this humble and lowly condition could be a challenge sent from God. We cannot say that it is or was the will of the Greeks that the Romanians should have a monastery of their own on Athos. Whoever says so, be they Greek or Romanian, excludes God and the Theotokos from the equation. Consequently, only one solution remains, so beautifully expressed by Stephan the Great in the inscription on a church that he built after a battle in which he had been defeated by the Turks: 'My Lord, because of my people's sins and especially because of my own sins, You permitted the pagans to defeat us!' Fr Dionysios, one of the last great Romanian fathers on Mount Athos, said, 'We Romanians are not united. That is why God and the Theotokos have not given us a monastery on Athos!' I am afraid that the Romanian diaspora can only confirm this painful truth.

There is a tension inside me. Although it is difficult, I almost want us to remain in this humble condition of Romanian monks continuing without a monastery. At the same time, I would make every effort to help them fulfil this desideratum. I once said to a Romanian monk: 'Don't compete with the Russians and the Greeks! Try to run in the opposite direction.

Basically, our Saviour's Gospel invites us to dispute the last place, not the first. From this point of view, it seems to me that the Romanians are in a better position!'

Fr Dionysios of Colciu, whom I had the pleasure to meet several times, said that he had one last battle to fight. He had turned ninety and had been a monk on Athos for over seventy years without ever having seen his country again. The battle he referred to was the temptation of nationalism: 'I left my country with the aim of leaving everything – my parents, my people, my country – for God. And here I have become nationalistic. All my life I have fought against this temptation!' I can assure you that Fr Dionysios was loved by all the Athonites: he was the spiritual father of many Greeks and Russians for the simple reason that he was first Athonite and secondly Romanian.

Bibliography

Bodogae, Pr. Teodor, *Ajutoarele româneşti la Mânăstirile din Sfântul Munte* (Sibiu, 1940).

Cioran, Gh., Σχέσεις των Ρουμανικών Χωρών μετά του Άθω και δη των μονών Κουτλουμουσίου, Λαύρας, Δοχειαρίου και Αγίου Παντελεήμονος η των Ρώσων (Athens, 1938).

Collection de documents diplomatiques et des pièces officielles concernant la question des monastères dédiées en Roumanie, 1858–1878 (Constantinople, 1880).

'Biserica Ortodoxă Română şi problema Sfântului Munte', *Ortodoxia*, 2 (1953).

Creţeanu, Radu, 'Traditions de famille dans les donations roumaines au Mont Athos', *Etudes byzantines et post byzantines* (Bucharest, 1979).

Iorga, Nicolae, 'Le Mont Athos et les pays roumains', *Bulletin de Section Historique d'Académie Roumaine*, 2 (1914).

——, *Roumains et grecs au cours de siècles* (Bucharest, 1921).

Marinescu, Florin, *Τα Ρουμανικά έγγραφα του Όρους. Αρχείο της Ιεράς Μονής Ξηροποτάμου* (Athens, 1997).

——, *Τα Ρουμανικά έγγραφα του Όρους. Αρχείο της Ιεράς Μονής Κουτλουμουσίου* (Athens, 1998).

Moldoveanu, Ioan, 'Contribuții la istoria relațiilor Țărilor Române cu Muntele Athos (1650–1863)' (PhD thesis, Bucharest, 2007).

Nandris, Gr., *Documente slavo-române din Mânăstirile Muntelui Athos* (Bucharest, 1936).

Năstase, D., 'Les documents roumains des archives du couvent de Simonopetra', Συμμεικτα, 1 (1983).

Năsturel, Petre, *Le Mont Athos et les roumains. Recherches sur leur relations du milieu du XIVe siècle à 1654*. Pont. Institutum Studiorum Orientalium (Rome, 1986).

Românii și Muntele Athos [Romanians and the Holy Mountain], Culegere de studii și articole, alcătuită de Prof. Gheorghe Vasilescu și Ignatie Monahul, 2 vols (Bucharest, 2007).

GRAHAM SPEAKE

'The Ark of Hellenism':
Mount Athos and the Greeks under Turkish Rule

Averil Cameron has already pointed out that when Constantinople eventually and inevitably fell to the Ottomans in 1453, the Holy Mountain was
able to represent a symbol of the continuity of Orthodox culture – not
exclusively, but none more so than, to the Greeks.[1] Most of the Greek-
speaking Byzantines had in fact been subjects of the sultan for decades,
if not centuries, before the fall of the City. For them the year 1453 was of
little significance in practical terms. Even on the Athonites the dissolution
of the empire made little impact. Since 1312 the monks had been under the
jurisdiction not of the emperor but of the ecumenical patriarch, and the
patriarchate was to become a key plank in the structure of the Ottoman
administration. While Macedonia as a whole was overrun by the Ottomans
in the late fourteenth century and again, after a brief Byzantine interlude,
in the early fifteenth century, the monasteries of Athos and their estates
remained inviolate. The monks in their wisdom had already come to an
arrangement with the sultan whereby in return for their submission to him
they would receive his protection; and in 1430 a delegation of Athonites
paid homage to Sultan Murat II in Adrianople. In this way they were able
to secure their survival under the infidel.

　　Other holy mountains had been less fortunate, or less perspicacious.
As Elizabeth Zachariadou has written, holy mountains were a characteristic
feature of Byzantine monasticism. Most of them were located in Asia Minor
(for example, Mount Olympos in Bithynia, Mount Latros near the ancient
city of Miletus, and Mount Galesion near Ephesus). After the defeat of the

1　　See above, p. 27.

Byzantines at Manzikert in 1071, the Seljuq Turks ravaged the newly won territory of Anatolia and, ignoring the rules of Islam, to which they had only recently and superficially been converted, saw no reason to spare the monasteries. Very few of them survived.

The decline of the monasteries of Asia Minor worked to the advantage of Mount Athos. Its monasteries were to emerge from the period of Latin rule after 1204 with an enhanced reputation for a pious way of life. They have preserved their unique character ever since. It served them well during the Ottoman conquest of Macedonia in the late fourteenth century, for the early Ottoman rulers were impressed by their spiritual authority and were anxious to fulfil the responsibilities expected of pious Muslim rulers.[2]

Before the year 1453 was out, a delegation of Athonites called on Sultan Mehmet II to pay their respects and in return he agreed to safeguard their rights and protect their independence. For a century and more the monks enjoyed the active support of successive sultans and the Mountain flourished as a 'symbol of divinely ordained religious authority'.[3] What did this mean in practice? Rather than attempt a broad sweep I propose to take two snapshots of Athos, in the sixteenth century and in the eighteenth century, and to observe the activities of two pairs of parallel lives.[4]

Sixteenth-century Athos

A clear indication of the continuing prosperity of the Holy Mountain in the sixteenth century is the foundation in 1541 of the monastery of Stavronikita. There are references in documents of the eleventh and twelfth centuries

2   E. A. Zachariadou, 'Mount Athos and the Ottomans c. 1350–1550', in M. Angold (ed.), *The Cambridge History of Christianity*, vol. 5: *Eastern Christianity* (Cambridge, 2006), p. 155.

3   Averil Cameron, above, p. 26.

4   For a more general survey of Athos under Turkish rule the reader is referred to the chapter on 'Ottoman Athos' in my book *Mount Athos: Renewal in Paradise* (New Haven, CT, and London, 2002), pp. 113–56.

to a monastery of that name, but it had clearly become deserted, perhaps during the Latin empire, and reverted to being a cell of Philotheou. In the 1530s monk Gregorios, abbot of a monastery in Thesprotia and a close friend of Ecumenical Patriarch Jeremias I (1522–46), purchased the cell from Philotheou for 4,000 piastres and set about restoring it as a monastery. But he did not live to complete his work and shortly after his death in 1536 the katholikon and newly built cells were destroyed by fire. The Holy Community then wrote to Patriarch Jeremias, asking him personally to undertake the restoration of Stavronikita, partly out of a desire to protect Karyes and the east coast of the peninsula from attack by pirates. This he agreed to do and by February 1540 he had assembled a group of monks and appointed an abbot. He endowed the monastery with estates on Kassandra and on Lemnos, he rebuilt the katholikon (completed in 1546), and he established the brotherhood on strict cenobitic lines, even though this was a period when most monasteries had adopted the idiorrhythmic way of life. In the manner of imperial founders Jeremias had himself portrayed in a fresco in the katholikon, dressed in his patriarchal robes and holding a model of the church that he had founded. His will survives and constitutes the *typikon* of the monastery. In it he writes:

> I appointed an abbot there and made good arrangement that there should be a coenobitic monastery, giving written instructions and laying down this canon, saying to the man chosen as abbot and to each of his successors: most reverend man and abbot of this my monastery, you shall in no way change the coenobitic rule and canon of the monastic community ... you shall not acquire any worldly goods or possessions, nor shall you lay up treasure for yourself personally, not even as much as one silver coin ... you shall not have any animal of the female sex for the use of the monastery, since you have renounced contact with the female ... you shall not allow any beardless youth to enter the monastery under your command, even for an hour ... you shall not have any different or valuable garment but shall go dressed and shod in the traditional manner like the other monks ... you shall not desert your flock to go to another, nor advance to higher office ... you shall put no man before the interests of the brotherhood in Christ ...[5]

5   C. Patrinelis, A. Karakatsanis, M. Theocharis, *Stavronikita Monastery: History, Icons, Embroidery* (Athens, 1974), pp. 23–4.

In short, this is every bit a traditional Byzantine foundation in a post-Byzantine world. But despite its generous endowments, which continued to accrue in subsequent centuries, it has remained throughout its history one of the poorest monasteries of the Holy Mountain and its population has always been small: 68 monks in 1615, 30 in 1666, 25 in 1808, 40 in 1873, 25 in 1903, 11 in 1965, 45 in 2000.

Cenobitic Stavronikita in the mid-sixteenth century was the exception to the idiorrhythmic rule. The transition to the latter had been a gradual one, and it had started before the end of the empire, but by the end of the sixteenth century every monastery had become idiorrhythmic and remained so at least until the late eighteenth century. Stavronikita was still idiorrhythmic in the 1960s when John Julius Norwich wrote of it:

> in the four centuries of its existence, so brief by local standards, its funds and its inhabitants have decreased to almost vanishing point. Discounting the tragic condition of the Russian cenobion of St Pantaleimon and of other smaller Slav houses not on the establishment as Ruling Monasteries, this will probably be the first to crumble altogether into ruins and die.[6]

In the event this prediction was not fulfilled, though the house was close to being abandoned in 1968 when the civil governor of the Mountain invited the hermit Fr Vasileios Gontikakis to take charge of it. Fr Vasileios accepted this invitation on condition that he was appointed abbot by the Holy Community and the monastery reverted to cenobitic rule. This was agreed and in the last forty years Stavronikita has become a model of Athonite renewal, though its numbers remain small.

Largely in response to the proliferation of the idiorrhythmic way of life among the monasteries, the first sketes were founded in the second half of the sixteenth century. They too were idiorrhythmic, inevitably because each comprised a scattered community living in separate houses grouped around a central church, but the intention of their founders was to provide a more ascetic way of life than was currently available in the monasteries, and they still retain something of that reputation for austerity even today. 'It is sometimes said', writes R. M. Dawkins who, as Professor of Byzantine and Modern Greek at Oxford, made several visits to Athos in the 1930s,

6   J. J. Norwich and R. Sitwell, *Mount Athos* (London, 1966), p. 146.

that the greatest severity of life may be found where there is the greatest freedom; even in the idiorrhythmic monasteries monks may live as hardly as any hermit. But it remains true in general that those who seek austerity prefer the sketes; they are ... the special resort of the wearers of the Great Habit, who live under a rule whose severity many monks are not willing to face.[7]

Far from contracting, then, the number and variety of monastic establishments on the Holy Mountain increased considerably during the first centuries of Ottoman rule. True, there was no longer a Christian emperor in Constantinople to provide financial support when this was needed, but instead the monasteries were able to turn to Orthodox rulers who were not under direct rule from the Sublime Porte, notably the Danubian principalities of Moldavia and Wallachia, but also to a lesser extent those of Russia and Georgia. For practical purposes it was business as usual for the monks, and the monasteries prospered. Let us look at two individuals who exemplified this prosperity.

Once the buildings of the new monastery of Stavronikita had been completed, they needed to be embellished. In Byzantine times the monks of Athos had regularly called on the finest artists currently available in Constantinople to beautify their buildings and write their icons. After the fall of the empire it was necessary to look elsewhere, notably to the island of Crete, which had been under Venetian rule since 1211 and during the fifteenth century became a favoured refuge for émigré Byzantine artists and scholars. A distinct Cretan school of painting emerged, of which the most prominent representative in the sixteenth century was Theophanes Strelitzas (c. 1490–1559), a native of Candia (modern Herakleion). Some of his early work survives at Meteora, but Mount Athos was still the place where artists' reputations were made and in 1535 he and his sons, Symeon and Neophytos, were invited to work on the katholikon and refectory at the Great Lavra. All three became monks and we know from archives of the Lavra that in 1536 Theophanes purchased a property for them near the monastery which he retained until 1559.

Needing an artist to paint the church and refectory of his brand new 'Byzantine' monastery of Stavronikita as well as the icons of the iconostasis,

7   R. M. Dawkins, *The Monks of Athos* (London, 1936), pp. 150–1.

it was natural that Patriarch Jeremias should turn to the most celebrated hagiographer of the day, Theophanes. With particular reference to the icons of the iconostasis, Fr Vasileios, abbot of Stavronikita from 1968 to 1990, has written:

> The maturity of our painter is evident: his lines are clear and crystallized, his colours are matched with reverence and harmony, the brush-strokes are simple, the figures are serene. The bodies are tall and slender, their movements gentle and dignified, and the composition is well-balanced. He reveals the whole inner world of each figure through the shaft of light on the dark modelling of a face. Through a small white brush-stroke and a black dot he gives to an eye an expression that a thousand words cannot describe. Wealth of simplicity and compassionate austerity characterize the art of the monk Theophanes. The contrite peace created by his iconographical world derives from the tranquillity that he possesses as a great artist and a true monk.[8]

With particular reference to the frescos of the katholikon at the Great Lavra, which predate those at Stavronikita, Manolis Chatzidakis has written:

> This Cretan painter, whose knowledge of grammar was somewhat wanting, shows marvellous skill in arranging and adapting his compositions to suit the available surfaces, and in harmonising the elegant, Hellenising figures and serene, balanced compositions he had inherited from fifteenth-century Cretan art – now of a monumental character – all in low relief against a black background with a ground-surface of green, in dominant earth colours and subtle harmonies. He created ensembles of an impeccably Orthodox character, befitting the good taste of the monastic public he was catering for and fulfilling the expectations of his patrons ... Endowed with these qualities – high art, a rich stock of iconographic material and, above all, representations of a doctrinally impeccable character – this Cretan emigrant painting radiated its influence beyond the bounds of Athos – becoming, it could be said, the official model art of the Church, whose fame endured until the late eighteenth century.[9]

---

8   Introduction to *Icons at the Monastery of Stavronikita Painted in 1546 by Theophanes the Cretan* (Athens, n.d.).

9   M. Chatzidakis, 'Byzantine Art on Mount Athos', in *Treasures of Mount Athos* (Thessaloniki, 1997), pp. 21–8 (pp. 24–5).

In short, what we see here is an artist of the first rank being attracted to Athos as the place to make his name and, in so doing, setting a style that became the model for Orthodox church art for the next two centuries. At his death he left a considerable fortune. Let us now turn from visual art to the world of books.

Michael Trivolis was born in Arta to a middle-class family of Laconian origin in about 1470. The family moved to Corfu when he was about ten years old, and in about 1492 Michael moved to Italy to continue his studies, first in Florence and later in Venice. Here he fell under the influence of such leading scholars of the Renaissance as Marsilio Ficino, Aldus Manutius, and Gianfrancesco Pico della Mirandola as well as emigré Greeks such as Janus Laskaris, Laonikos Chalkokondylis, and Constantine Laskaris. But perhaps the most influential of all was the Dominican friar Savonarola (1452–98) whose preaching affected him deeply and persuaded him, in 1502, to enter the Dominican order. But after only two years he left the order and returned to Greece. By 1506 he had joined the brotherhood of Vatopedi on Mount Athos and adopted the name of Maximos. It is clear from his later writings that he had become disenchanted with many of the doctrines of the Latin Church and it may have been the influence of his teacher Janus Laskaris that directed him to Athos. Laskaris was fully aware of the rich contents of certain Athonite libraries from his own travels, and this may have been what led Maximos to choose Vatopedi in particular.[10] Whatever the reason for the choice, it was clearly a happy one and for the rest of his life Maximos was to regard Vatopedi as his spiritual home.

The library of Vatopedi provided Maximos with the opportunity to immerse himself in the study of patristic literature, especially the works of St John of Damascus, whom he later described as having achieved 'the summit of philosophy and theology', and St Gregory of Nazianzus.[11] He may also have enjoyed the cosmopolitan nature of Athonite society which now embraced considerable numbers of men from Russia, Serbia, Bulgaria,

10   See G. Speake, 'Janus Laskaris' Visit to Mount Athos in 1491', *Greek, Roman and Byzantine Studies*, 34: 3 (1993), 325–30.
11   See D. Obolensky, *Six Byzantine Portraits* (Oxford, 1988), pp. 201–19 (p. 206).

and Romania, attracted by the revival of hesychasm in the late Byzantine period. Certainly this will have prepared him to some extent for his future life in Russia.

In 1516 an embassy arrived on Athos from the Russian ruler Basil III with the aim of inviting to Moscow a skilled translator of Greek. During the Byzantine period, when the Russian Church had been under the jurisdiction of the Constantinople patriarchate, the royal library had acquired a large number of manuscripts in Greek which, by the early sixteenth century, very few Russians could read. They therefore needed a scholar who could read them and translate them into Slavonic. The abbot of Vatopedi recommended Maximos because, as he wrote to the metropolitan of Moscow, he was

> proficient in divine Scripture and adept in interpreting all kinds of books, both ecclesiastical and those called Hellenic [i.e. secular], because from his early youth he has grown up in them and learned [to understand] them through the practice of virtue, and not simply by reading them often, as others do.[12]

There is no doubt that he was also expected to raise funds for his monastery. On his way he stopped in Constantinople where we may be sure that the patriarch briefed him on the two most pressing issues of the day: the wish to restore his authority over the Russian Church and his hope that Russia might provide aid for the Greek subjects of the sultan.

Maximos arrived in Moscow in March 1518, accompanied by the Greek monk Neophytos and the Bulgarian monk Lavrentii, and was received with honour. His first assignment was to translate some patristic commentaries on the Psalms. Since he did not yet know Russian, his method was first to translate the texts into Latin, which his collaborators then translated into Slavonic. This was not an ideal procedure and inevitably mistakes were made, but in his introduction to the work when it was finally completed Maximos assured his patron that it would be a useful aid to defeating heresy. So-called 'Judaizers' were thought to have tampered with the text of certain passages in the Psalms, and though the heretics had been denounced in 1504, Russian society was still divided over how to respond to them and so Maximos's work was a hot potato.

---

12   Ibid., p. 208.

On completion of this translation Maximos expected to be able to return to Mount Athos, but this was not to be. Now he was employed in translating various biblical and patristic texts and also in correcting the liturgical books, which he found to be full of errors. 'It became obvious to him', writes Dimitri Obolensky,

> that the howlers committed by early translators, compounded by scribal errors, had led to mistranslations which at best were absurd, and at worst heretical. Some of the most glaring he corrected himself, unaware of the trouble he was storing up for the future.[13]

Maximos also allowed himself to be drawn into other controversial debates. At the request of his friend Vassian Patrikeev, a former general and diplomat who had become a monk, he wrote in praise of the virtues of cenobitic monasticism as practised by the monasteries of Athos. He left unstated his opposition to the very different approach of the larger monasteries of Russia which had become immensely wealthy by their possession of enormous estates and exploitation of peasant labour. But if Maximos was restrained in his writing, his friend Vassian went to the opposite extreme in declaring:

> All our books are false ones, and were written by the devil and not by the Holy Spirit. Until Maxim we used these books to blaspheme God, and not to glorify or pray to him. Now, through Maxim, we have come to know God.[14]

Not everyone agreed. In 1522 Daniel, abbot of Volokolamsk, one of the wealthiest of the monasteries that Maximos had tacitly impugned, was appointed bishop of Moscow and primate of the Russian Church. Most provocatively, Daniel invited Maximos to translate a book that supported monastic landownership and contained other texts of a heretical nature. Maximos declined, and went on to criticize the divorce and remarriage of the ruler, earning himself enemies both ecclesiastical and princely. In the winter of 1524/5 he was arrested on charges of heresy (for making changes to the liturgical books), sorcery, and treason (for allegedly entertaining rela-

---

13   Ibid., p. 211.
14   V. S. Ikonnikov, *Maksim Grek i ego vremya*, 2nd edn (Kiev, 1915), p. 409, quoted in Obolensky, op. cit., p. 213.

tions with the Sublime Porte). He was also accused of maintaining that the independence of the Russian Church from the Constantinople patriarchate was illegal and of criticizing the Russian monasteries for their ownership of land and serfs. While the first three charges were clearly unjust, the last two were no doubt true and Maximos would not have denied them. The court, presided over by Grand Prince Basil III and Metropolitan Daniel, sentenced Maximos to solitary confinement in the monastery of Volokolamsk where he was put in chains, excommunicated, and deprived of the means to read and write. After a second trial, in 1531, convened to silence the prisoner's protests at his unjust treatment, he was moved to Tver where gradually some of his privations were relaxed. He asked repeatedly to be allowed to return to Mount Athos but all such requests were refused.

Maximos was finally released from prison in about 1548, his excommunication was annulled, and he was allowed to reside in St Sergius's monastery of the Holy Trinity near Moscow (formerly Zagorsk, now Sergiev Posad). Here he spent his last years reading, writing, and teaching and here he died, at the age of eighty-six, on 21 January 1556. His entry in the *Synaxarion*, a compendium of saints' lives first put together by St Nikodimos of the Holy Mountain, ends with these words:

> Saint Maximus the Greek was the most prolific of all the writers of Old Russia. Opposed with good reason to the infiltration of western humanism, he conveyed the treasures of the Byzantine spirit and literature to the Russian people. Soon after his decease, he was recognized and venerated as a holy Martyr and 'Enlightener of Russia'.[15]

Dimitri Obolensky, who had championed the cause of Maximos and was instrumental in his eventual canonization, concludes his portrait with a judiciously balanced assessment:

---

15   Hieromonk Makarios of Simonos Petra, *The Synaxarion: The Lives of the Saints of the Orthodox Church*, trans. C. Hookway, vol. 3: January, February (Ormylia, 2001), p. 252. But it was not until 1988 that the Moscow Patriarchate formally added Maximos to the calendar of saints.

Maximos, though not a creative thinker, was at least a sound and wide-ranging scholar, with an excellent training in ancient philosophy and textual criticism; though he played an important role in the controversies that shook sixteenth-century Muscovite society, his learning was, with a few notable exceptions, above its head; and he lived in a cosmopolitan world where the Byzantine heritage, the late medieval Italo-Greek connections, and the traditional links between Russia, Mount Athos, and Constantinople were still to some extent living realities. He was one of the last of his kind.[16]

It was the Russian scholar Elie Denissoff who succeeded in identifying Maximos the Greek with the Greek émigré Michael Trivolis and was therefore able to suggest that his life took the shape of a diptych with Mount Athos as its hinge and Italy and Russia as its two leaves.[17] This attractive image would surely have appealed to Maximos who throughout his Russian exile longed to be allowed to return to the Holy Mountain. It was not until 1997 that the final denouement of the drama was to be played out. In July of that year Abbot Ephraim of Vatopedi travelled to Moscow to be presented with a portion of the relics of Maximos by Patriarch Alexis II. After concelebrating the Divine Liturgy with the Patriarch in the church of the Intercession (St Basil's) in Red Square, the abbot returned to Athos with the relics and placed them in the Katholikon of the Annunciation at Vatopedi. This joyful event, by which some of the physical remains of Maximos were at last laid to rest in his spiritual home some 480 years after he had left it, was seen as symbolic of the increasingly close relationship between Vatopedi and the rest of the Orthodox world.

16   Op. cit., p. 219.
17   E. Denissoff, *Maxime le Grec et l'Occident: Contribution à l'histoire de la pensée religieuse et philosophique de Michel Trivolis* (Paris, 1943). Hence the title of Obolensky's 1981 Raleigh Lecture on History, 'Italy, Mount Athos, and Muscovy: The Three Worlds of Maximos the Greek (*c.* 1470–1556)', published in the *Proceedings of the British Academy*, 67 (1981), 143–61, which preceded the publication of his book, *Six Byzantine Portraits*, by seven years.

Eighteenth-century Athos

For long periods of its history we have precious little information about what life was really like for the average monk on the Holy Mountain. Since for the most part there was nothing particularly remarkable about it, there was no reason to write it down. We only know about the stars who shine out by reason of their exceptional qualities, their enduring writings, or their adventurous exploits. 'When exploring Athonite spirituality,' writes Metropolitan Kallistos, 'we are like children gathering sea shells on the margin of an uncharted ocean.'[18] Certainly for the seventeenth century and the early part of the eighteenth there was a mood of gloom and despondency throughout much of the Greek world and Athos was no exception to this trend. Economic decline set in as a result of punitive taxes imposed by the Ottoman authorities, followed by intellectual decline which manifested itself particularly in neglect of the libraries and their contents. There is also some evidence of spiritual decline, though standards of asceticism were upheld and vows were strictly observed, despite the universal adoption of the idiorrhythmic system.

We gain some idea of conditions for monks on Athos at the time from the accounts of pilgrims. The Russian traveller Vasily Barsky (1702–47), for example, visited the Mountain as a pilgrim in 1725 and again in 1744, leaving copious accounts of both journeys. When he arrived at the Russian monastery of St Panteleimon in 1725, he found just four monks, two Russians and two Bulgarians; on his second visit, in 1744, he noted that the monastery was now in Greek hands, that it was idiorrhythmic, and that its buildings were in a serious state of disrepair.[19] He observed Russian monks 'wandering hither and thither about the hills, living by manual labour, eating scraps and being despised by all', though he suggested that they only had

---

18   K. Ware, 'St Nikodimos and the *Philokalia*', in D. Conomos and G. Speake, eds, *Mount Athos the Sacred Bridge: The Spirituality of the Holy Mountain* (Oxford, 2005), pp. 69–121 (p. 74).
19   N. Fennell, *The Russians on Athos* (Oxford, 2001), p. 58.

themselves to blame for this sorry state of affairs: 'for in Russia, where all labour is carried out by dedicated Christians, the monks live in great ease and comfort'.[20] Spiritual life on the Holy Mountain had clearly reached a pretty low ebb, especially for the Slavs.

Despite the prevailing gloom, or perhaps because of it, one or two stars emerge; and as the century wore on, a veritable galaxy bears witness to an intellectual and spiritual revival in which Athos was to play a leading role. Once again we shall focus our attention on just two parallel but contrasting lives, both remarkable examples of Athonite outreach.

The initiative for the foundation of an academy of higher learning on Mount Athos in the mid-eighteenth century seems to have come from the idiorrhythmic fathers of Vatopedi under the enlightened leadership of their Prohegoumenos Meletios. The school on Patmos, which had been a major centre of Orthodox education for the Greek world in the early part of the century, was now in decline and when Cyril V was appointed to the patriarchal throne in 1748 he soon became aware of the need for a new one. The Holy Synod therefore welcomed the suggestion of the Vatopedi fathers and entrusted the task of establishing the academy to Meletios. A site was chosen on high ground overlooking the monastery and handsome buildings were erected at Vatopedi's expense. The aim of this institute of higher learning, both religious and philosophical, was to produce suitably qualified leaders for the Church and for the Orthodox world as a whole. Its first director, monk Neophytos of Kafsokalyvia, perhaps the most learned Athonite of the time, was appointed in December 1749. But by the end of his term of office the school still had no more than twenty students and in 1753 the patriarchate appointed Evgenios Voulgaris (1716–1806) to take over as director and to provide instruction in philosophy and mathematics as well as ethics and theology.

---

20 V. G. Barsky, *Travel Diary* (St Petersburg, 1793), pp. 296, 300. For Barsky's two journeys to Athos see further R. Gothóni, *Tales and Truth: Pilgrimage on Mount Athos Past and Present* (Helsinki, 1994), pp. 73–80, and A. Grishin, 'Bars'kyj and the Orthodox Community', in Angold (ed.), *Eastern Christianity*, pp. 210–28.

This was an inspired appointment, and a bold one. Voulgaris was a Corfiot who had studied in Italy where he learned Latin as well as French and Italian. He was a devout deacon who had served the church in Venice, but he was also a student of modern philosophy and the sciences. Returning to Greece to teach in schools in Ioannina and Kozani, he had aroused controversy among traditionalists who were suspicious of his rationalist views and even accused him of heresy. None of this deterred the patriarchate from appointing him to Athos since he was clearly the best candidate for the post. Paschalis Kitromilides has described the Athonias, as the academy came to be known, as 'undoubtedly the most important initiative of the Church in the field of education during the eighteenth century'.[21]

> When Voulgaris was called by patriarchal sigil, in 1753, to improve the Athonite Academy, to 'change and reform it', certainly the Church's expectation was that by modernizing the education of its leading personnel, it would be able to respond more effectively to the challenges of the times.[22]

With the backing of both the patriarch and the Vatopedi fathers, Voulgaris seemed destined for a stellar career that would test the extent and the strength of the encounter between Orthodoxy and the Enlightenment. For a while all seemed to go well, and in a letter written in 1756 to a former pupil, Kyprianos the Cypriot, whom he had taught in Ioannina, he wrote lyrically of the delights of the school's location and went on to give a rather poetic description of the curriculum:

> There Demosthenes struggles, encouraging the Athenians against the Macedonians; there Homer in his rhapsodies sings the heroic deeds around Ilion; there Thucydides narrates in sublime style the civil strife of the Greeks; there the father of history in Ionic

21   P. Kitromilides, 'Initiatives of the Great Church in the Mid-Eighteenth Century: Hypotheses on the Factors of Orthodox Ecclesiastical Strategy', Ch. V in *An Orthodox Commonwealth: Symbolic Legacies and Cultural Encounters in Southeastern Europe* (Aldershot, 2007), p. 5.
22   Ibid., p. 3.

style narrates earlier history and victories against the barbarians; here Plato expounds theology and Aristotle in multiple ways unravels the mysteries of nature; and the French, the Germans, and the English teach their novel philosophical systems.[23]

There is no reference to religious instruction (apart from Plato); and 'the French, the Germans, and the English' who did form part of the curriculum were presumably Descartes, Leibniz and Wolff, and John Locke. As in Ioannina, it was these 'novel philosophical systems' that were to be the director's undoing.

Despite his impeccable Orthodox credentials, his serious interests in hesychasm and apophatic theology, and his receipt of a cure from a miracle-working icon of the Mother of God at Dionysiou, Voulgaris soon encountered opposition. It came first from the monks who found his teaching to be at odds with their own conservative traditions. Then his own students (who had greatly increased in numbers since his arrival at the school) divided into factions and a group turned against him. Finally in 1757 Patriarch Cyril himself was deprived of his throne and retired to Athos where he proceeded to meddle in the business of the school. Having been Voulgaris's staunchest supporter, Cyril became his most hostile opponent and set the whole Mountain against him. Under attack on all fronts, from colleagues, students, and his former patron, Voulgaris felt obliged to resign. In a letter to Cyril dated 29 January 1759 Voulgaris cites the behaviour of the former patriarch as the principal reason for his resignation and in February he left Athos for good.

Thus ended the Holy Mountain's experiment with Enlightenment. For the best part of a decade the Athonias had shone as a model institution, attracting pupils not only from the Greek world but from as far afield as Italy and Russia, drawn no doubt by the international reputation of its director as well as by the thirst for knowledge that characterized the eighteenth century in general. Among them were Athanasios Parios, Iosipos Moisiodax, and Kosmas the Aetolian, all of whom went on to enjoy distinguished careers as scholars and evangelists. The school itself survived for a

---

23   Quoted by P. Kitromilides, 'Orthodoxy and the West: Reformation to Enlightenment', in M. Angold (ed.), *Eastern Christianity*, p. 203.

year or two. The appointment of Nikolaos Zerzoulis, a philosopher from Metsovo who had introduced the Greek world to Newtonian physics, as successor to Voulgaris demonstrates the determination of the patriarchate to persevere with its original intention of creating a modern institute of higher learning. But he too encountered problems similar to those of his predecessor and within two years he was back in Metsovo. Those students that remained followed Voulgaris to Constantinople and the school on Athos was closed. Revisiting his *alma mater* in 1765, Iosipos Moisiodax described it as a 'nest of ravens'.[24]

Voulgaris's career, however, was far from being at an end. After a short stint in Constantinople, where he was invited by Patriarch Seraphim II to reform the patriarchal academy and to modernize its curriculum, in 1763 he returned to the west and continued his studies in Leipzig and Halle, immersing himself in German rationalism and publishing works of his own including his influential *Logic* (Leipzig, 1766). Then in 1771 came an invitation to Russia from no less a person than Empress Catherine II to join her court in St Petersburg as librarian and curator of antiquities.[25] Voulgaris's acceptance of this invitation should be seen in the context of his vision of the advantages that were to be gained from the adoption of western philosophy and science in the education system of the Orthodox world. As Kitromilides has written,

> Voulgaris visualised that intellectual reform would supply the appropriate moral substratum for the attainment of political change and the re-establishment of an enlightened Christian monarchy over the Orthodox peoples of south-eastern Europe in the place of Ottoman autocracy. His predilection for a Christian monarchy eventually attached Voulgaris to the policies of Catherine the Great, who in her turn saw the expectations of the Christian subjects of the Ottoman Empire as a convenient vehicle for Russian imperial expansion toward the warm seas of the South.[26]

---

24   I. Moisiodax, *Apologia* (Vienna, 1780), p. 128; quoted by P. Kitromilides, 'Athos and the Enlightenment', Ch. VII in *An Orthodox Commonwealth*, p. 261.

25   See S. K. Batalden, *Catherine II's Greek Prelate: Eugenios Voulgaris in Russia, 1771–1806* (New York, 1982).

26   P. Kitromilides, 'Europe and the Dilemmas of Greek Conscience', Ch. XI in *An Orthodox Commonwealth*, p. 5.

From 1775 to 1779 Voulgaris served as Archbishop of Kherson and Slaviansk in Novorussia, territory ceded to Russia as a result of the Russo-Ottoman war of 1768–74. In retirement he remained for some years in Kherson and Poltava before returning to St Petersburg in 1788. There he spent his old age, studying the philosophers, but remaining ever loyal to his church, until his death in 1806. Variously labelled 'the dean of the Enlightenment in south-eastern Europe' (by Kitromilides) and 'the living library of polymathy' (by Moisiadax), Voulgaris was one of the greatest intellectuals and theologians of the eighteenth-century Orthodox world. If his principal achievements lay in the extension of the political dimension of Greco-Russian cultural relations, his motivation is neatly summarized by Kitromilides:

> Despite his receptivity to several of the fundamental philosophical and scientific principles of the European Enlightenment, the broader context of his thought was determined by the Orthodox tradition and by Orthodox doctrine. He thus remained within the bounds of Orthodoxy, which he saw as the common denominator to the aspirations of the Russians and the Greeks.[27]

My fourth and final Athonite star is Kosmas the Aetolian (1714–79). Born to a pious family of weavers in the village of Megadendron near Naupaktos, he was educated locally before moving to Mount Athos and finally enrolling as a student at the newly founded Athonias in 1749. On leaving the academy, probably shortly before the arrival there of Voulgaris, Kosmas was tonsured a monk at the monastery of Philotheou and later ordained priest. After thirty-five years of study he was finally convinced that Orthodoxy was the one true faith.

Having reached this conclusion, Kosmas felt a calling to share his faith with his fellow Greeks and asked permission of his elders to leave the monastery and travel to Constantinople. There he obtained the blessing of Patriarch Seraphim II (1757–61) to become a missionary and a permit in

---

27   P. Kitromilides, 'From Orthodox Commonwealth to National Communities: Greek-Russian Intellectual and Ecclesiastical Ties in the Ottoman Era', Ch. VI in *An Orthodox Commonwealth*, p. 13.

writing that would ensure his safe passage among local bishops and Otto-man officials. Kosmas was deeply conscious of the widespread ignorance of his fellow countrymen in matters of religion and alarmed by the rate at which they were abandoning Orthodoxy and converting to Islam. His aim was to counter this by taking his knowledge of the Bible and of the Church Fathers and of Athonite spirituality to the people of Greece and the Balkans.

Kosmas began his ministry in 1760 in the churches around Constan-tinople. He was clearly a charismatic preacher and attracted huge crowds who came to hear his message. Wherever he went – and in the course of nearly two decades he covered more or less the whole of Greece including the Dodecanese and the Ionian islands – he founded schools that would promote both the study of Orthodox Christianity and the knowledge of Greek as the language of the Bible and the Fathers, saying:

> My beloved children in Christ, bravely and fearlessly preserve our holy faith and the language of our Fathers, because both of these characterize our most beloved homeland, and without them our nation is destroyed.[28]

From time to time Kosmas returned to the Holy Mountain, but only for brief periods, no doubt to recharge his spiritual batteries. But it is inter-esting to note that he had acquired the Athonite practice of the Jesus prayer and that this formed part of his teaching. At a time when hesychastic tra-ditions are thought to have more or less died out on Athos, Kosmas was exhorting people to pray continually: 'Lord Jesus Christ, Son and *Logos* of the living God, by the intercessions of the Theotokos and all the saints, have mercy on me the sinner and unworthy servant of Thee.'[29] Perhaps Philotheou, a strict monastery (then as now), had succeeded in preserving spiritual traditions that had been lost elsewhere on the Mountain.

28   N. M. Vaporis, *Father Kosmas, the Apostle of the Poor: The Life of St Kosmas Aitolon together with an English Translation of his Teaching and Letters* (Brookline, MA, 1977), p. 146.
29   C. Cavarnos, *St Cosmas Aitolos*, 3rd edn (Belmont, MA, 1985), p. 71.

Kosmas's missionary journeys and the impact that he made on his hearers are described in detail by his disciple Sapphiros Christodoulidis in the *New Martyrologion*, of which an English translation is included in Constantine Cavarnos's book, *St Cosmas Aitolos*.

> Wherever this thrice-blessed man went [writes Christodoulidis], people listened with great contrition and devoutness to his grace-imbued and sweet words, and there resulted great improvement in their ways and great benefit to their souls ... Aided by Divine grace, he tamed the fierce, rendered brigands gentle, made the pitiless and unmerciful compassionate and merciful, the impious pious, instructed those who were ignorant in divine things and made them attend the church services, and briefly he brought the sinners to great repentance and correction, so that everybody was saying that in our times there has appeared a new Apostle.[30]

By the Greeks he was labelled 'Isapostolos', 'equal to the Apostles', but he was equally revered by Muslims who were deeply moved by his sermons, his piety, and the miracles that occurred wherever he went. There is no doubt about the spiritual effect that his missionary activities aroused, but Kitromilides, doyen of the study of eighteenth-century Greece, is surely wise to be cautious about the anachronistic contribution some see him as making towards the arousal of Greek national consciousness.[31] He concludes his survey of the initiatives of the Great Church in the mid-eighteenth century thus:

> The activities [of the Church] in the sectors of education [in the hands of Voul-garis], pastoral care [in the hands of Kosmas] and administration [in the hands of Patriarch Samuel I] ... appear to aim at safeguarding the Orthodox community as a whole, and do not seem to issue from any nationalist motives or from expediencies of secular power politics. For this reason, the systematic effort that has been made in Greek historiography to elevate Kosmas the Aetolian to this status of 'awakener

---

30   *Neon Martyrologion*, 3rd edn (Athens, 1961), pp. 202–3; quoted in C. Cavarnos, *The Holy Mountain*, 2nd edn. (Belmont, MA, 1977), p. 58.

31   P. Kitromilides, 'Orthodox Culture and Collective Identity', Ch. II in *An Orthodox Commonwealth*, p. 141 n. 22.

of the nation' and to dub him a 'national apostle' of the political interests of Hellenism in the Balkans is not only a misinterpretation but also a suppression of the significance of the Church's solicitude for the weal of Orthodoxy.[32]

On the contrary, Kosmas belonged to the school of thought that regarded Turkish rule as a punishment sent by God for the sins of the Greeks: 'And why did God bring the Turks and not some other race? For our good, because the other nations would have caused detriment to our Faith.'[33] This line of thought, by which the hierarchs of the Church could be seen to have identified their own interests with those of the Ottoman government, was to manifest itself later in the declaration of Patriarch Anthimos of Jerusalem, causing great resentment in the ranks of the embryonic nationalist intelligentsia in the decades before 1821:

> Our Lord ... raised out of nothing this powerful Empire of the Ottomans in the place of our Roman [Byzantine] Empire which had begun, in certain ways, to deviate from the beliefs of the Orthodox faith, and He raised up the Empire of the Ottomans higher than any other Kingdom so as to show without doubt that it came about by Divine Will.[34]

As Richard Clogg comments, 'The argument advanced by the Patriarch Anthimos of Jerusalem in 1798 that Christians should not challenge the established order because the Ottoman Empire had been raised up by God to protect Orthodoxy from the taint of the heretical, Catholic West was by no means untypical of the views of the hierarchy at large.'[35] Indeed it was being propounded by Kosmas the Aetolian thirty years earlier.[36]

32   P. Kitromilides, 'Initiatives of the Great Church in the Mid-Eighteenth Century', Ch. V in *An Orthodox Commonwealth*, p. 6.

33   Id., 'Orthodox Culture and Collective Identity', Ch. II in *An Orthodox Commonwealth*, p. 23.

34   Anthimos, Patriarch of Jerusalem, *Didaskalia Patriki* (1798), quoted in R. Clogg, *A Concise History of Greece* (Cambridge, 1992), p. 13.

35   Ibid. See also R. Clogg, ed. and trans., *The Movement for Greek Independence 1770–1821: A Collection of Documents* (London, 1976), pp. 56–62.

36   The same view is stated by St Nikodimos of the Holy Mountain who in his collection of the Holy Canons entitled *Pedalion* ('Rudder') writes, 'Divine Providence has set a guardian over us', that 'guardian' being none other than the Ottoman empire. See K. Ware, 'St Nikodimos and the *Philokalia*', p. 81.

In fact Kosmas was careful always to ask permission to preach not only of the local bishop but also of the Turkish authorities wherever he travelled. Having obtained it, he did not hold back from references to the Antichrist, the end of the world, and (despite his belief in the Ottoman empire as the bulwark of Orthodoxy) the liberation of Greece which he predicted would come about within three generations. Not surprisingly, such comments aroused the suspicions of the authorities who were easily persuaded that Kosmas and his followers were associated with the declared aims of the Russian government to liberate the Orthodox peoples of south-eastern Europe from the Ottoman yoke. One day, when visiting the Albanian village of Kolikontasi, he was seized by agents of the local pasha and, realizing that the moment had come for his work to be crowned with martyrdom, he gave thanks to Christ for deeming him worthy of so great an honour. The next day, 24 August 1779, he was hanged from a tree beside the road to Berat. 'Thus', comments Christodoulidis, 'the thrice-blessed Kosmas, that great benefactor of men, became worthy of receiving, at the age of sixty-five, a double crown from the Lord, one as a Peer of the Apostles and the other as a holy Martyr.'[37]

Kosmas's tomb became the site of many miracles, and in 1813 Ali Pasha of Ioannina, whose glittering career the saint had predicted thirty years before, built a church and monastery there in his honour. Having been officially canonized by the patriarchate of Constantinople in 1961, his relics are now the object of fervent veneration by the Orthodox and a symbol of the restoration of the faith in the land of Albania.

So we see that the power of Athos as symbol of continuity for the Orthodox lives on even today. If after the fall of the Byzantine empire the Holy Mountain represented a symbol of the continuity of Orthodox culture, it has never lost sight of this role. If the symbol was shining with all the brilliance of a new creation in the sixteenth century, it had lost none of its lustre in the eighteenth, and in the twenty-first century, when the need for it is greater than ever before, it shines just as brightly as ever.

37 Cavarnos, *St Cosmas Aitolos*, p. 45.

Similarly, throughout its history Athos has never ceased to attract men of outstanding ability, endowing them on their arrival with the full panoply of its own spiritual gifts, then sending them out into the world to live and work to God's praise and glory. The careers that we have briefly charted above have been among the most celebrated: Theophanes the artist, drawn to Athos to make his name, only to find his work raised to the status of a model for the art of the Church for centuries to come; Maximos the scholar, lured by the prospect of studying the famed contents of Athonite libraries, only to find himself exporting the treasures of Byzantine spirituality and culture to the Russian people; Voulgaris, one of the greatest intellectuals and theologians of the eighteenth-century Orthodox world, appointed to Athos to mastermind the pet project of the patriarch, then translated to the court of Catherine the Great with a vision to re-establish an enlightened Christian monarchy over the Orthodox peoples of south-eastern Europe; finally Kosmas, the humble monk, blessed with a compulsive missionary urge to enlighten his fellow Greeks, equal of the Apostles and holy martyr. It would be hard to imagine a starker contrast than that between Voulgaris, doyen of the Enlightenment, and the arch-traditionalist Kosmas. That both could be accommodated on Athos at more or less the same time is testimony to the Mountain's astonishing vitality in the second half of the eighteenth century. These are just four examples from an endless stream of witnesses to the power of Athos to preserve and transmit its traditions, 'at once landmark and generator of spiritual movement, known to fourteenth-century writers as "the workshop of virtue"'.[38]

Athos has survived because it transcends national borders. It remains the centre of spirituality for all the Eastern Orthodox Churches. As could be said of all the lands of Byzantium (and according to Anthony Bryer can be said by a villager in north-eastern Turkey to this day), 'this was Roman country; they spoke Christian here.'[39] It is no accident that all four of the

---

38   J. Shepard, 'The Byzantine Commonwealth 1000–1500', in M. Angold (ed.), *Eastern Christianity*, pp. 3–52 (p. 36).

39   A. Bryer, 'The Roman Orthodox World (1393–1492)', in J. Shepard (ed.), *The Cambridge History of the Byzantine Empire c. 500–1492* (Cambridge, 2008), p. 853.

stars whose careers we have traced have been Greeks. Apart from a brief period of Slav domination at the turn of the nineteenth century, Greeks have always formed a majority on Athos. But three of them died outside the borders of modern Greece, and all of them exerted an influence that spread throughout the Orthodox world. Between them they transmitted the elements of Greek art, Greek scholarship, Greek philosophy, and Greek language to a world that was ravenously hungry for them. Not without reason is Athos celebrated as 'the ark of Hellenism'. This is the principal legacy of the post-Byzantine Greeks on the Holy Mountain.

Bibliography

Batalden, S. K., *Catherine II's Greek Prelate: Eugenios Voulgaris in Russia, 1771–1806* (New York, 1982).

Bryer, A., 'The Roman Orthodox World (1393–1492)', in J. Shepard (ed.), *The Cambridge History of the Byzantine Empire c. 500–1492* (Cambridge, 2008), pp. 852–80.

Cavarnos, C., *The Holy Mountain*, 2nd edn (Belmont, MA, 1977).

——, *St Cosmas Aitolos*, 3rd edn (Belmont, MA, 1985).

Chatzidakis, M., 'Byzantine Art on Mount Athos', in *Treasures of Mount Athos* (Thessaloniki, 1997).

Clogg, R., *A Concise History of Greece* (Cambridge, 1992).

——, ed. and trans., *The Movement for Greek Independence 1770–1821: A Collection of Documents* (London, 1976).

Dawkins, R. M., *The Monks of Athos* (London, 1936).

Denissoff, E., *Maxime le Grec et l'Occident: Contribution à l'histoire de la pensée religieuse et philosophique de Michel Trivolis* (Paris, 1943).

Fennell, N., *The Russians on Athos* (Oxford, 2001).

Gothóni, R., *Tales and Truth: Pilgrimage on Mount Athos Past and Present* (Helsinki, 1994).

Grishin, A., 'Bars'kyj and the Orthodox Community', in M. Angold (ed.), *The Cambridge History of Christianity*, vol. 5: *Eastern Christianity* (Cambridge, 2006), pp. 210–28.

Icons at the Monastery of Stavronikita Painted in 1546 by Theophanes the Cretan (Athens, n.d.).

Kitromilides, P., *An Orthodox Commonwealth: Symbolic Legacies and Cultural Encounters in Southeastern Europe* (Aldershot, 2007).

——, 'Orthodoxy and the West: Reformation to Enlightenment', in M. Angold (ed.), *The Cambridge History of Christianity*, vol. 5: *Eastern Christianity* (Cambridge, 2006), pp. 187–209.

Hieromonk Makarios of Simonos Petra, *The Synaxarion: The Lives of the Saints of the Orthodox Church*, trans. C. Hookway, vol. 3: January, February (Ormylia, 2001).

Norwich, J., J., and R. Sitwell, *Mount Athos* (London, 1966).

Obolensky, D., 'Italy, Mount Athos, and Muscovy: The Three Worlds of Maximos the Greek (c. 1470–1556)', *Proceedings of the British Academy*, 67 (1981), 143–61.

——, *Six Byzantine Portraits* (Oxford, 1988).

Patrinelis, C., A. Karakatsanis, M Theocharis, *Stavronikita Monastery: History, Icons, Embroidery* (Athens, 1974).

Shepard, J., 'The Byzantine Commonwealth 1000–1500', in M. Angold (ed.), *The Cambridge History of Christianity*, vol. 5: *Eastern Christianity* (Cambridge, 2006), pp. 3–52.

Speake, G., 'Janus Laskaris' Visit to Mount Athos in 1491', *Greek, Roman and Byzantine Studies*, 34: 3 (1993), 325–30.

——, *Mount Athos: Renewal in Paradise* (New Haven, CT, and London, 2002).

Vaporis, N. M., *Father Kosmas, the Apostle of the Poor: The Life of St Kosmas Aitolon together with an English Translation of his Teaching and Letters* (Brookline, MA, 1977).

Ware, K., 'St Nikodimos and the *Philokalia*', in D. Conomos and G. Speake (eds), *Mount Athos the Sacred Bridge: The Spirituality of the Holy Mountain* (Oxford, 2005), pp. 69–121.

Zachariadou, E. A., 'Mount Athos and the Ottomans c. 1350–1550', in M. Angold (ed.), *The Cambridge History of Christianity*, vol. 5: *Eastern Christianity* (Cambridge, 2006), pp. 154–68.

NICHOLAS FENNELL

The Russians on Mount Athos

In October 2006 the Moscow Patriarchate hosted a conference entitled 'Moscow-Athos: A Millennium of Spiritual Unity'. Greek scholars and clerics participated, and Archimandrite Ephraim of Vatopedi was a guest of honour. The late Patriarch Alexis II chaired the opening plenary session, at which keynote speeches were made by Archimandrite Ephraim, a metropolitan representing the Ecumenical Patriarch, and two Russian politicians, including the Foreign Minister. Orthodox unity was being showcased.

Some one hundred papers were delivered, three-quarters of which were published two years later.[1] As would be expected, the publication speaks positively of the link between Russia and Athos. Discreetly placed half-way through the papers, however, is a short article by Metropolitan Iuvenaly of Krutitsk and Kolomna entitled 'The Mutual Relations between the Russian Orthodox Church and Athos in the Twentieth Century'.[2] The metropolitan delivered this text as his keynote speech at the opening ceremony, but the editorial board thought it best not to give it such prominence. With the minimum of preamble, he writes:

> The Greek government ... contrary to the guarantees of the League of Nations, kept introducing with impunity a series of legal and administrative measures in contravention of the Treaty of Lausanne. The Greek authorities took every step to stem the flow of Russian monks to St Panteleimon monastery ... Athos started to turn into an association of exclusively Greek monasteries.

1   *Rossiya-Afon: tysyacheletie dukhovnogo edinstva* (Moscow, 2008).
2   Metropolitan Yuvenaly of Kolomna and Krutitsk, ibid., pp. 236–40: 'Vzaimnootnosheniya Russkoy Pravoslavnoy Tserkvii i Afona v XX veke'.

The paper continues in this bellicose vein. Repeated pleas on behalf of the Moscow Patriarchate, explains the metropolitan, were ignored. Today, he concludes, there are sixty brethren in St Panteleimon. Thus, 'the sacred authority of the Russian Orthodox Church, by dint of dogged efforts lasting many years, managed at the most critical moment in the history of Russian Athos to stave off its physical demise.'

Metropolitan Iuvenaly's address caused a stir and a number of the Greek delegates were offended.[3] Of course, the overwhelming message from the conference was of the strength of ties between Russia and Athos. For all their careless slips, the Moscow hosts were generous and warm, especially towards their Greeks guests. No fewer than four papers were delivered on the Greek Elder Joseph the Hesychast.[4] They extolled the virtues of Greek Athos and had no direct link with the conference's central theme. Archimandrite Ephraim, who delivered two of these papers as well as his keynote speech, was greeted with genuine interest and enthusiasm. Many young Russians flocked to hear him and to catch their first glimpse of a real Athonite elder.

For their part, the Greeks spoke positively about the Russian contribution to the unity. Priest-Monk Athanasios Simonopetritis spoke with gratitude about the material and moral support Simonopetra monastery has been receiving from Russia since the time of Ivan IV. In striking contrast with Metropolitan Iuvenaly, he observes that ties with Russia are stronger than ever, especially since Perestroika. 'May Almighty God', concludes Fr

---

3   The metropolitan representing the Ecumenical Patriarch spoke next in the opening ceremony. He prefaced his speech with the acerbic observation that according to protocol he should have been asked to speak before any Russian metropolitan. To make matters worse, about half-way through Metropolitan Iuvenaly's speech the simultaneous translation into Greek inexplicably ground to a halt. Many of the Greek delegates were shocked by what they considered as hostility on his part. After dinner on the same day in the Daniilov Monastery Hotel they discussed whether to boycott the rest of the conference, but it was decided that the metropolitan's inhospitality was due to characteristically Russian bluntness and tactlessness, which were unfortunate but would have to be put up with. Greek displeasure was firmly but discreetly voiced more publicly subsequently, although this is not evident in the published articles.

4   Ibid., pp. 25–55. Two of the papers were delivered by Abbot Ephraim; the others by Protopresbyter Vasilios Kalliamanis and G. Manzaridis.

Athanasios, 'rest the souls of all our departed Russian brethren, who in one way or another have helped to prolong to this day the existence of the habitation of [our holy monastery].'[5]

Much was also said at the conference about the Russian Elder Sophrony (Sakharov), the disciple of St Silouan the Athonite, a monk of the Russian monastery of St Panteleimon.[6] Fr Sophrony founded the monastery of St John the Baptist in the English county of Essex. One of the delegates described it in Fr Sophrony's time as a model of pan-Orthodoxy:

> The monastery was multinational: the representatives of fifteen nationalities coexisted side by side; services and communication were mainly carried out in various languages; and the elder strictly saw to it that life did not veer towards any kind of Hellenization or Russification, both of which he considered to be a deviation from and corruption of the true spirit of Orthodoxy.[7]

Russia's relationship with Athos has never been straightforward. It has been a mixture of conflict, contradiction, envy, and rivalry on the one hand; and inspiration, mutual support, and spiritual regeneration on the other. Over the last 300 years the Holy Mountain did indeed veer towards both Hellenization and Russification.

Its remoteness and otherworldliness make its askesis an intense one. Physical and spiritual trials often invite discord: a monk undergoing the hardships of self-denial and vigilance is likely to find the presence of certain of his brethren a temptation. Tensions between the Russian and the Greek Athonite communities have in the past been exacerbated by their sharply contrasting ethnic characteristics. The Holy Mountain has always been at the heart of the Hellenic world. From the beginning, the Greeks have been in the majority on Athos. Serbs, Romanians, and Bulgarians have blended in with relative ease to the Athonite world because they are close neighbours of the Greeks; they have a common background of the mainly rural Mediterranean peoples. The Russians, on the other hand,

---

5   Monk Athanasios Simenopetritis, ibid., pp. 240–5: 'Svyazi monastyrya Simonopetra s Rossiyey'.

6   Abbot of the Great Schema Serafim (Pokrovsky), ibid., pp. 55–66: 'Molitvenny i literaturny opyt startsa Sofroniya (Sakharova) v svete russkoy i afonskoy traditsiy'.

7   Ibid., p. 57.

come from the remote north, beyond the Black Sea. Russian Athonite architecture, food, church singing, nineteenth-century iconography, vestments, and even liturgical tradition differ from those of the Greeks and of their Balkan neighbours.

A more striking difference setting the Russians apart from the Greeks, Bulgarians, Serbs, and Romanians is political. The Russian empire repeatedly defeated the Ottomans and, until 1829, the Russians alone on Athos represented an independent Orthodox nation. The Greeks had been under the Turkish yoke since the fall of Constantinople and without the Russians they would not have been granted their own sovereign nation. Especially in the nineteenth century, the Russians were seen to enjoy special privileges from the Athonite Turkish civil authorities, who seemed to respect them more than anyone else. For instance, only the Russians were allowed to ring bells and a special customs shed was set up in the latter half of the nineteenth century on the quayside of the Russian monastery of St Panteleimon to cope with the increasing numbers of Russian visitors.

The greater the influx of pilgrims, the wealthier the Russian community became. Russian Athonite architecture was not merely outlandishly different; it was a display of wealth. The central church of the St Andrew skete was the largest in the Christian Orthodox Near East. By the 1860s over sixty *kellia* (hermitages) had been converted into thriving cenobitic houses, several of which were as wealthy and populous as some of the ruling monasteries themselves. These *kellia* had been bought from the non-Russian ruling monasteries mostly by rich Russian merchants. The Greeks by comparison were poor. From the 1860s even the wealthier Greek monasteries, such as Vatopedi, were feeling the pinch, owing to the requisition of dedicated monastic property in Romania and Bessarabia. Little wonder that the Greeks looked with disapproval tinged with envy at the burgeoning Russian houses with their imposing stone buildings, gold ornamentation, and coloured cupolas.

Both ethnic and political differences were exacerbated by overcrowding on the Holy Mountain. When the Russian community was at its height it represented half of the total Athonite population of some 10,000 monks. Mount Athos was rapidly ceasing to be a haven of peace and contemplation. Before the latter half of the nineteenth century the Russians had coexisted more easily with the Greeks, and perhaps as well as any other ethnic group on Athos: there had never been many Russians present (their numbers probably did not significantly exceed 200 at any one time) and the Greeks had been in the majority. When the Russian Athonite population dramatically increased from the end of the Crimean War (1856), the Greeks for the first time in centuries found themselves faced with the prospect of being in the minority. They have not forgotten that the Russians threatened to outnumber them, even now that Russian numbers have shrunk to their previous levels, a process that began in the wake of the October Revolution when ties between Russia and Athos were temporarily severed. Until 1917 the Greeks so resented being challenged in an area they considered theirs by right that they thought the Russians were attempting to oust them from the Holy Mountain. After the formation of their independent state in 1829 the Greeks were anxious to annex Macedonia, in the east of which is Mount Athos. Part of Macedonia was wrested from the Turks in 1912 and Mount Athos was liberated by the Greeks on St Demetrios's day after the Bulgarians had been beaten in the race for Thesssaloniki. Thus the overwhelming Russian presence on Athos was seen as a threat to a proud fledgling nation that had been contending with its Balkan Slav rivals for the prize of Macedonia. Moreover, the Ecumenical Patriarch of Constantinople has always been Greek; and the Greeks are considered to be, like the Ecumenical Patriarch, *primi inter pares* on Mount Athos.

Even before Russian numbers started dramatically increasing, there were occasional spectacular clashes with the Greeks. On his first visit to the Holy Mountain in 1726, Monk Vasily Grigorovich-Barsky spent some time in the Russian monastery of St Panteleimon, where he saw several Russian brethren, and heard Russian singing and reading. He begins his chapter on St Panteleimon, written after his second visit (1744–7), with the oddly emphatic assertion that 'this monastery is universally called Russian by everyone – by the Greeks, Serbs, and Bulgarians.' In other words, Russian ownership of the monastery was in doubt: it was Russian only in name.[8]

---

8   This is a view commonly held by some Greeks since the nineteenth century; they claim that the monastery had never originally belonged to the Russians. See Nicholas Fennell, *The Russians on Athos* (Oxford, 2001), pp. 52–5.

Barsky goes on to explain that the Russians had lived there from the beginning, and in great numbers, until 1735. Thereafter their numbers dwindled until the monastery was abandoned and taken over by the Greeks, who refused to allow any Slavs to live in it, 'for fear that they might rightfully repossess it as their own ancient habitation'.

Barsky's account now becomes disturbing.

> There I heard from the Serbs and Bulgarians, and from Russians who had lived there many years, a terrible tale. The Greeks do not wish to hear about it, for they say it is lies. Once, many years ago, but already during Turkish rule, the monastery belonged to the Russians ... and initially the Greeks cohabited with them. The Russians accused the Greeks of some misdeed – which I have no time to specify. The latter, being in the majority and unable to bear the indignity [of the] accusation, were goaded by demons into a rage, and a great fight broke out between them both. [The Greeks] fell on [the Russians]; they caught them unawares, slaying every one of them and losing many of their own numbers. Those who survived fled nobody knows whither, out of fear of punishment.[9]

This incident, Barsky explains, happened a century before the monastery became deserted in 1735. More violence was to follow. On Easter Day 1765, after Barsky had left, there was a scandalous fracas between Greek and Slav monks which ended in bloodshed and the destruction of the already dilapidated buildings by arson. They had to move out of the monastery buildings and settled in to a new site by the sea.[10]

It should be emphasized that these clashes which took place in the eighteenth century were exceptional. Until the 1850s the story of Russian Athos had mainly been one of asceticism and spiritual achievement. The greatest and most influential Russian Athonites have been saintly examples of humility, poverty, and prayer. The foremost of these were St Antony Pechersky, who came to Athos shortly after 1051, and St Paisy Velichkovsky, who was there from 1746 to 1762. Both made their way via Kiev to

9   Vasily Grigorovich-Barsky, *Vtoroe paseschenie svyatoy Afonskoy gory vasiliya Grigorovicha-Barskogo im samim opisannoe* (Moscow, 2004), pp. 296–8.
10 Gerasimos Smyrnakis, *To Aghion Oros* (Mount Athos, repr. 1988), p. 662.

the Holy Mountain on foot. They were tonsured after they had arrived; they lived there in extreme self-denial, and then they left to continue the Athonite tradition in monastic communities at home.

St Antony, the founder of the great Kievan monastery of the Caves, is considered the father of Russian monasticism. In the seventeen short years St Paisy spent on Mount Athos he became spiritual father to monks of many nationalities, one of whom was Patriarch Seraphim I. St Paisy's personal qualities transcended ethnic barriers. He knew that the ability to maintain harmonious inter-ethnic relations was a gift others did not have. He was in charge of ethnically mixed brotherhoods: in the Prophet Elijah skete of Athos,[11] and, once he had left for the Danubian principalities, in the monasteries of Neamţ and Secul. In all three houses his brethren were Slav and Romanian; divine office was read and sung in both languages. St Paisy knew that maintaining harmony in an ethnically diverse community was possible only with great cenobitic discipline, and that only leaders with exceptional gifts could enforce it.[12]

On Athos, St Paisy was at the forefront of spiritual revival: he espoused the traditionalists' side in the Kollyvades debate and resurrected ancient patristic texts hidden away on dusty shelves of Athonite libraries. A little over a decade after his departure, Sts Nikodimos of the Holy Mountain and Makarios of Corinth were instrumental in reviving Greek Orthodox patristic traditions, the *Philokalia*, and cenobitic monasticism on the Holy Mountain. All three saints were crucially influential in the latter half of the eighteenth century when feelings of revolutionary independence were stirring in all Greeks. Turkish oppression seemed at its worst; but, just as in the Peloponnese, church schools were opening and the Athoniada was founded. It is remarkable that St Paisy, a Slav, should be associated in this way with the resurgence of the Greek national Church.

---

11 And possibly in Simonopetra monastery, where he arrived in 1762 and stayed for only a year before leaving for Moldavia.

12 When he gave the rule to Abbot George of Chernica, Moldavia, he told him to accept only Romanians into the brotherhood in order to avoid misunderstandings and conflicts.

St Paisy was also the reviver in Russia of *starchestvo*, the tradition of the spiritual elder to whom disciples would subject themselves in total obedience. His spiritual descendants were the great elders of the Optina Pustyn.[13] In the nineteenth century there lived on the Holy Mountain another spiritual descendant of St Paisy's, the great Russian *starets*, Elder Arseny. He was on Athos from 1821 until his death in 1846. Few knew of him outside Russian Athos, but he had immense influence. He was the spiritual father of the entire Russian community. The first great and successful leader and organizer of the Russians in the nineteenth century, Priest Schema-Monk Ieronim, came to the Russian monastery and became the Russians' father-confessor because the elder had instructed him to do so. Fr Ieronim initially resisted, for he wished to spend his days in eremitical seclusion and tried at all costs to avoid being ordained a priest. The elder insisted, prophesying: 'You must care for everyone; it behoves you to set up the Russian monastery, and through you it will be glorified ... The blessing of the Lord will be with you.'[14] Once Fr Ieronim was installed, the formerly destitute monastery of St Panteleimon, whose brethren were by now Greek, became the largest and wealthiest of Athonite houses, and home to almost 2,000 Russians.

Elder Arseny, meanwhile, continued to live the ascetic life Fr Ieronim had longed for. Like Sts Antony and Paisy, Elder Arseny came to the Holy Mountain on foot and was tonsured there. He travelled first via Kiev, where he was joined by Nikita (later Nikolai of the Great Schema). Then they continued on their journey, stopping in Moldavia, where, like St Paisy, they were tonsured into the Small Schema. Once on Athos, they settled down to an eremitical life, speaking to each other as little as possible and reciting the Jesus prayer. By day they carved wooden spoons which they hoped to sell. They emulated the first years on the Holy Mountain of St Paisy, who lived four years in great poverty and hesychastic silence, carving spoons by day for a living. Both Arseny and Nikolai, like St Paisy and his brother

---

13   In Kozel'sk, south of Moscow. The Optina elders were a source of inspiration and religious renewal for Dostoyevsky, Solovyev, and many other Russians, especially members of the Russian intelligentsia.

14   Schema-Monk Parfeny Aggeev, *Skazanie o stranstvii i puteshestvii po Rossii, Moldavii, Turtsii i Svyatoy zemle* (Moscow, 2008), Vol. I, Pt. II, p. 373.

in Christ Vissarion, were tonsured into the Great Schema after a similar number of years on the Holy Mountain; and Arseny was also reluctantly ordained to the priesthood.

Arseny fasted as strictly as St Paisy. The life of Arseny and his companion was so harshly ascetic that he discouraged others later on from joining them in their hermitage. The writer and missionary, Schema-Monk Parfeny Aggeev, who had chosen Fr Arseny as his own elder and knew him personally, gives a detailed description. Unlike the eleventh-century Chronicle account of St Antony or the Lives of St Paisy, it is sufficiently personal and immediate to be convincingly realistic.

> [The Elder explained:] 'Nobody can live with us. We have barely managed to attain this level of existence after thirty years, yet we are still prey to temptation and exhaustion ....' Since their arrival on the Holy Mountain they tasted neither fish nor cheese nor wine nor oil. Their food was rusks dipped in water.

These they supplemented with pickled or raw vegetables.

> And they always ate once a day, in the third hour of the afternoon; but on Wednesdays and Fridays they had no food. Their daily rule was as follows: after eating until vespers they read spiritual works in their cells. Then they served vespers according to the *Typikon*; they always read attentively and with weeping, not hurriedly, but quietly and humbly. Then followed compline with a canon to the Mother of God. The whole night was spent in vigil, prayer, and prostrations. If they were weighed down with sleep, they would allow it to take hold while they sat, but not for more than an hour and hardly perceptibly, for they mostly forced themselves to keep awake – often by pacing up and down. They had no clock, but they always knew the time, for at the foot of the mountain the clock strikes on the belfry of Iviron monastery and they always heard it. At midnight itself they would meet in the [*kellion*] church, where they would read the midnight office followed by matins according to the *Typikon*. After matins they always read the canon with the Akathist Hymn to the Mother of God. [Next] they would devote themselves to hesychastic prayer until dawn. Then they would do handicraft and work to a schedule producing ten spoons each, but each sitting in a separate place. They never held any conversations with each other, but spoke only about essentials when it was unavoidable, for they always kept quiet. They preserved their hearts from distraction and kept up a ceaseless internal prayer. The spoons they made were of the simplest kind.[15]

---

15   Ibid., Vol. II, Part IV, pp. 208–9.

The elder Arseny would weep copiously during the divine office. As we have seen, the elder could foretell the future and was able to reveal the innermost secrets of those who consulted him. He knew on which day he was to die and was able to prepare for it. He was also reputed to have the power of telekinesis. As a spiritual father he insisted on obedience to his instructions, for he received them directly from God. Monk Parfeny found the elder's commands hard to follow, as did Fr Ieronim, but such was their power that disobedience was impossible.

The elder was completely unattached to material possessions and generous to a fault. He always quoted Matthew 6: 26 and 33,[16] for he knew that God would provide for their material needs. When Monk Parfeny arrived on Athos penniless, the elder advised him to carve spoons for a living, but the young man had no carving knife. A new instrument cost 50 leva, so the elder gave him 30 leva, then 'went into the church, brought a book from there and gave it to me saying "Go and pawn it with the Korenev brothers, and take as much money as you need. I'll buy it back later."' Monk Parfeny was moved to tears by this generosity and observed of the elder: 'His first question of everyone was "Well, have you enough? Is there anything you need?"'[17]

Elder Arseny as depicted by Monk Parfeny strikingly resembles Elder Joseph the Hesychast. Both underwent extreme abstinence and poverty, and devoted themselves to hesychastic prayer, but the same is true of many Athonite ascetics. Few Athonites, however, possessed powers of telekinesis, or foresight bordering on prophecy, as they both did. Following the tradition of the Fathers of the Church, Joseph the Hesychast wept copiously during prayer, like the Elder Arseny:

---

16   'Look at the birds of the air: they neither sow nor reap nor gather into barns, and yet your heavenly Father feeds them'; and 'But seek first His kingdom and His righteousness, and all these things shall be yours as well'.

17   Ibid., Vol. II, Part IV, pp. 210–11.

Like a true hesychast and imitator of Sts Arsenios the Great and Isaac the Syrian, Elder Joseph shed copious tears during vigils and prayers. For he supposed that, should tears not flow whenever God is remembered, then ignorance, pride, and stony indifference will be locked away in the heart.[18]

As we can see, the great Athonite ascetics were all alike and followed in the footsteps of their illustrious Fathers of the Church. Priest Schema-Monk Ieronim would have liked to emulate his elder's eremitical life. He endured great physical hardship, but of a worldly kind: he manfully put up with an untreated double hernia so painful that in his last years he could hardly sit or sleep. He was so busy that he had little time for himself, let alone for sleep. However, as the leader of a vast and burgeoning cenobitic community, his life was by comparison full of worldly cares. Unlike the elder, he was a high-profile figure, constantly in the gaze of the Athonite community. Coming from a wealthy family of merchants, he knew the value of money and would probably not have been able to subject himself to complete poverty and abstinence. When on the command of the elder he left his *kellion* to move in to St Panteleimon monastery, he gave away to the poor most of his possessions:

> It was like a feast for two weeks in our *kellion*. Two men cooked food; everyone was fed and offered wine, for we had plenty of everything: there were sufficient supplies for a year of flour, fish, oil, and wine. And by God's grace we gave all away and exhausted everything, leaving only what was needed for the monastery – the essential books and costly vestments and essential clothing for ourselves. Then we sold the *kellion*.[19]

Once he was installed in St Panteleimon he devoted himself wholly to the task of securing the Russians' place there. A St Panteleimon monk recently characterized Fr Ieronim's mission thus: 'He gathered Russian monks in the Russian House, which was "their own habitation of

---

18   Archimandrite Ephraim (Kutsu), 'Lichnost' i trudy startsa Iosifa Isikhasta', *Rossiya-Afon*, p. 34.
19   Monk Parfeny Aggeev, op. cit., Vol. I, Book II, p. 374.

old"; he defended their right to an independent existence on Athos.'[20] Fr Ieronim achieved his aims by attracting generous donations from wealthy benefactors, many of whom he knew from the time when he worked in his father's tannery business before he came to Athos. He also chose as his helper and deputy the young Mikhail Sushkin, the son of a millionaire merchant from Tula. Sushkin was tonsured to the Great Schema with the name of Makary and was installed as the first Russian abbot of St Panteleimon in modern times, in 1875.

Being in charge of a vast and growing brotherhood meant that Fr Ieronim and Archimandrite Makary had constantly to work. They were wholly dedicated to their cause and operated as a team: Makary was relatively young and inexperienced; he was initially impulsive and prone to make rash decisions. Ieronim was the old head on young shoulders; he was always calm and focused. His steely resolve and clear-headedness impressed all who knew him. The Russian consul in Macedonia, K. N. Leontyev, characterized him thus:

> Firm, unwavering, fearless, and enterprising; bold and cautious at the same time; a profound idealist and thoroughly practical; as strong in body as in spirit ... – Fr Ieronim effortlessly imposed his will on people.[21]

Fathers Ieronim and Makary were good men. St Panteleimon monastery enjoyed a golden age from 1875 until the death of the latter in 1889, four years after that of Fr Ieronim. They were perhaps the principal reason why so many Russians flocked to the Holy Mountain: all knew that they would be welcomed in an edenic monastic world in which a 2,000-strong community of monks lived a life of order, decorum, and prayer. Yet neither Ieronim nor Makary was truly ascetic; they cannot be compared with those saintly men who all followed a remarkably similar path of self-denial and prayer. At the height of the struggle between Greeks and Russians for

---

20   Priest-Monk Ioakim (Sabel'nikov), *Velikaya Strazha* (Moscow, 2001), p. 62.
21   K. N. Leontyev, *Polnoe sobraniye sochineniy i pisem v dvadtsati tomakh*, Vol. 6 (1), 'Vospominanie ob arkhimandrite Makarii, igumene russkogo monastyrya sv. Panteleymona na gore Afonskoy' (St Petersburg, n.d. [2003]), p. 760.

supremacy in the monastery preceding Archimandrite Makary's enthrone-ment as abbot, Fr Ieronim knew he had the upper hand. He famously said: 'I hold the purse strings, so I can do as I please – *koshelek v moikh rukakh* – *takzhe i volya.*' [22]

Money and power belong to the world. If asceticism and prayer alone were striven for on the Holy Mountain, there would be no phyletic bias, envy, or quarrels. Then Mount Athos would be a truly pan-Orthodox Eden. The Russians and Greeks frequently clashed. Only the true ascetics were able to overcome or were simply not prone to ethnic differences. On the Holy Mountain askesis alone is proof against ethnic divisions.

Bibliography

Dmitrievsky, A. A., *Russkie na Afone: ocherk zhizni i deyatel'nosti igumena russkago Panteleymonovskago monastyrya svyaschenno-arkhimandrita Makariya (Sushkina)* (St Petersburg, 1895).

Fennell, Nicholas, *The Russians on Athos* (Oxford, 2001).

Grigorovich-Barsky, Monk Vasily, *Vtoroe paseschenie svyatoy Afonskoy gory vasiliya Grigorovicha-Barskogo im samim opisannoe* (Moscow, 2004).

Ioakim (Sabel'nikov), Priest-Monk, *Velikaya Strazha* (Moscow, 2001).

Leontyev, K. N., *Polnoe sobraniye sochineniy i pisem v dvadtsati tomakh*, Vol. 6 (1), 'Vospominanie ob arkhimandrite Makarii, igumene russkogo monastyrya sv. Panteleymona na gore Afonskoy' (St Petersburg, 2003).

Parfeny Aggeev, Schema-Monk, *Skazanie o stranstvii i puteshestvii po Rossii, Moldavii, Turtsii i Svyatoy zemle* (Moscow, 2008).

Rossiya-Afon: tysyacheletie dukhovnogo edinstva (Moscow, 2008). Athanasios Simenopetritis, Monk, 'Svyazi monastyrya Simonopetra s Rossiyey'. Ephraim (Kutsu), Archimandrite, 'Lichnost' i trudy startsa Iosifa Isikhasta'. Serafim (Pokrovsky), Abbot of the Great Schema, 'Molitvenny i literaturny opyt startsa

22 A. A. Dmitrievsky, *Russkie na Afone: ocherk zhizni i deyatel'nosti igumena russkago Panteleymonovskago monastyrya svyaschenno-arkhimandrita Makariya (Sushkina)* (St Petersburg, 1895), p. 142.

Sofroniya (Sakharova) v svete russkoy i afonskoy traditsiy'. Yuvenaly, Metropolitan of Kolomna and Krutitsk, 'Vzaimnootnosheniya Russkoy Pravoslavnoy Tserkvii i Afona v XX veke'.

Smyrnakis, Abbot Gerasimos, *To Aghion Oros* (Mount Athos, repr. 1988).

KALLISTOS WARE

The Holy Mountain: Universality and Uniqueness

The One and the Many

It is our practice, when speaking of Mount Athos, to call it not merely *a* holy mountain but *the* Holy Mountain. Why should this be so? Throughout the world, whether Eastern or Western, whether Christian or non-Christian, there are in fact numerous mountains that are regarded as holy. Moreover, besides those that exist in actual space, there are in literature many imaginary mountains that are invested with numinous power, such as the invisible *Mount Analogue* in René Daumal's parable. 'O the mind, mind has mountains', exclaimed Gerard Manley Hopkins, 'cliffs of fall frightful, sheer, no-man-fathomed.'[1] Why, then, among all these mountains, real and imaginary, should one in particular have been singled out as *the* Holy Mountain *par excellence*? Why, in the title of his recent book on Mount Athos, should Metropolitan Nikolaos of Mesogaia describe it as, not simply 'a high place', but 'the highest place on earth'?[2] What makes Athos, if not unique, then certainly exceptional and distinctive?

Let me offer four different kinds of answer to these questions; but my list of four makes no claim to be exhaustive.

1   From the poem 'No worst, there is none': *Poems of Gerard Manley Hopkins*, 3rd edition by W. H. Gardner (London, 1948), p. 107. Robert Macfarlane used Hopkins's words for the title of his book *Mountains of the Mind: A History of a Fascination* (London, 2003).

2   Metropolitan Nikolaos (Hatzinikolaou) of Mesogaia, *Mount Athos: The Highest Place on Earth*, translated by Caroline Makropoulos (Athens, 2007). The original Greek appeared in 2000 (Athens).

The World as Sacrament

First of all, Athos is not just a mountain of holy men, but in itself a mountain that is holy. Before we speak of the monastic vocation pursued by the human persons who dwell on Athos, we do well to reflect upon the intrinsic sacredness of the material environment within which these persons live. Our starting-point, then, should be the physical reality of the Holy Mountain itself.

All visitors to Athos have surely been amazed by the astonishing natural beauty of the Mountain: by the rocks on the sea shore, by the flowers and the trees, by the abundance of the wild life, and above all by the vast triangular outline of the peak that dominates the southern extremity of the Athonite peninsula. As the monks said in the 1840s to the German visitor Jakob Fallmerayer (the passage is quoted by Philip Sherrard):

> Forsake the world and join us; with us you will find your happiness. Do but look at the retreat there with its fair walls, at the hermitage on the mountain, how the westering sun flashes on its window panes! How charmingly the chapel peeps out from the bright green of the leafy chestnut forest, in the midst of vine branches, laurel hedges, valerian, and myrtle! How the water bubbles forth, bright as silver, from beneath the stones, how it murmurs among the oleander bushes! Here you will find soft breezes, and the greatest of all blessings – freedom and inward peace. For he alone is free, who has overcome the world, and has his dwelling in the laboratory of all virtues on Mount Athos.[3]

In common with other pilgrims, I have my own special memories of the landscape and of the flora and fauna of the Holy Mountain. I recall, for example, meeting a family of wild boar, father, mother, and two children, on the deserted uplands north-west of Hilandar. I found them courteous and friendly. On another occasion, near the skete of the Prophet Elijah –

---

3   Philip Sherrard, *Athos the Mountain of Silence* (London, 1960), p. 2. On Fallmerayer and the Holy Mountain, see Veronica della Dora, *Imagining Mount Athos: Visions of a Holy Place from Homer to World War II* (Charlottesville/London, 2011), pp. 192–3.

at that time, still Russian – I encountered a lynx or wild cat, who was less amiable; but it was after dusk, and no doubt he felt that I was transgressing Athonite etiquette, which prescribes that no humans should wander outside the monasteries after sunset. In the words of the introductory psalm at Vespers, 'Man goes forth to his work and to his labour until the evening', and then comes the darkness 'wherein all the beasts of the forest do move' (Ps. 103 [104]: 20–3).

I achieved a better working relationship with a snake, some 3 metres in length, close to Hilandar. While I was engaged there on the translation of the *Philokalia*, going out for my habitual mid-day walk I found him on the path enjoying the sunshine. When I banged with my stick three times on the ground, he surveyed me with a fixed stare but did not move. Then, knowing that snakes are fluent linguists, I addressed him in English, 'Could you kindly move aside?', which he did at once, disappearing into a cranny in the stone wall beside the path. No sooner had I passed than I heard a swish immediately behind me, as he re-emerged into the sunshine. Next day at the same hour I found the snake in the same place. This time I did not bang with my stick but simply asked him to move aside, and he complied. On the third day I did not even have to ask, for he slipped into the wall of his own accord.

I have never actually seen wolves on Mount Athos, although in the past I have noted what I took to be their footprints in the sandy paths not far from the northern frontier of the monastic territory. No doubt they were observing me from the undergrowth nearby. The presence of wolves on the Mountain, at least as recently as the 1970s, always struck me as a reassuring sign. For wolves in their own way are hesychasts, who dislike disturbance and noisy intrusion from human beings. So long as they continued to make their home on Athos, this was an indication that the Mountain remained still a place of silence and seclusion. Their disappearance troubles me.

Among the non-human denizens of the Mountain, I value in particular the presence of frogs. Their singing at certain seasons of the year surpasses that of any *protopsaltis* in the monasteries. I recollect sitting on a balcony at one of the hermitages in the skete of Great St Anne, around sunset shortly before Pentecost. Each *kellion* of St Anne has its own garden with a cistern, and each cistern has its *synodia* of frogs. On that evening, first a group began to sing hundreds of feet below me, and then another group commenced hundreds of feet above. Soon dozens of other companies of frogs had taken up the chant to the right and to the left, and the entire hillside re-echoed with their voices.

It was a magical moment. There came to my mind an Athonite anecdote, typical of the monastic sense of humour, about an elder who was celebrating the pre-dawn service with his disciples. Disturbed by the noise of the nearby frogs, he went out of the chapel to remonstrate. 'Frogs,' he said, 'we've just completed the Midnight Office and are starting Matins: would you mind keeping quiet until we've finished.' Whereupon the frogs replied, 'We've just completed Matins and are starting the First Hour: would *you* mind keeping quiet until *we've* finished.' It has always distressed me that St Gregory of Nyssa – among all the Greek Fathers, the one with whom I feel the closest sympathy – should speak about frogs in disapproving terms.[4]

Complementing the Athonite frogs, there are also the many birds on the Holy Mountain. A friend of mine, who has the gift of imitating bird-song, was once walking through the woods of Athos in the company of a monk. Eager to display his talent, my friend twittered, and the birds promptly responded. The monk was not impressed. 'Would you please stop doing that', he said. 'All right,' my friend answered, 'but what's wrong?' The monk replied, 'You are disturbing the natural order.' This illustrates the way in which monasticism at its best – alas! not always in practice – displays a respect for the integrity of creation, for the proper dignity of the birds and beasts.

As for my memories of the mountain itself, these are associated above all with my second ascent to the 2,000-metre peak of Athos, in the year 1971. I climbed up alone during the night – there was a full moon – so as to arrive at the summit by sunrise. I reached the top at the exact moment when the great red disk of the sun emerged from the low clouds over the

---

4   *The Life of Moses* 2. 68 : 'ugly and noisy amphibians, leaping about, not only unpleasant to the sight, but also having a foul-smelling skin'. But Gregory had in mind here the plagues of Egypt (Exod. 8: 2).

sea. After gazing for some time at the sun in the east, rapidly moving up the sky, I turned and looked northward. In the clarity of the morning light, I saw the whole Athonite peninsula spread out before me more than 1,000 metres below, stretching away to the distant mainland of Thrace. It was like a relief map, in which every feature stood out with startling sharpness. I could distinguish the various footpaths that I had been taking during the previous days, and could even make out the exact points where I had missed the right turning. Then, with my back to the rising sun, I looked westward over the sea. I was met by a sight that I had not expected, and that I shall never forget. I saw the shadow of the mountain as a vast pyramid of darkness, extending many kilometres across the waters, and shrinking visibly minute by minute as the sun behind my back rose higher.[5] At length, defeated by the piercing cold, I commenced the long descent. During the eleven hours on the way up and then down, I did not meet a single person.

Now it could be objected that the words of the monks, as reported by Fallmerayer, and equally my own delight in the panoramic view from the peak of Athos, are no more than the expression of aesthetic sentiments that are subjective and 'romantic' in character. It is possible, someone might argue, to be emotionally moved by the beauty of nature – by the sunset or the sunrise – without such an experience possessing any specifically Christian content and, more precisely, without it shedding any light on the spiritual meaning of Athonite monasticism.

This objection misses a vital point. It is indeed true that an agnostic or atheist can be deeply inspired by the beauty of nature, without being thereby drawn to any kind of faith in God. Yet to one who does in fact believe in God, such engagement with natural beauty possesses not merely a sentimental but a genuinely theological significance. Beauty transforms the world into a sacrament of the divine presence. Responding to the glory of creation, suddenly we apprehend the immediacy of the Creator. Renewing our sense of wonder, cleansing the doors of perception, we see all things in God, and God in all things. This is not pantheism but panentheism;

---

5   On the shadow of Athos (in the evening, not the morning), see Apollonius Rhodius
    1. 601–6, quoted in della Dora, *Imagining Mount Athos*, p. 20.

the distinction between the two is vital.[6] The material world around us, without losing any of its characteristic 'isness', becomes at the same time transparent. In it and through it we discern the Infinite and the Eternal. We acquire what William Blake termed 'double vision'.[7]

Viewed in this perspective, the natural beauty of Athos possesses more than a purely aesthetic importance. It enables us to experience the Holy Mountain as a frontier land between earth and heaven. We need to think in terms not only of sacred history but equally of sacred geography. There are on this globe certain points within space that act as a burning glass, concentrating the rays of the noetic sun and mediating God's presence to us: 'thin' places such as Jerusalem or Sinai, Patmos or Assisi, Walsingham or Iona. One such place is precisely the Holy Mountain of Athos. Often, though not always, the spiritual potency of the place in question is enhanced by its natural beauty; and this is exactly the case with Athos. Such natural beauty has deep value in itself, but much more significant is the manner in which the beauty points beyond itself to the Divine.

Visiting Athos, then, and opening our hearts to its visible beauty, we understand in a new way the words attributed to Jesus Christ by the early Christians, although not to be found in the canonical Gospels: 'Cut the wood in two, and I am there; lift up the stone, and there you will find Me.'[8] As the Russian hermit of Karoulia Fr Nikon (+1963) used to say of the Mountain, 'Here every stone breathes prayers.'[9] A young Anglo-Russian, returning from his first pilgrimage, told me that, when walking alone on the Athonite paths, for the first time in his life he was conscious of God all the time. Such is exactly the way in which the material environment of Athos can act as a sacrament, transforming physical space into sacred space.

---

6   See Philip Clayton and Arthur Peacocke (eds), *In Whom We Live and Move and Have Our Being: Panentheistic Reflections on God's Presence in a Scientific World* (Grand Rapids, MI/Cambridge, UK, 2004), especially the essays by Niels Henrik Gregersen and David Ray Griffin; and compare my own comments on pp. 157–9.

7   Letter to Thomas Butts (22 November 1802), in Geoffrey Keynes (ed.), *Poetry and Prose of William Blake* (London, 1948), p. 860.

8   *The Gospel according to Thomas*, Logion 77.

9   For a photograph of Fr Nikon, see Graham Speake, *Mount Athos: Renewal in Paradise* (New Haven/London, 2002), p. 228.

Note that my young friend, when he experienced the divine presence on Athos, was walking alone on the traditional footpaths. Doubtless when we circumnavigate the Mountain in a motor-boat full of cigarette smoke and engine fumes, or when we hurry from monastery to monastery in a crowded Jeep, we can still feel the presence of the Eternal. But it is far more difficult. To every prospective visitor to Athos, this is my advice. Take with you no more than a light knapsack, stout walking boots, and a staff. Travel on foot. Walk alone. You will have to endure the steepness of the way, the sharpness of the stones, the heat, sweat, and exhaustion. But you will also begin to understand the Psalmist's words, 'Be still, and know that I am God' (Ps. 45 [46]: 10).

Philip Sherrard, in a prophetic article on 'The Paths of Athos', has rightly drawn attention to the singular benefit that comes from walking along the ancient mule-tracks that link each monastic settlement to its neighbour.[10] In his eyes, the progressive neglect and obliteration of these paths from the 1960s onwards was a fateful sign of an inner and spiritual deterioration. Fortunately the decline has been in part reversed by the successful programme for the restoration of the Athonite paths, pursued in recent years under the auspices of the Friends of Mount Athos. This venture possesses more than simply a practical purpose, in assisting people to move more easily from one place to another. To every visitor it also affords the opportunity to discover the intrinsic holiness of the Mountain. Long may this work continue!

In 1973 I walked, without undue difficulty, up the ridgeway from Hilandar to Karyes. It is a journey of some 22 kilometres, and it took me nearly five hours, but every moment of those five hours was a time of gifts. In 1982 I attempted the same walk, but after some 3 kilometres I turned back, defeated by the barrier of thorns and brambles. Now I learn that, through the efforts of the Friends of Mount Athos working party in 2010, the ridgeway path has been reopened. The journey now lies, I fear, beyond my own physical capacity, but I commend it warmly to younger and more agile pilgrims.

---

10 'The Paths of Athos', *Eastern Churches Review*, 9: 1–2 (1977), 100–7. The main substance of this article is included in the second edition of Sherrard's book *Athos the Mountain of Silence* (see note 3), which appeared under the slightly different title *Athos the Holy Mountain* (London, 1982); see pp. 48–53.

Yet the answer to our initial question – what makes the Holy Mountain exceptional? – remains as yet incomplete. For there are other places
of outstanding natural beauty – such as the Cairngorms or the Pyrenees,
the rivers Tweed or Wye, Derwentwater or Lake Ochrid – that can also
act as a sacrament of the divine presence. What sets the Holy Mountain
on a level higher than these others, and confers on it an especial sanctity?
To answer that question, it is necessary to turn our attention from the
Mountain itself to the monks who inhabit it.

Ecumenical Orthodoxy

A second distinctive feature of the Holy Mountain, alongside its sacra-
mental beauty, is its universality. From the later tenth century – when the
first fully organized cenobitic houses were established on the peninsula
– without interruption until the present time Athonite monasticism has
always possessed an international character. St Athanasios of Athos, founder
(c. 963) of the earliest cenobitic house on the Holy Mountain, the Great
Lavra, is said to have assembled in his monastery numerous monks 'from
different nationalities, tongues, races and cities, not only from those living
near at hand, but also from very distant regions, from Rome itself, from
Italy, Calabria, Amalfi, Iberia [Georgia], Armenia, and from yet further
afield'.[11] It is a striking fact that, among the four most senior of the 'ruling'
monasteries – Lavra, Vatopedi, Iviron, and Hilandar – two are, or were
originally, non-Greek. Thus Iviron was founded by the Georgians St John
and St Euthymios around 979–80,[12] only seventeen years after the inau-
guration of the Great Lavra by St Athanasios, although sadly there are no

11   *First Life of Athanasios the Athonite* 158 (ed. J. Noret, pp. 74–5).
12   See Tamara Grdzelidze, *Georgian Monks on Mount Athos: Two Eleventh-Century
     Lives of the Hegoumenoi of Iviron* (London, 2009), pp. 53–94. For an eighteenth-
     century description of Athos by a Georgian archbishop, see Mzia Ebanoizde and
     John Wilkinson, *Pilgrimage to Mount Athos, Constantinople and Jerusalem 1755–1759:*

longer any Georgians resident within the walls of Iviron, while Hilandar was refounded by the Serbs St Simeon (Stefan) Nemanja and his son St Sava in 1198.[13] Indeed, in the fifteenth century, besides Hilandar, as many as five other monasteries were predominantly Serbian.[14] There is evidence for a monastery 'of the Rus' as early as 1016, and the Bulgarian presence at Zographou dates back at least to the twelfth century.

In this way Athos was from the start, and remains today, a spiritual centre for all Orthodox (provided, of course, that they are male).[15] It is truly ecumenical in character, in the sense that it embraces in principle the entire *oikoumeni* or inhabited earth. Although, according to the Constitutional Charter approved by the Athonite Holy Community in 1924 and ratified by the Greek government in 1926, Athos is 'a self-governing part of the Greek state', this does not in any way imply it is limited to persons of Greek ethnic origin. While, as the Charter states, 'All persons leading a monastic life there acquire Greek citizenship without further formalities upon admission as novices or monks',[16] at the same time Athos is genuinely pan-Orthodox, a home not only for Greeks but equally for Georgians, Serbs, Bulgarians, Russians, and Romanians. Truly, so far at least as Chalcedonian Orthodoxy is concerned – for there are no Copts, Ethiopians, or Armenians on the Mountain – Athos is indeed a microcosm of the Christian East. And not of the Christian East only, for during the tenth to thirteenth centuries there was also a Latin house on the Mountain, 'St Mary of the Amalfitans', where the monks followed the rule of St Benedict.[17]

Timothy Gabashvili, Georgian Studies on the Holy Land, vol. 1, Caucasus World Series (Richmond, 2001).

13   For an interesting portrayal of Hilandar, with some reference to its early history, see Sydney Loch, *Athos: the Holy Mountain* (London, 1957), pp. 27–45.

14   Speake, *Mount Athos*, p. 81.

15   On the exclusion of women from the Holy Mountain, see Alice-Mary Talbot, 'Women and Mt Athos', in Anthony Bryer and Mary Cunningham (eds), *Mount Athos and Byzantine Monasticism*, Papers from the Twenty-eighth Spring Symposium of Byzantine Studies, Birmingham, March 1994 (Aldershot, 1996), pp. 67–79.

16   See Article 5 of the 1975 Constitution, cited in Speake, *Mount Athos*, p. 162.

17   See Dom Leo Bonsall, OSB, 'The Benedictine Monastery of St Mary on Mount Athos', *Eastern Churches Review*, 2: 3 (1969), 262–7; Marcus Plested, above pp. 97–106; and

Athonite monasticism, however, in thus possessing an international character, is not in itself unique. So far from innovating, it reflects in this regard a tradition that marked the Christian monastic movement from its inception. Fourth-century monasticism in Egypt included not only Copts and Greeks but Syrians and a sprinkling of westerners. In the *lavra* of St Sabas in the sixth-century Judaean wilderness, besides those who spoke Greek there were Armenians who had a special oratory where they celebrated the Divine Office in their own language; there were also then, or somewhat later, Georgians and Syrians who likewise recited the Divine Office in their own chapels and their own languages, although the whole community came together in the main church for the celebration of the Eucharist.[18] At Sinai in the sixth and following centuries there were Greeks, Armenians, and Georgians, along with Syriac and Arabic speakers, all living alongside each other.[19]

Yet, if Eastern Christian monasticism has long been international in character, this pan-Orthodox dimension has been developed and maintained to an exceptional degree on Athos. This ethnic universality is certainly one of the reasons why it is regarded throughout the Orthodox world as *the* Holy Mountain. For many centuries the various nationalities on Athos appear to have lived side by side in a reasonably peaceful manner. Care should be taken not to read back into an earlier period the more acute sense of ethnic identity that only emerged in the Balkans, among both Greeks and Slavs, from the late eighteenth century onwards. As Dimitri Obolensky observes with reference to Athos, 'National antagonisms were not unknown; yet the sense of solidarity rooted in a common tradition of ascetic endeavour and spirituality seems to have been more important.' In this connection he notes that the Byzantines, 'aware of this supranational bond', referred to the different peoples on Athos not as 'nations' (*ethni*)

---

idem, 'Athos and the West: Benedictines, Crusaders, and Philosophers', in Graham Speake (ed.), *Friends of Mount Athos: Annual Report 2007* (published in 2008), pp. 43–54.

18   Cyril of Scythopolis, *Life of Sabas* 20; cf. John Binns, *Ascetics and Ambassadors of Christ: The Monasteries of Palestine, 314–631* (Oxford, 1994), p. 171.

19   Derwas Chitty, *The Desert a City* (Oxford, 1966), p. 170.

but as 'tongues' (*glossai*).²⁰ This cosmopolitan spirit on the Holy Mountain is readily intelligible when it is borne in mind that the Byzantine empire itself was multi-ethnic. Greek was the language of government, education, and church worship,²¹ but within the bounds of the empire there were also Syrians and Armenians, as well as many Slavs.

This supranational mentality continued during the Tourkokratia, at least until the end of the eighteenth century. Greek-speaking Christians thought of themselves not as 'Hellenes' but as *Romaioi*, 'Romans', heirs not so much to classical Hellas as to the universal Roman empire of Augustus, Constantine, and Justinian. Those Christians in the Ottoman empire who used some dialect of Slavonic, Vlach, or Albanian also shared this 'Romaic' spirit, albeit in a less articulate fashion. Paschalis Kitromilides remarks that the period up to 1800 was 'an epoch marked by the absence of national divisions from the Balkans'. 'There of course existed elements of ethnic differentiation,' he continues, 'expressed primarily in the multiplicity of Balkan vernacular languages. What is surprising, however, for a premodern era was the facility with which people crossed linguistic frontiers.' Balkan society was 'culturally homogenised'; there were 'social and class divisions', but these cut across 'ethnolinguistic demarcation lines'.²² This general cultural situation in the Ottoman domains naturally made it easier for the different 'tongues' on the Holy Mountain to coexist in harmony.

Professor Kitromilides illustrates the existence of this cosmopolitan spirit in the Ottoman world, and more particularly on Athos, by describing the career of Constantine (Kaisarios) Dapontes (1713/14–84), monk of the Athonite house of Xeropotamou. Dapontes is the author of a lengthy narrative poem, describing the nine-year peregrination that he undertook

---

20 Dimitri Obolensky, *Six Byzantine Portraits* (Oxford, 1988), p. 120.

21 The Slavonic translations of the liturgical texts made by Cyril and Methodios, and by their disciples, were used only outside the frontiers of the Byzantine empire, not within it.

22 Paschalis M. Kitromilides, '"Balkan Mentality": History, Legend, Imagination', *Nations and Nationalism*, 2 (1996), 170–1, 181; reprinted in Paschalis M. Kitromilides, *An Orthodox Commonwealth: Symbolic Legacies and Cultural Encounters in Southeastern Europe*, Variorum Collected Studies Series CS 891 (Aldershot, 2007), article 1.

throughout the Ottoman empire in order to raise money for his monastery. Dapontes was passionately devoted to his native island of Skopelos, his 'golden homeland', as he called it; but beyond this particular locality he had no sense of a national motherland. He regarded 'the entire space of Southeast Europe as an integral whole, unfragmented by political or national divisions'.[23] What mattered to him, as he journeyed through the Ottoman territories, was not primarily whether the inhabitants spoke Greek, Albanian, Vlach, or a Slavonic dialect, but whether they were Christians or Muslims. He had no sense of 'Greece' as a political entity or of the 'Greek nation' in the modern sense.

This consciousness of a supranational 'Orthodox commonwealth', inherited from Byzantium and persisting during the Tourkokratia, helped the monastic communities on Athos to preserve a pan-Orthodox spirit. Regrettably, however, during the nineteenth century this was replaced throughout the Balkans by a growing sense of distinctive national particularity; and this had a sadly negative impact upon the peace and unity of the Holy Mountain. Already in the eighteenth century two monks of Hilandar, Jovan Rajić and Paisy Hilandarsky, awakened among the Serbs and Bulgars an awareness of their medieval past: Jovan emphasized the glories of the Serbian empire in the fourteenth century, while under his influence Paisy wrote about the First and Second Bulgarian empires.[24] In the early years of the nineteenth century a similar tendency emerged among the Greeks, on Athos and elsewhere, as they developed a heightened consciousness of their roots in classical Hellas; and this sense of Hellenic identity was greatly increased by the Greek uprising of 1821.

23   Kitromilides, "'Balkan Mentality'", p. 176. On Dapontes, see also R. M. Dawkins, *The Monks of Athos* (London, 1936), pp. 65–73.

24   On Rajić, see Paschalis M. Kitromilides, 'The Enlightenment East and West: A Comparative Perspective on the Ideological Origins of the Balkan Political Traditions', *Canadian Review of Studies in Nationalism*, 10: 1 (Charlottetown, PEI, 1983), 58; reprinted in Paschalis M. Kitromilides, *Enlightenment, Nationalism, Orthodoxy: Studies in the Culture and Political Thought of South-eastern Europe*, Variorum Collected Studies Series CS 453 (Aldershot, 1994), article I. On Paisy, see Paschalis M. Kitromilides, 'Athos and the Enlightenment', in Bryer and Cunningham (eds), *Mount Athos and Byzantine Monasticism*, p. 271; reprinted in Kitromilides, *An Orthodox Commonwealth*, article VII.

While all of this had its effect upon the monks of Athos, what chiefly led to a sharp deterioration in interethnic relations on the Holy Mountain was the dramatic increase in the number of Russians.[25] By the start of the twentieth century they had come to outnumber the Greeks: thus in 1902 there were on Athos no fewer than 3,496 Russians, but only 3,276 Greeks (there were also 307 Bulgarians, 286 Romanians, 51 Georgians, and 16 Serbs: a total of 7,432).[26] Although the Greeks remained in control of seventeen out of the twenty 'ruling' monasteries, they felt threatened by a Russian 'takeover', and this led them to react with hostility. A vivid account of the bitterness between Greeks and Russians in this period is provided by Athelstan Riley, who sees an 'amusing side' to the story. But the humour leaves a nasty taste in the mouth.[27]

Nationalism still continues today to exercise a baneful influence on the Orthodox Church throughout the world. But, at least so far as Athos is concerned, interethnic suspicions now exist only on a greatly diminished scale. The Russians no longer present a realistic threat to the Greek dominance on the Holy Mountain. Indeed, the pan-Orthodox universality of Athos has been reaffirmed in a new way during my own lifetime. On my early visits to Athos as an Orthodox layman in 1961 and 1962, I did not meet Western converts in any of the monasteries. Although at that time I was already seriously thinking of becoming a monk, never once did it occur to me that I might do so on the Holy Mountain, nor did any of the monks there suggest such a possibility to me. But from the 1970s onwards, on my visits to Athos I began to meet Western converts wherever I went – French, Germans, Swiss, English, Americans, and even a Peruvian – and today there is scarcely a single Greek house that does not contain Westerners who have adopted the Orthodox faith as adults.

25　The story is well recounted by Nicholas Fennell, *The Russians on Athos* (Oxford/ Bern, 2001), chapters 2–5.

26　I take these figures from Gerasimos Smyrnakis, *To Agion Oros* (Athens, 1903), p. 707. For Athonite statistics in the twentieth century, see Speake, *Mount Athos*, pp. 169, 174; René Gothóni, *Paradise within Reach: Monasticism and Pilgrimage on Mt Athos* (Helsinki, 1993), pp. 30–2.

27　Athelstan Riley, *Athos or the Mountain of the Monks* (London, 1887), pp. 241–50.

In my case, however, there would certainly have been an obstacle. It is required of any convert who seeks to take monastic vows on Athos that he should have been received into Orthodoxy by baptism. As I had been admitted into the Church by 'economy' through the sacrament of chrismation, I would have needed to be rebaptized. Yet this has not prevented me from receiving invitations, whenever I visit Athos, to celebrate the Divine Liturgy. Recently, after I had officiated in one of the Greek monasteries, the abbot – a man of great personal kindness – suggested that I might wish to settle there in my declining years. I wondered whether I would have to be rebaptized in my episcopal vestments. But I kept this thought to myself.

Embracing as it does not only the traditional Orthodox nations but also the West, Athos is indeed a microcosm of the Orthodox world, a pan-Orthodox diversity-in-unity.

The Threefold Way

It is time to turn from the outward aspect of monastic Athos to its inner life, and this brings me to a third noteworthy feature of the Holy Mountain. Athonite monasticism can justly claim to be a microcosm, not only because of its national and ethnic diversity, but also because it includes within its boundaries examples of all three forms of the monastic life, as found in the Christian East: of the eremitic life, of the cenobitic, and of the middle way that can be described either as semi-eremitic or as semi-cenobitic. St John Climacus in his *Ladder of Divine Ascent*, written at Sinai around the middle of the seventh century, clearly distinguishes these three forms, and himself expresses a preference for the semi-eremitic form, which he terms 'the King's highway':

> All monastic life may be said to take one of three forms. There is the path of withdrawal and solitude for the spiritual athlete; there is the life of stillness shared with one or two others; and there is the practice of patient endurance in a community. 'Turn neither to the right hand nor to the left', says Ecclesiastes (Prov. 4: 27), but

rather follow the King's highway; for the second of these ways is suitable for many people ... 'For where two or three are gathered together in My name, there am I in the midst of them' (Matt. 18: 20).[28]

All three of these forms are to be found side-by-side in fourth-century Egypt; all three forms had emerged on Athos by the end of the tenth century; and all three forms likewise coexist on the Holy Mountain today. This is a remarkable example of the continuity of Eastern monasticism, and more particularly of continuity on Mount Athos itself.[29]

The hermit life – what Climacus calls 'the path of withdrawal and solitude for the spiritual athlete' – flourishes on Athos above all in the wooded valleys and steep rock faces of the southern part of the peninsula. Here a monk can dwell in entire isolation, or perhaps with a few other hermits in the near vicinity. There even survives on Athos the most radical expression of the eremitic life, that of the 'pasturing monks' or *boskoi*, who have no roof over their heads, no fixed habitation, and who wear no monastic habit but go about naked like the wild animals, living on wild plants and berries. My friend Gerald Palmer (1904–84) was talking one day, back in the 1950s, with Fr Nikon of Karoulia, when the latter's disciple Fr Zosima arrived in a state of some confusion. Fr Zosima's handiwork was to make baskets, and he had gone out into the woods to gather withies. Wandering beyond his habitual haunts, he had espied three naked figures on a nearby crag. 'Were they demons?' asked Fr Zosima. 'No', Fr Nikon replied; and he said that he knew of 'pasturing monks' who dwelt in that particular region.[30]

---

28 *The Ladder of Divine Ascent*, Step 1 (*PG* 88: 641D).

29 For a careful analysis of the various types of monastic life on Athos, see N. F. Robinson, SSJE, *Monasticism in the Orthodox Churches* (London/Milwaukee, 1916), pp. 3–24; compare Emmanuel Amand de Mendieta, *Mount Athos the Garden of the Panagia* (Berlin/Amsterdam, 1972), pp. 177–213. The idiorrhythmic form of life has now disappeared from the twenty 'ruling' monasteries (Speake, *Mount Athos*, pp. 181–2), but there still exist what are known as 'idiorrhythmic sketes', such as Great St Anne.

30 Jacques Valentin, in his book *The Monks of Mount Athos* (London, 1960), p. 37, claims to have seen one such naked *boskos* on a balcony in the monastery of St Panteleimon. In general, however, Athonite monks display a deep reserve towards the naked human body, as visitors who bathe in the sea within sight of a monastery will quickly discover to their cost.

At the other extreme from the hermit life there is the cenobitic life in a fully organized monastery, 'the practice of patient endurance in a community', as Climacus terms it. This is represented on Athos primarily by the twenty 'ruling' monasteries. Also in this category are the cenobitic sketes, such as the Romanian house of Prodromou. Examples of such cenobitic sketes from the past include the Russian sketes of St Andrew and of the Prophet Elijah.

Thirdly, there is what Climacus describes as 'the life of stillness shared with one or two others', the semi-eremitic or semi-cenobitic form. This is to be found in the idiorrhythmic sketes of, for instance, Great St Anne or Kafsokalyvia. These are monastic villages, with scattered cottages surrounding a central church; and within each cottage there are between two and six monks – occasionally even more – sharing a common life. In practice the first and the third ways, the eremitic and the semi-cenobitic, are not always sharply distinct.

The spiritual ideal of each of these three monastic types is plainly expressed in the lives of their respective founders in fourth-century Egypt; and the same understanding of each form still prevails on Athos today. The pioneer of the first way, the eremitic, is St Antony the Great (c. 251–356). His conversion to the monastic life is recounted in somewhat iconic terms by his biographer and contemporary St Athanasios of Alexandria. Antony was the child of Christian parents. Aged about eighteen or twenty, he was listening in church one Sunday to the Gospel reading: 'If you want to be perfect, go and sell all you have, and give the money to the poor ... then come and follow Me' (Matt. 19: 21). These words changed his life. He heard them as if they had been spoken for the first time personally to him alone. He took Christ's commandment literally, giving everything away, devoting himself to a life of asceticism and prayer, and withdrawing gradually further and further into the uninhabited desert, so as to be alone with God.[31] *If you want to be perfect* ...: Antony's thirst for perfection, his all-consuming love for God, was so compelling, so total and uncompromising, that for God's sake he renounced everything else.

31   Athanasios, *Life of Antony* 2.

St Pachomios (286–346), the founder of the earliest cenobitic monastery – or, more exactly, of the earliest cenobitic order, for he founded a series of monasteries integrated into a single federation – was also about twenty when he first heard God's call. At the time he was still a pagan. Drafted into the army, he and the other recruits were taken down the Nile to Alexandria. As they journeyed, they were shut up at night in the local prison, presumably to prevent them from running away. After dark the Christians of the place came to them with food and drink. Pachomios asked who these unexpected visitors might be; it was the first time that he had ever heard the name 'Christian'. Deeply moved by their practical compassion, at once he resolved to become himself a Christian on his release from military service.

'O God', Pachomios prayed that same night in the prison, '... if You deliver me from my present troubles, I shall obey Your will all the days of my life; and, loving all men, I shall serve them according to Your commandment.'[32] He kept his promise. Dismissed from the army a few months later, he received baptism and at the same time embraced the ascetic life: his conversion to Christianity was simultaneously a conversion to the monastic vocation. *Loving all men, I shall serve them* ...: faithful to the ideal of loving compassion which his initial contact with the Christians had revealed to him, he did not choose to be a hermit like Antony but he founded a community, in which he and his brother monks might express their love through a shared life and through acts of daily service to one another. So, in its spirit of mutual sharing, the monastery was to be an image of the first apostolic community at Jerusalem, in which the Christians 'shared all things in common' (Acts 2: 42).

As for the third or middle way, in fourth-century Egypt this is exemplified in particular by the semi-eremitic settlements of Nitria and Scetis, where the pioneering figures were Pambo, Makarios the Egyptian, and Makarios the Alexandrian. It is from this milieu that there chiefly emerge the collections of stories and aphorisms known variously as the *Gerontikon*,

32　*First Greek Life of Pachomios* 4–5; compare *Bohairic Life* 7–8. See Armand Veilleux, *Pachomian Koinonia*, vol. 1, Cistercian Studies Series 45 (Kalamazoo, MI, 1980), pp. 27–8, 300.

the *Apophthegmata*, or the *Sayings of the Desert Fathers*.[33] This seminal work is essential reading for anyone who seeks to understand the meaning of Athonite monasticism.

The monastic ideal of the third way is summed up in a story told by Palladios of Helenopolis about his spiritual father Makarios the Alexandrian. One day, in a state of discouragement, Palladios went to Makarios and said, 'Father, what shall I do? For my thoughts oppress me, saying, "You are making no progress; go away from here".' And the old man answered, 'Tell your thoughts, "For Christ's sake I am guarding the walls".'[34] *I am guarding the walls*: with what weapons? The early monks had a precise answer: with the weapon of prayer. And against whom were they guarding the walls? Once more, the early monks replied in specific terms: against the demons. And since the demons are the common enemies of all humankind, it follows that the monks, by withdrawing into the desert that is the home of the demons, are not acting selfishly, for the invisible warfare in which they are engaged benefits the human race as a whole. Incidentally, if the desert is understood in this sense, as the abode of the forces of evil, it may well be asked: where is the desert today – in the countryside or in the inner city?

Palladios' image of guarding the walls – which applies, indeed, not only to the semi-eremitic life but to all forms of monasticism – is taken up by the anonymous author of *The History of the Monks in Egypt* (late fourth century). 'There is no town or village in Egypt and the Thebaid', he writes, 'that is not surrounded by hermitages as if by walls, and the people depend on the prayers of these monks as if on God Himself ... Through them the world is kept in being, and through them too human life is preserved and honoured by God.'[35]

---

33   These exist in two main redactions, the 'alphabetical' (under the names of specific persons) and the 'systematic' (under particular themes). Both have been translated by Sister Benedicta Ward, SLG: *The Sayings of the Desert Fathers: The Alphabetical Collection*, revised edition (London/Oxford, 1981); *The Desert Fathers: Sayings of the Early Christian Monks* (London, 2003). Compare Kallistos Ware, 'The Desert Fathers and the Love of Others', in Graham Speake (ed.), *Friends of Mount Athos: Annual Report 2009* (published in 2010), pp. 21–37.

34   Palladios, *Lausiac History* 18.

35   *Historia Monachorum in Aegypto*, Prologue §§ 10 and 9: in *The Lives of the Desert Fathers*, tr. Norman Russell, Cistercian Studies Series 34 (London/Oxford/Kalamazoo, MI, 1981), p. 50.

Now it has been objected that this notion of 'guarding the walls' reflects an external opinion, expressing what outsiders thought about the monks rather than what the monks thought about themselves.[36] There may be some truth in this. Doubtless most of the early monks, if challenged to epitomize the meaning of their vocation, would have hesitated to describe themselves as guardians of the walls or to claim that they were keeping the world in being. They might have preferred to answer, in less ambitious terms, 'I am here to repent of my sins.' As St Antony said, 'This is a man's chief task: always to blame himself before God for his sins.'[37] 'Why are you weeping?' Abba Dioskoros was asked by his disciple; and he replied, 'I am weeping for my sins.'[38] Present-day Athonite monks would give the same answer.

Yet this second way of interpreting the monastic vocation does not necessarily contradict the first. Even if, in repenting, a monk thinks only of his own indigence and helplessness in God's sight, even if he does not think that he is guarding the walls and supporting others, none the less through his repentance or 'change of mind' (*metanoia*) he is in fact doing precisely that. In the words of Fr Irénée Hausherr, SJ, 'All progress in sanctity realized by one member profits every member; each ascent to God establishes a new point of contact between Him and humankind as such; every oasis of spirituality renders the desert of this world less savage and uninhabitable.'[39] St Seraphim of Sarov (1754–1833) made the same point more succinctly: 'Acquire inner peace, and thousands around you will find salvation.'[40]

It is here, in the words of Fr Irénée and St Seraphim, that we find the answer to an objection often made against monasticism, whether on Athos or elsewhere. What service, it is asked, does the monk render to society at large? Is not the monastic life selfish? Various answers can of course be

---

36 See Sister Benedicta Ward, introduction to *The Lives of the Desert Fathers*, pp. 12–13.

37 *Apophthegmata*, alphabetical collection, Antony 4.

38 *Apophthegmata*, alphabetical collection, Dioskoros 2.

39 'L'hésychasme. Etude de spiritualité', *Orientalia Christiana Periodica*, 22 (1956), 23; reprinted in Irénée Hausherr, *Hésychasme et prière*, Orientalia Christiana Analecta 176 (1966), p. 181.

40 See Archimandrite Lazarus Moore, *An Extraordinary Peace: St Seraphim, Flame of Sarov* (Port Townsend, WA, 2009), pp. 30, 83.

offered. First, through their writings on theology and spirituality, many
monks have given support to the Church as a whole. So far as Athos is concerned, one of the most encouraging fruits of the renewal that has taken
place since the late 1960s has been the marked increase in the number of
valuable books that the monks have produced. Second, hospitality has
always been regarded as an essential part of the monastic vocation. By
opening its doors to pilgrims and visitors of all kinds, the monastery reaches
out to the stranger, the unchurched, the outcast. Even if the vast increase
in visitors in recent decades has meant that Athonite hospitality is now
sometimes distant and perfunctory, yet in principle every guest is to be
received 'as if he were Christ Himself', as the rule of St Benedict states,[41]
and as the Athonite tradition also affirms.

A third and more fundamental service rendered by monks to the
outside world is the ministry of spiritual counsel. The hermit who, like St
Antony, withdraws into solitude solely because of his thirst for perfection,
often becomes in later life, exactly as St Antony did, a guide to others, an
'elder' (*geron, starets*), bringing hope and healing not only to his fellow
monks but equally to a multitude of lay people.[42] Significantly, the present
Athonite renewal has been blessed by a group of outstanding spiritual
fathers, such as Fr Vasileios of Iviron (formerly of Stavronikita), Fr Aimil-
ianos of Simonopetra, Fr George of Grigoriou, Fr Ephraim, formerly of
Philotheou (now in America), the late Fr Joseph of Vatopedi, and the late
Fr Paisios, to mention but a few. Without the presence of such 'elders', the
Athonite renaissance could never have taken place. Their sphere of influence
has extended throughout the whole of Greece, and indeed far beyond.

None of these answers, however, goes to the heart of the matter. The
basic and primary service rendered by the monk to humankind as a whole
is quite simply to pray. He helps others not just through explicit prayers of
intercession but through all his prayer, through his communion with God
at every level of his daily life. As Fr Irénée and St Seraphim appreciated,

41   The rule of St Benedict, §53.
42   See Kallistos Ware, 'What do we mean by Spiritual Guidance?' in Graham Speake
     (ed.), *Friends of Mount Athos: Annual Report 2010* (published 2011), pp. 22–8.

such communion with God operates dynamically as a positive force, transfiguring the world. It is prayer that makes both monk and layman a 'man for others'; and if the monasteries are *par excellence* houses of prayer, they are most certainly serving society at large. Olivier Clément was right to claim that if a few people, whether monastics or lay persons, turn their lives into prayer – prayer that is 'pure' and to all appearances quite useless – they transform the world by the sole fact of their presence, by their very existence.[43]

This threefold ideal, as set forth by the monastic pioneers in fourth-century Egypt, still remains the ideal of Athonite monasticism in the twenty-first century. The monks of contemporary Athos, in common with their predecessors seventeen centuries ago, are engaged on the pursuit of perfection; they are seeking to love and serve their brethren; and they are guarding the walls of the human city through their repentance and their continual prayer. Underlying all three forms of the monastic life – the eremitic, the cenobitic and the middle way – there is a single leitmotif, the quest for freedom. As the Athonite monks said to Jakob Fallmerayer, 'Here you will find ... the greatest of all blessings – freedom and inward peace.' The monastic discipline of poverty, chastity, and obedience can easily be formulated in negative terms – no money, no wife, no independence – yet in reality its purpose is supremely positive: it is the doorway to personal liberation.

This point is rightly emphasized in the 'Announcement' issued by the Athonite monastery of Koutloumousiou early in 2009. The monk, it is said here, 'possesses nothing', and so 'he is possessed by nothing'.[44] 'The Holy Mountain', continue the Fathers of Koutloumousiou, '... professes freedom of spirit – an axial point in Orthodoxy.' Every monastic commu-

---

43 *Byzance et le christianisme* (Paris, 1964), p. 18.
44 It is true that many of the cenobitic houses on the Holy Mountain own landed property or urban apartment buildings; but these are not personal but collective possessions, and the income from them helps the monasteries to keep their buildings in repair and to meet the heavy expense of entertaining visitors. Yet, as the recent difficulties at Vatopedi indicate, there is always a danger that such collective possessions may interfere with the inner freedom of the monks.

nity is 'a miniature of the Church'. 'The Holy Mountain does not belong to anyone .... It belongs to the Mother of God .... It is the centuries-old fruit of the collaboration between God and His saints.' As an expression of the *synergeia* or 'co-working' between divine grace and human freedom (see 1 Cor. 3: 9), Athos initiates its members into what St Paul terms 'the glorious liberty of the children of God' (Rom. 8: 21).

Creative Silence

Such, then, is a third distinctive feature, manifesting the universality of the Holy Mountain: its comprehensive character, embracing as it does the three paradigmatic forms of the monastic vocation. There remains a fourth feature that makes Athos exceptional, if not unique: the special protection that the Holy Mountain enjoys from the Mother of God, its privileged status as the Garden and Sanctuary of the Panagia.

The Theotokos signifies many different things for the Athonite monk, but she may be seen above all as the defender and patron of one thing in particular: creative silence. This aspect of Athonite spirituality is developed especially by St Gregory Palamas in a homily written around 1334, while he was still living on the Mountain, in honour of the feast of the Entry of the Mother of God into the Temple (21 November).[45] How, asks Palamas,

---

45   *Homily* 53, ed. P. K. Christou, *Ellines Pateres tis Ekklesias*, vol. 79 (Thessaloniki, 1986), pp. 260–346; English translation by Christopher Veniamin, *Saint Gregory Palamas: The Homilies* (Waymart, PA, 2009), pp. 414–44. *Homily* 52 (Christou, pp. 238–56; Veniamin, pp. 407–13) is also devoted to the Mother of God. Briefer and later in date, composed in the 1350s when Palamas was Archbishop of Thessaloniki, it does not however develop the theme of Mary's *hesychia*, as is done in *Homily* 53. See Kallistos Ware, 'The Feast of Mary's Silence: The Entry into the Temple (21 Nov)', in Dom Alberic Stacpoole, OSB, *Mary in Doctrine and Devotion*, Papers of the Liverpool Congress, 1989, of the Ecumenical Society of the Blessed Virgin Mary (Dublin, 1990), pp. 34–41.

are we to understand the childhood years that Mary spent, according to ancient tradition, in the Temple at Jerusalem, secluded in the profound silence of the Holy of Holies? We are to see her, he answers, as a model of the contemplative life, as the supreme hesychast, the one who more than any other person has attained genuine *hesychia*, stillness, or silence of heart.

Entering the Temple, states Palamas, Mary severed all links with secular and earthly things, renouncing the world, 'living for God alone', choosing a hidden existence invisible to outside eyes, a 'life of stillness'. Enclosed within the Holy of Holies, her situation was like that of the hermits and ascetics who dwell in 'mountains and deserts and caves of the earth' (cf. Heb. 11: 38). Her residence in the Temple, interpreted in this way as a 'desert' experience, was an anticipation of monasticism. There she learnt to subject her 'ruling intellect' (*nous*) to God, leading an angelic life, initiated into *theoria* or contemplation, and practising continual prayer. Transfigured by the divine light, she saw the uncreated God reflected in the purity of her heart as in a mirror.[46] And her means of access to all these mysteries of inner prayer was precisely *hesychia*, stillness:

> It was holy stillness that guided her on her path; the stillness that signifies cessation of the intellect and of the world, forgetfulness of things below, initiation into things above, the shedding and transcending of thoughts. Such stillness is true action, the ascent to genuine contemplation or, to speak more truly, to the vision of God ... She alone among all humankind from such an early age practised stillness to a surpassing degree ... She made a new and secret road to heaven, the road – if I may so express it – of noetic silence.[47]

Reading these words of Palamas about the inner stillness of the Mother of God, we are led to ask: what then is the true meaning of silence, whether for the Athonite monk or for the Christian in the midst of society? Evidently, for Palamas it is not merely negative, a pause between words, an absence of sound. He views it on the contrary in highly positive terms: it

---

46 *Homily* 53, §§ 18, 21, 22, 45, 47, 49, 50, 53, 59 (Christou, pp. 282, 286, 288, 318, 322, 324, 326, 328, 338; Veniamin, pp. 422, 423, 424, 434, 435, 436, 438, 441).

47 *Homily* 53, §§ 52, 53, 59 (Christou, pp. 328, 330, 338; Veniamin, pp. 437–8 [translation altered]).

is not emptiness but fullness, not an absence but a presence. There are of course many different kinds of silence, and some of them are indeed highly negative, signifying not openness but closure and exclusion. But the *hesychia* of the Holy Virgin, about which Palamas speaks, denotes not rejection of the Other but relationship, not distance but communion. Stillness of heart is basically nothing else than an attitude of listening. In the words of Max Picard, 'Listening is only possible when there is silence in man: listening and silence belong together.'[48] The Psalmist does not simply say, 'Be still', but 'Be still and *know that I am God*' (Ps. 45 [46]: 10): stillness is not vacancy but precisely God-awareness, listening to God. In the Gospels the Virgin Mary is in fact presented to us precisely as the one who listens, who waits on God in attentive silence, pondering things in her heart (Luke 2: 19; 2: 51; cf. 11: 28), who tells others to hearken to her Son (John 2: 5).

This creative stillness, this silent God-awareness, that characterizes the Mother of God is at the same time one of the most precious qualities of the Holy Mountain. If Mary is protector of Athos, then she is above all protector of the stillness, both outer and inner, that marks Athonite spirituality. Few if any have described this Athonite stillness better than the English Orthodox Gerald Palmer, who was over several decades an annual pilgrim to the Holy Mountain:

> It was midday on 6 August 1968. The motorboat from Daphni stopped at the harbour of Simonopetra. No one else landed, so after a friendly greeting from the monk on the jetty, I started climbing alone up the steep path as the motorboat went down the coast. After some twenty minutes or so, I reached the point where the path from the monastery of Grigoriou joins the track from the right. Here, at the junction, there is a small shrine with a Cross and stone seats under the shade of a roof; the open sides of the little building give wide views over the sea to the next peninsula. Having reverenced the Cross, I sat down in the shade and looked out across the sea, listening to the silence.
>
> *All was still.*
>
> Immediately, I felt that now at last I was back on the Holy Mountain, and thanked God for once again giving me this immense privilege.
>
> *All was still.*

48   *The World of Silence* (London, no date), p. 177.

This stillness, this silence, is everywhere, pervades all, is the very essence of the Holy Mountain. The distant sound of a motorboat serves only to punctuate the intensity of the quiet; the lizard's sudden rustling among the dry leaves, a frog plopping into a fountain, are loud and startling sounds, but merely emphasize the immense stillness. Often as one walks over the great stretches of wild country which form much of this sacred ground, following paths where every stone breathes prayers, it is impossible to hear a sound of any kind. Even in the monastery churches, where the silence is, as it were, made more profound by the darkness, by the beauty and by the sacred quality of the place, it seems that the reading and chanting of priests and monks in the endless rhythm of their daily and nightly ritual is no more than a thin fringe of a limitless ocean of silence.

But this stillness, this silence, is far more than a mere absence of sound. It has a positive quality, a quality of fullness, of plenitude, of the eternal Peace which is there reflected in the Veil of the Mother of God, enshrouding and protecting her Holy Mountain, offering inner silence, peace of heart, to those who dwell there and to those who come with openness of heart to seek this blessing.

May many be blessed to guard here this peace or to bear it away as a lasting gift of grace.[49]

Threats and Hopes

It would be comforting, yet at the same time seriously misleading, to end our discussion of the distinctive features of the Holy Mountain with this moving testimony. But if Gerald Palmer could return to Athos today, some forty-three years later, would he find the same stillness? How far are this particular characteristic of Athonite monasticism, and indeed the other three distinctive features that have been mentioned, to be seen as safe and secure under present-day conditions? Or are they under threat?

There is little or no need to express anxiety about the third of the distinctive features, namely the diversity of monastic vocations that coexist

---

49 Quoted in Kallistos Ware, 'Mount Athos Today', *Christian*, 3: 4 (1976), 324–5. This text was originally published anonymously in *Orthodox Life* (Jordanville, NY), Nov.–Dec. 1968, p. 33.

on the Holy Mountain. All three forms of life – the eremitic, the cenobitic, and the middle way – continue to thrive on Athos today as in the
past, and there is every reason to expect that they will do so in the future.
Back in the 1960s it was the Greek sketes such as Great St Anne or New
Skete that displayed the greatest vitality, whereas a number of the twenty
'ruling' monasteries were in a state of perilous decline. Today there has
been a renewal in almost all the 'ruling' monasteries, and none of them
is in danger of extinction; at the same time the Greek sketes remain fully
active. The Mountain, so it may be hoped with reasonable confidence, will
not cease to be in this way a genuine microcosm of the varied monastic
vocations to be found in the Christian East.

Sadly, as regards the other three features of Athonite monasticism, the
situation is more problematic. Let us take first the second feature, the pan-
Orthodox character of the Holy Mountain. There is a substantial body of
evidence, dating from the period 1970–2000, which indicates that persons
of non-Greek origin, particularly Romanians and Russians, confront obsta-
cles when seeking to become monks on Athos, such as are not encountered
by Greeks.[50] Why should this be so? Certainly the opposition does not
come from the Greek houses on the Holy Mountain; on the contrary, on
several occasions the Holy Community has protested against the difficulties created for non-Greeks. It may be that the Greek Foreign Office has
reasons to discourage the admission of Slavs and Romanians, but precise
information on this matter is hard to obtain. Unfortunately there is direct
evidence to suggest that the present Ecumenical Patriarch Bartholomew
has obstructed the entry of non-Greeks. During the past decade the situation seems to have grown somewhat easier, and there has been a modest
yet significant increase in numbers at all the non-Greek houses.

Any attempt to turn Athos into a Greek enclave, if such an attempt is
indeed being made, would be directly contrary to the international treaties

50   See Speake, *Mount Athos*, pp. 184–92; also Kallistos Ware, 'Athos after Ten Years: The
      Good News and the Bad', in Graham Speake (ed.), *Friends of Mount Athos: Annual
      Report 1992* (published in 1993), pp. 8–17, especially pp. 15–16; reprinted in *Sobornost
      Incorporating Eastern Churches Review*, 15: 1 (1993), 27–37, especially pp. 34–5.

governing the Holy Mountain. It would also be directly contrary to the 1924/26 Constitutional Charter of Athos, ratified by the Greek state. It would likewise contravene the principles of the European Union, of which Greece is a member. Above all it contradicts, in a blatant and shameful manner, the pan-Orthodox spirit that has prevailed from the beginning in the monastic republic of Athos. The Mountain has never been the exclusive preserve of any national group. For ten centuries it has been a centre of ecumenical Orthodoxy, and may it always remain so. Yet, to ensure this, there is need of continuing vigilance.

If there are grounds for disquiet concerning the second of our four distinctive features, our misgivings are greatly increased when we turn to the first and the fourth features. The natural beauty of the Holy Mountain is being eroded, and so also is the quality of its silence. I am glad that I first visited Athos as long ago as 1961 and 1962, and so I was able to see the Mountain in its 'pre-industrial' state. There were at that time virtually no motorized vehicles on the Mountain. The Russian monastery had a lorry, to transport logs from its upland woods, and I was told that Hilandar had a tractor, donated by Tito, but I never saw it. That, I think, was all. There were no dirt tracks leading from one monastery to another, and there was no bus between the port of Daphni and the monastic capital of Karyes. Pilgrims in the early 1960s used the cobbled mule-paths, or travelled in small motor boats, far more modest than the bulky ships that now ply along the Athonite coasts.

Now undoubtedly Athos could not remain indefinitely in this 'pre-industrial' condition. Some sort of modernization was inevitable and, indeed, desirable. There is, after all, nothing intrinsically sacred about oil lamps or transport by mules. It is possible to lead a genuinely ascetic life, while at the same time making use of electricity, hot water, and central heating. Roads can be constructed and maintained with ecological sensitivity. Buildings can be restored with a proper use of traditional materials. If this did not always happen in the 1950s and 1960s, with the imposition of a concrete roof on the Protaton in Karyes and the destruction of the wooden balconies at Dionysiou, it may be hoped that such mistakes will not be repeated in the future. Fortunately there are no motor roads on the southern tip of the peninsula, between Lavra and Prodromou, on the one

side, and Great St Anne on the other. In view of the precipitous character
of the terrain, it is likely that this region, which forms the very heart of
Athos, its Holy of Holies, will remain for ever a non-motorized 'temenos'.
Yet here again there is great need for vigilance.

Vigilance is needed still more to safeguard the stillness of the Mountain. 'If I were a doctor,' said Søren Kierkegaard, 'and were asked for my
advice, I should reply: Create silence!'[51] Is there not need for such a doctor
on the Holy Mountain today? The proliferation of mobile phones, the
coming and going of motor vehicles, the whining of chain saws in the
depths of the forest – all these are making it more difficult to listen to
the silence, in the way that Gerald Palmer could do back in 1968. Journey-
ing on Athonite soil, it is still possible to feel with Fr Nikon, 'Here every
stone breathes prayers.' But the 'eloquent silence' – to borrow a phrase
from Marius Victorinus (fourth century)[52] – which has always been such
an outstanding characteristic of the Holy Mountain, is now growing more
and more elusive.

Robert Byron, in a famous phrase, referred to the Holy Mountain as
'station of a faith where all the years have stopped'.[53] Is that still true? Yes
and no. The Mountain has indeed continued to be a bastion of Holy Tradition, a treasure house of the past. Yet the tradition that Athos embodies has
never ceased to be a living tradition, in which conservatism is mixed with
change, and ritual goes hand-in-hand with renewal. In the past half-century
during which it has been my privilege to make regular visits to Athos,
there have in fact been many new developments on the Mountain, and
most of them have been for the good. In particular, the positive influence
of Athos on the outside world, non-Orthodox as well as Orthodox, has
markedly increased.

Yet at least three of the four distinctive features that I have singled out
as serving to set Athos apart as *the* Holy Mountain, unequalled and unique,

---

51   Quoted in Picard, *The World of Silence*, p. 231.
52   Marius Victorinus, *Against the Heresies* 3. 16.
53   *The Station. Athos: Treasures and Men*, with an introduction by Christopher Sykes
      (London, 1949), p. 256 (first published in 1928).

are today under threat to a greater or lesser degree. The heritage of Athos is not only a gift but a challenge and a summons. Today, as never before, there is a need for all who value Athos to become consciously aware of what this heritage signifies and how it must be constantly defended. And yet in the last resort it is not we who protect the Holy Mountain but the Holy Mountain that protects us.

Bibliography

Amand de Mendieta, E., *Mount Athos the Garden of the Panagia* (Berlin/Amsterdam, 1972).

Athanasios the Athonite, *First Life*, ed. J. Noret, Corpus Christianorum Series Graeca 9 (Turnhout/Leuven, 1982).

Bonsall, L., 'The Benedictine Monastery of St Mary on Mount Athos', *Eastern Churches Review*, 2:3 (1969), 262–7.

Bryer, A., and Cunningham, M. (eds), *Mount Athos and Byzantine Monasticism*, Papers from the Twenty-eighth Spring Symposium of Byzantine Studies, Birmingham, March, 1994 (Aldershot, 1996).

Byron, R., *The Station. Athos: Treasures and Men* (London, 1949).

Dawkins, R. M., *The Monks of Athos* (London, 1936).

della Dora, V., *Imagining Mount Athos: Visions of a Holy Place from Homer to World War II* (Charlottesville/London, 2011).

Ebanoizde, M., and Wilkinson, J., *Pilgrimage to Mount Athos, Constantinople and Jerusalem 1755–1759: Timothy Gabashvili*, Georgian Studies on the Holy Land, vol. 1 (Richmond, 2001).

Fennell, N., *The Russians on Athos* (Oxford/Bern, 2001).

Gothóni, R., *Paradise within Reach: Monasticism and Pilgrimage on Mt Athos* (Helsinki, 1993).

Grdzelidze, T., *Georgian Monks on Mount Athos. Two Eleventh-Century Lives of the Hegoumenoi of Iviron* (London, 2009).

Kitromilides, P. M., *Enlightenment, Nationalism, Orthodoxy: Studies in the Culture and Political Thought of South-eastern Europe*, Variorum Collected Studies Series CS 453 (Aldershot, 1994).

——, *An Orthodox Commonwealth: Symbolic Legacies and Cultural Encounters in Southeastern Europe*, Variorum Collected Studies Series CS 891 (Aldershot, 2007).

Loch, S., *Athos: the Holy Mountain* (London, 1957).

Nikolaos (Hatzinikolaou), Metropolitan of Mesogaia, *Mount Athos: The Highest Place on Earth* (Athens, 2007).

Plested, M., 'Athos and the West: Benedictines, Crusaders, and Philosophers', in Graham Speake (ed.), *Friends of Mount Athos: Annual Report 2007* (2008), pp. 43–54.

Riley, A., *Athos or the Mountain of the Monks* (London, 1887).

Robinson, N. F., *Monasticism in the Orthodox Churches* (London/Milwaukee, 1916).

Sherrard, P., *Athos the Mountain of Silence* (London, 1960); 2nd ed., *Athos the Holy Mountain* (London, 1982).

——, 'The Paths of Athos', *Eastern Churches Review*, 9:1–2 (1977), 100–7.

Smyrnakis, G., *To Agion Oros* (Athens, 1903).

Speake, Graham, *Mount Athos: Renewal in Paradise* (New Haven/London, 2002).

Valentin, J., *The Monks of Mount Athos* (London, 1960).

Ware, Kallistos, 'Athos after Ten Years: The Good News and the Bad', in Graham Speake (ed.), *Friends of Mount Athos: Annual Report 1992* (1993), pp. 8–17; reprinted in *Sobornost Incorporating Eastern Churches Review*, 15:1 (1993), 27–37.

——, 'Mount Athos Today', *Christian*, 3:4 (1976), 322–33.

——, 'St Nikodimos and the *Philokalia*', in D. Conomos and G. Speake (eds), *Mount Athos the Sacred Bridge: The Spirituality of the Holy Mountain* (Oxford/Bern, 2005), pp. 69–121.

——, 'Three Different Views of the Holy Mountain: Athos through the Eyes of F. W. Hasluck, R. M. Dawkins and P. Sherrard', in M. Llewellyn Smith, P. M. Kitromilides and E. Calligas (eds), *Scholars, Travels, Archives: Greek History and Culture through the British School at Athens*, British School at Athens Studies 17 (London, 2009), pp. 111–23.

——, 'Two British Pilgrims to the Holy Mountain: Gerald Palmer and Philip Sherrard', in R. Gothóni and G. Speake (eds), *The Monastic Magnet: Roads to and from Mount Athos* (Oxford/Bern, 2008), pp. 143–57.

——, 'Wolves and Monks: Life on the Holy Mountain Today', *Sobornost Incorporating Eastern Churches Review*, 5:2 (1983), 56–68.

Notes on Contributors

AVERIL CAMERON has recently retired as Warden of Keble College, Oxford, and is the chair of the newly established Oxford Centre for Byzantine Research. Her most recent book was *The Byzantines* (Oxford, 2006), for which she was awarded the Criticos Prize.

CONSTANTIN COMAN is a graduate of the Theology Faculty in Bucharest and gained a PhD in theology from the University of Athens. He is Professor of New Testament at the Theology Faculty of Bucharest University, specializing in biblical hermeneutics, and also serves as a parish priest.

NICHOLAS FENNELL studied Russian and Italian at Trinity College, Cambridge, and gained a PhD from the University of Southampton. Since 1974 he has taught Russian and French literature and language at Winchester College. He is the author of *The Russians on Athos* (Oxford, 2001) and numerous articles on Russian Athos.

TAMARA GRDZELIDZE works for the Faith and Order Secretariat of the World Council of Churches in Geneva. She holds a DPhil from the University of Oxford, a doctorate in medieval Georgian literature from the Tbilisi State University, and an honorary doctorate from the University of Bern.

VLADETA JANKOVIC is a retired professor of classical literature at the University of Belgrade. He was formerly Ambassador of Yugoslavia to the United Kingdom and currently serves as Ambassador of Serbia to the Holy See.

KYRILL PAVLIKIANOV is Professor of Byzantine Philology and Palaeography at the University of Sofia. His doctoral dissertation (University of Athens, 1997) was concerned with the Slavic monastic presence on Mount Athos during the Middle Ages and he has published widely on the history of the Holy Mountain as well as its medieval cultural and documentary heritage.

MARCUS PLESTED is Vice-Principal and Academic Director of the Institute for Orthodox Christian Studies (Cambridge Theological Federation). He was schooled in London, educated at Oxford, and received into the Orthodox Church on Athos. He is the author of *The Macarian Legacy* (Oxford, 2004) and of many articles on Patristics and Eastern Orthodoxy. He is also a Member of the Institute for Advanced Study in Princeton, New Jersey.

GRAHAM SPEAKE studied classics at Trinity College, Cambridge, and gained a DPhil at Oxford for a thesis on the Byzantine transmission of ancient Greek literature. He is the founder and secretary of the Friends of Mount Athos and author of *Mount Athos: Renewal in Paradise* (New Haven, CT, and London, 2002), for which he was awarded the Criticos Prize. He too was received into the Orthodox Church on Athos and is also a Fellow of the Society of Antiquaries of London.

KALLISTOS WARE holds a doctorate in theology from the University of Oxford where from 1966 to 2001 he was a Fellow of Pembroke College and Spalding Lecturer in Eastern Orthodox Studies. He is a monk of the monastery of St John the Theologian, Patmos, and an assistant bishop in the Greek Orthodox Archdiocese of Thyateira and Great Britain. In 2007 he was raised to the rank of metropolitan. His publications include *The Orthodox Church*, 2nd edn (London, 1993) and *The Orthodox Way*, 2nd edn (Crestwood, NY, 1995).

Index